Clive Sinclair's

True Tales of the

WILD
WEST

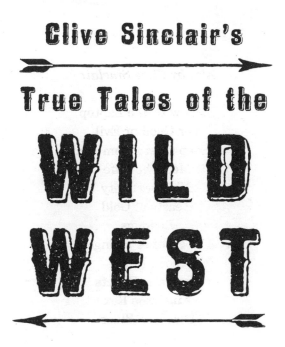

Clive Sinclair's

True Tales of the

WILD
WEST

PICADOR

First published 2008 by Picador
an imprint of Pan Macmillan Ltd
Pan Macmillan, 20 New Wharf Road, London N1 9RR
Basingstoke and Oxford
Associated companies throughout the world
www.panmacmillan.com

ISBN 978-0-330-42643-5

Printed and bound in the UK by
CPI Mackays, Chatham ME5 8TD

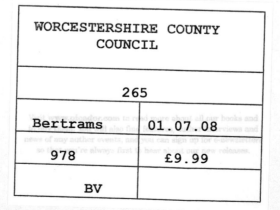

For Seth & Haidee

'I wandered over the land, and good people did not neglect me. After many years I became old and white: I heard a great deal, many lies and falsehoods, but the longer I lived the more I understood that there were really no lies. Whatever doesn't really happen is dreamed at night. It happens to one if it doesn't happen to another, tomorrow if not today, or a century hence if not next year.'

From *Gimpel the Fool* by
Isaac Bashevis Singer (trans. Saul Bellow)

'I remember Townes van Zandt, the great storywriter, telling me how he could completely re-enact Custer's Last Stand with salt and pepper shakers, because he grew playing Cowboys & Indians with those things . . . We all grew up putting together our own little miniture Wests . . . I think mine was a little darker.'

Tom Russell, *The Cowboy's Last Ride*
BBC Radio 2

ACKNOWLEDGEMENTS

The Author should like to express publicly his appreciation to the following people.

To Amity Bacon, Haidee Becker Kenedy, Rachel Kenedy, Seth Sinclair, Ben Vardi; all of whom accompanied him on a seven-thousand-mile drive across the Western States of the Union in the summer of 2003.

To Murray & Sheila Baumgarten, who provided shelter in Santa Cruz, California, in the spring of the same year.

To Maureen Droz and Vicky Engelhaupt of the South Dakota Department of Tourism; Philys Reller of the Deadwood Chamber of Commerce & Visitors Bureau; and Bill Walsh, erstwhile owner of Deadwood's Franklin Hotel; all of whom afforded him help and hospitality above the call of duty. None, needless to say, bear any responsibility for the ways in which their generosity was used (and maybe abused).

To Sarah Spankie, Deputy Editor of *Condé Nast Traveller*, who commissioned some of his first pieces on the Wild West, and emboldened him to write more.

To Jan Shure, Travel Editor of the *Jewish Chronicle*; and Andy Pietrasik, Travel Editor of the *Guardian*.

To Will Eaves, who accommodated his reviews of Westerns in the *TLS*; and Boyd Tonkin, who found room for his reviews of Western books in the *Independent*.

ACKNOWLEDGEMENTS

To Anne Mounic, who commissioned a story for her French on-line magazine, *Temporel*, and found herself with True Tale No. 6.

To Yosl & Audrey Bergner, Pamela & Jonathan Lubell, Josanne Ben Hur, Cecil Helman, all of whom read the work in progress and made encouraging noises.

To Sam Humphreys and Andrew Kidd of Picador, whose enthusiasm and patience were a sine qua non.

To David Sinclair, his late father, who took him to his first Western.

To Philip French, who continues to write about them so inspiringly.

CONTENTS

INTRODUCTION

Five years ago I resolved to concoct a history of the Wild West by visiting the sites where that history was made, and often re-enacted on a daily or annual basis. Thus it was that on 3 August 2003 I drove from Mesilla to Lincoln, New Mexico, to watch a dramatic reconstruction of Billy the Kid's bloody escape from the local jail. It was scheduled to take place on a baseball field beside the original courthouse and prison. But an unscheduled downpour of biblical proportions ended that entertainment before it began. Alas for the promoters, alas for the spectators, alas for me. Without the re-enactment it seemed that all I could do was offer yet another rewriting of Billy the Kid's brief career. A dull prospect, for writer and reader alike. Then I recalled two miniature tragedies that had occurred on the road to Lincoln: in brief succession I had seen a gorgeous yellow bird run over by a RV, and a dead dog (made unusually poignant by the fact that it was still wearing its collar and leash). Perhaps their deaths were not in vain, I thought, if I could only use both to set a story in motion. As it turned out I felt more comfortable writing in this manner than I had been when writing in a more straightforward mode about the cold-blooded murder of Wild Bill Hickok, the horrible massacre of General Custer, and the indiscreet charms of Calamity Jane. So I decided to upgrade those narratives too, to let them unfasten their seat belts, and stretch their legs. Some may call the resultant hybrid Creative Nonfiction. I prefer Dodgy Realism (you'll see why). All I can promise is that such liberties as I have taken are true to the spirit of the Wild West.

True Tales of the
WILD WEST Nº1

The Man Who Killed
Randolph Scott

Peppercorn took off for the States at the tail end of September. When asked why, his wife replied that he had gone to find his inner cowboy. But in reality Peppercorn, a photojournalist more familiar with deadlines than front lines, had been commissioned by *Terra Incognita*, the travel magazine, to turn in an article on the Buffalo Roundup at Custer State Park.

His destination was Rapid City, South Dakota, which he finally reached, via Denver, at twilight. He scanned the airport for the promised rep from the Department of Tourism, but could see only fatigued army volunteers slouched against their kitbags. Most were so exhausted they lacked the energy to raise their crew-cut heads when a rare new arrival burst through the swing doors. Peppercorn, however, was entranced. The newcomer was wearing a pearly-white

Stetson and a powder-blue blouse alive with sequins, and was shapely too. Seeing him, she squealed and jumped a foot in the air. 'Wow!' he said. 'Thank God you're still here,' she said. 'I've come straight from this year's Miss Rodeo South Dakota contest in Belle Fourche. I didn't win it, but I was a runner-up in Appearance, Personality and Photogenics.' 'You were robbed,' observed Peppercorn, extending his right hand. 'Mercy Sweetbriar,' said the young woman, shaking it. Her vitality branched up his arm like electricity. 'You really like my outfit?' she asked. 'Like it?' cried Peppercorn. 'I want to be buried in it.' 'Flattery will get you everywhere,' she said.

That night it got him to the Alex Johnson, where Alfred Hitchcock and Cary Grant had stayed while shooting *North by Northwest*. The old hotel's lobby was dominated by a mighty fireplace made of local granite. Above it hung a portrait of the hotel's founder, arrayed in buckskin and warbonnet, though he was no more a Sioux than Peppercorn. Buffalo heads hung on either side of the painting. 'That's it for tonight,' said Mercy, 'unless you want to help me clean out my horse stalls.' Waking in the small hours, Peppercorn telephoned his wife. 'Have you found your inner cowboy yet?' she asked. 'No,' he replied, 'but I've found a rhinestone cowgirl who's just right for him when I do.'

Once upon a time Mrs Peppercorn would have been beside her husband in bed, not on the far end of a telephone connection. But she had vowed to boycott the United States so long as Bush was its president. To tell the truth, she was beginning to feel increasingly queasy about his predecessors too, especially those who had peddled manifest destiny. In her opinion the pioneers and the descendants of pioneers

who peopled South Dakota were all tainted by the same original sin; they all had the blood of Crazy Horse upon their
hands. Not excluding the beautiful innocent who stood waiting for Peppercorn in front of the Alex Johnson, all gloried
and gilded by the new-minted sun.

She took her charge to the Journey Museum out on
Rapid City's New York Street, where photographic evidence
of her ancestors' sins was prominently displayed, though of
course it was not presented as such. In the beginning the sin
was merely one of trespass, the most consequential of which
was committed by George Armstrong Custer, Civil War hero,
enthusiastic Indian fighter, and leader of the 1874 Black
Hills Expedition (the subject of the most significant display).
'I expect to visit a region of country as yet unseen by human
eyes except those of the Indian,' he wrote as he made his
final preparations, 'a country described by the latter as
abounding in game of all varieties, rich in scientific interest,
and of surpassing beauty in natural scenery.' Perhaps it was
on account of the anticipated beauty that Custer chose to
employ a photographer to record his progress.

The Expedition was to be the high-point of Yorkshire-
born William Henry Illingworth's life. He got along famously with the notoriously vain and photogenic General.
'Our photographer has obtained a complete set of magnificent
stereoscopic views of Black Hills scenery,' Custer wrote to
his devoted wife, 'so I will not allude to the beautiful scenery
until I can view it with you by aid of the photographs.' He
was right to praise them; the photographs amazed Pepper
corn, as they had Mrs Custer. But what Custer had failed to
mention was the inconvenient fact that the apparently innocent images provided indubitable proof of both trespass and

3

– worse – treaty violation. For the Black Hills – Jerusalem to the Sioux – had been ceded to them in perpetuity by the 1868 Fort Laramie Treaty. Nor did he spell out that the chief object of scientific interest was gold, hence the presence of prospectors in his party. Some have since argued that they went at the behest of the railroad owners, who needed a new gold rush to repay their massive investment.

Examining a view entitled, 'Golden Park, where Gold was first found', Peppercorn could see four tiny figures (probably the successful prospectors themselves) making their way across a meadow, overshadowed by the granite bulk of a bulbous peak. The photograph was taken on August 2. The following day Custer sent a rider named Lonesome Charley Reynolds to Fort Laramie (of all places) with news of the find, news that immediately made the 1868 treaty a dead letter. 'Calamity followed close on Lonesome Charley's heels,' mused Peppercorn, and he didn't mean Calamity Jane.

Despite this knowledge he was not immune to Custer's glamour (damn his eyes), and envied Illingworth his part in the adventure. Not only did the Yorkshireman have luck, it seemed he had talent too. Peppercorn was particularly impressed by an image entitled, 'Wagon train passing through Castle Creek Valley', which appeared to have been taken from some mountain redoubt. He was leaning forward to get a better look when darkness suddenly descended, or at least an unknown person covered his eyes with their hands. 'If I'd a been a Native American,' said Mercy, 'you'da been dead by now.' 'I was miles away,' said Peppercorn, 'trying to imagine myself in Illingworth's shoes.' 'I'm no miracle worker and can't introduce you to the man himself,' said Mercy, 'but I can arrange for you to meet a photographer who followed in his footsteps. In fact, he has just published a book of photographs that duplicate Illingworth's points of view. He's as near as you'll get to the real thing.'

Turned out the man in question wasn't so keen on such a close identification. Indeed, his initial response to the idea of recreating Illingworth's photographs had been to resist it. Paul Horsted was already an established photographer, had his own way of looking at things, and saw no benefit in mimicking another's. So what had won him over? Not sophistry, but a simple photograph of some rocks. He recognized the rocks immediately. Why not? They were practically in his own backyard. As a matter of fact he had photographed them many times himself. Thereafter the idea of copying Illingworth did not seem such a betrayal of self after all. Peppercorn and Horsted were breakfasting in the Bank Coffee House and Gaming Parlor (opened in 1881 as the First National Bank of Dakota Territory) in the latter's home town of Custer, a mile or so north of Custer State Park. 'There's no escaping that man hereabouts,' said Horsted. 'Had we been sitting here in 1874 we'd have been facing his so-called permanent encampment. It was in the adjacent creek that they found the gold, though the exact spot is something of a mystery. The miner who made the discovery – or so he claimed – used to take the curious to a place about three miles out of town. Here's the odd thing: the place was always on the move. The older he became the nearer it got.' 'Did the project change your view of Custer?' asked Peppercorn. 'You're assuming I already had one,' said Horsted. 'I certainly knew that the man had passionate admirers and equally passionate detractors, but I'd always been an agnostic on the subject. If I thought of him at all, it was as a vainglorious soldier who brought most of his troubles on his own head. However, when I came to understand the enormity of the task he'd been set, I had to applaud his achievement.'

'And what about Illingworth's?' asked Peppercorn. 'Not just applause, but a standing ovation,' replied Horsted. 'Modern photographers like us carry lightweight SLRs, and if we still use film, it fits in our pockets. We flit from place to place in 4 x 4s. But he . . . he had a wagon, a badly sprung box on wheels, inside which he would coat his glass plates with light-sensitive chemicals, and slot them into his weighty camera. Then he would have to lug all his equipment to some distant spot. Shot taken, he would immediately retreat to his dark wagon, in order to develop and fix the image. After all that he still had to preserve the precious but fragile plates for the duration.' 'What happened to him afterwards?' asked Peppercorn. 'Did he share Custer's fate at the Little Bighorn?' 'It might have been better for him if he had,' said Horsted. 'He found life increasingly difficult as his glory days receded and he approached his fifties. Like many men in similar circumstances he became an alcoholic. Nor did his private life provide stability. He was thrice married: once bereaved, twice divorced. On March 16 1893 he picked up his favourite hunting gun, and turned it on himself.' Illingworth's end gave Peppercorn the willies. He was glad when Mercy reappeared to exorcise his unquiet spirit. 'Time to go, Peppercorn,' she said, 'people are waiting for you in the Park.'

The Black Hills therein lived up to their name, courtesy of massed thickets of ponderosa pine and blue spruce. The wide valley which bisected them was aglow, however, thanks to the fiery foliage of sumacs and golden-leafed aspen. Looking out of the sidelight as Mercy Sweetbriar drove, Peppercorn saw pronghorn antelope pogo-stick into the distance, while white-tailed deer demonstrated their distinguishing feature. Only the longhorn sheep remained as indifferent to their passage as the mountains. Mercy followed the road deep into the woods, until she came to a green meadow in which cowboys were unloading horses from several trailers. Their leader was the spitting image of Walter Brennan. Mercy stuck her head out of the window and cried, 'Howdy, Bob!' 'Why, look who's here,' he said. 'I love that man,' said Mercy. 'If I didn't have a daddy already, I'd want him to be mine.' As if to prove she meant every word, she leapt from the automobile and jumped screaming straight into his open arms. 'Slow down, darlin,' he said, 'or you'll be spookin the animals.' 'Don't pretend you're not pleased to see me, you old grump,' said Mercy. 'Course I am,' said Bob, putting her down. 'Now don't go away, I've got something to show you.' He strode towards the cab of his truck, and came back waving a glossy magazine. 'Oh my Lord,' cried Mercy, 'you've made the cover of *Today's Horse*. You're a celebrity, Bob!' The old cowboy tried unsuccessfully to conceal his pride. 'Keep it,' he said. 'If you want.' 'Keep it?' said Mercy. 'I intend to frame it and hang it over my bed.' Turning to the auto she yelled, 'Peppercorn, come and meet the famous Bob Lantis.'

Close up he looked even more the archetypal Westerner, with his hat, his faded shirt, and his leathery complexion. 'Mostly Bob leads packing trips through Yellowstone's back country, where he's known as "The Man who Runs Bears out of Camp with a Stick",' said Mercy, 'but he always finds time to help out with the Buffalo Roundup.' 'Pleased to meet you,' said Peppercorn, conscious that Bob's attention had shifted elsewhere. A couple of buffalo had been grazing on some distant greenery, but now one of them, a big old bull, was trotting determinedly in their direction. The horses didn't like it. Neither did Bob. He picked up a black-handled whip of vast dimensions and cast it, as though angling for flying fish. The endless thong flew out, and cracked the silent air like a thunderclap. The bull immediately backed off, requiring no second warning. 'That was one big son of a bitch,' said Peppercorn. 'You betcha,' said Bob. 'Six-six at the shoulder. Two thousand pounds and rising on the scales. Speeds of up to thirty-five miles an hour.

8

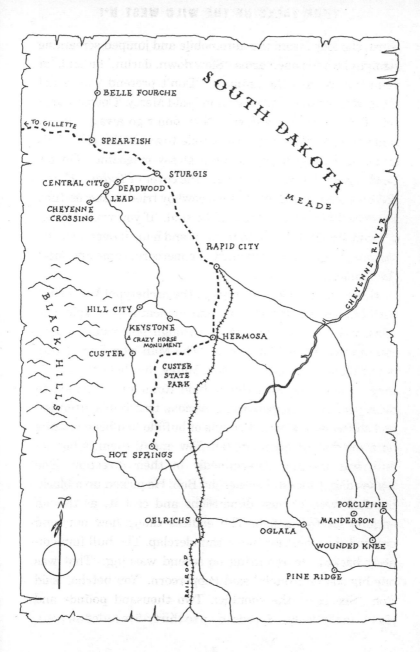

A head like a battering ram. And that's just one of em. On Monday there'll be fifteen hundred.'

Then he went over to help the cowboys calm the horses. Having re-established tranquillity he threw a blanket over the back of his favourite, smoothed out its furrows, and placed a saddle upon it, quietly singing all the while, 'A-ridin ole Paint, and a-leadin ole Dan . . . goin to Montana, for to throw the hoolihan . . .' In the meantime, Peppercorn took photographs. 'I hope you turn out to be just like him,' he whispered to his inner cowboy.

Among the real cowboys were a pair of dudes, pegged as such by their branded leather flasks, their spotless Stetsons, their ironed shirts, their uncreased chaps, their silver spurs, and their shiny tooled boots. Peppercorn felt protected by their play-acting, but not for long. 'Bob,' said Mercy, when all the mounts were ready, 'have you got a quiet horse for my friend to ride?' 'As quiet as he likes,' said Bob. Babies were born bow-legged in South Dakota. They could ride before they could walk. There was maybe a single person in the whole State who was frightened of horses. 'Why does it have to be me?' groaned Peppercorn. One by one all the cowboys mounted, even the dudes. 'Are you ready, Peppercorn?' asked Mercy. He looked at the stirrup and at the placid piebald to which it was attached. Mercy was holding the reins, but in truth it was so still it could have been stuffed. Peppercorn felt his inner cowboy champing at the bit. He tried to lift his foot. Nothing happened. Instead he heard himself uttering the magic words: 'Jet lag.' Bob shrugged. It made no difference to him. But Mercy Sweetbriar looked disappointed. Peppercorn watched her follow Bob along a path that descended into woodland. She was leading the rid-

erless piebald. Behind her were the dudes, evidently packing a good supply of Coors. The last thing he heard was Bob
warning them, 'You'd better be very positively sure not to
leave any trash on this trail.' Left alone, Peppercorn sank to
his knees. 'Let me outta here,' demanded his inner cowboy.
'I don't need a host who's got a yellow streak wider than the
Missouri.' Shamed, Peppercorn sneaked back to the hotel.
It was evening in England, so he telephoned his wife. 'Well,'
she said, 'has your inner cowboy made any headway with
the rhinestone cowgirl?' 'Fuck off,' he said. 'I'll take that as
a no,' she said.

The people of South Dakota might have been natural-
born riders, but on the whole they were not frequent flyers.
To Mercy Sweetbriar – who had never boarded an aircraft
in her life – jet lag was something as exotic and unlikely as
beriberi. Returning rosy-cheeked and ravenous from the
ride, she sought out Peppercorn and asked solicitously if he
felt well enough to join her in the Pheasant Dining Room.
And so, instead of being an object of derision, Peppercorn
found himself the recipient of undeserved sympathy.
Granted this reprieve he became charm personified: that is,
he asked Mercy Sweetbriar numerous questions about herself, and listened attentively to the answers. She was a
native of Spearfish, near Deadwood, where her daddy was a
rancher, and her mother – though a registered nurse – a
ranch wife. She had reckoned her father the handsomest
man in the world until her early teens, when she had
watched Kevin Costner shoot the winter scenes for *Dances
with Wolves* in beautiful Spearfish Canyon. At high school
she was very active in gymnastics, wrestling statistics and
cheerleading. The previous June she had graduated with an

Associate of Applied Science degree in Agricultural Business Management from South Dakota State University. Since then she had been an intern in the office of Maureen Droz, international marketing manager at the Department of Tourism, and a great role model. Peppercorn was her first solo flight, so to speak. 'I'll do my best not to give you jet lag,' he promised.

In the bar after dinner they found an empty table, and Peppercorn offered to buy his eye-catching companion a drink. Mercy's order was modest: Diet Pepsi. 'Nothing stronger?' he asked. 'No way,' she said. 'State officials are not allowed to touch alcohol while on duty. The rule sucks, but there are too many witnesses to risk breaking it.' A TV was bracketed to the wall just above the bartender's head, tuned to Fox News. Its small screen barely contained the features of President George W. Bush. The first anniversary of 9/11 had just passed, and the president was letting his fellow Americans know how the War on Terror was getting along. Conscious that the Buffalo Roundup's full title was Governor Bill Janklow's Buffalo Roundup, and conscious also that Governor Janklow and the vast majority of his guests were Republicans, Peppercorn decided to keep his smart-ass remarks to himself. This self-denying ordinance came under immediate strain when a couple asked if they could share the table. Peppercorn didn't need to be a semiotician to deduce their politics. She was sporting a denim jacket, upon which Old Glory was embossed in sequins of red, white and blue; he was wearing a tie from which beamed the face of Ronald Reagan. They introduced themselves as buddies of the Governor, the one a corporate lawyer, the other a plastic surgeon over at Sioux Falls. Once seated, they raised their glasses and toasted Bush. Then they thanked the Lord that it was him and not Al Gore in the White House. Would Gore have squared up to Osama? They thought not. Bush, on the other hand, had grown into the job after a shaky start, and – as events had proved – had no fear of man's work. The couple had visited with him more than once, and found him to be courageous, honest and very smart. What's more, he was a genuinely nice guy. And modest enough to recognize that there was always a higher authority than the President. With him the Godless years were over for good, years when the White House was an out-post of Sodom and Gomorrah, was host to adultery and even murder. 'Murder?' echoed Peppercorn. 'Most foul,' replied the lawyer, alluding to convenient plane crashes and apparent suicides. When punch-drunk Peppercorn finally returned to his room, having escorted Mercy to hers, he found a note on his bed. It read: 'Strap this on and shoot the sites.' Near it was a disposable Instamatic. The note was signed: 'Bill.' Not Clinton, Peppercorn presumed.

On Sunday morning there was a frisson in the hotel, as word spread that the Governor was on his way. All were instructed to reassemble at 10.45 precisely. 'Time enough to check out the Arts Festival,' said Mercy, 'it's bound to pro-vide a few good photo-ops.' Well, there was a white-faced singer in a black shirt conducting what he called a 'cowboy service' in a marquee. There were trestle tables groaning with plates of pancakes and bowls of maple syrup. There were local artists, who had set up shop for the day. And there was the 7th Cavalry Drum and Bugle Corps, most of whose players looked old enough to have ridden with Custer. Nonetheless, they marched around the meadow blowing

their bugles, their tubas and their flutes, and bashing the hell out their drums. For the finale, they entered the marquee and offered a rousing version of 'God Bless America', which prompted every man, woman and child to rise and stand to attention, right fist on heart. And finally there was Miss Rodeo South Dakota herself, from whose hat shone the insignia of royalty, an intricate silver heart. Her bust shone even more brightly, however, being encased in a mosaic of mirrors, in whose many facets Peppercorn saw himself multiplied. He had to admit, if only very quietly, that Miss Rodeo South Dakota looked even more splendid than had Miss Sweetbriar when she'd made her grand entrance at Rapid City's metropolitan airport. Seeing Mercy she squealed, hopped, and hugged her. 'Hello, Jennifer,' said Mercy, squealing no less. Passing a tent sponsored by the Governor, where visitors could have their blood tested for excess sugar, Mercy Sweetbriar said to Peppercorn, 'That little madam would be off the scale.'

When they returned to the hotel at 10.45 someone was already assigning all the guests to waiting autos. Unlike the Rodeo Queen he wore no signs of office, but he was just as clearly its king, though it was hard to pinpoint exactly why.

His visage was not that of a lean and hungry Western hero
– if anything, it was on the pudgy side. But it didn't signify,
for Governor Bill Janklow was surrounded like Saturn by
an atmospheric belt of charisma. Even Peppercorn felt its
gravitational pull, and wondered whether poor Illingworth
had experienced the same sensation when he first set eyes
on General Custer.

Not that their assignments were comparable, alas. Illingworth was bound for terra incognita, whereas Peppercorn
was just bound into its pages. It was equally true that heading a column of some dozen SUVs – Governor Janklow's
present responsibility – was rather less taxing than guiding
a hundred and ten wagons through hostile territory. Moreover, as soon as the convoy hit the main road a black-
and-white with flashing lights moved to the head. At its
approach private cars pulled to the side so it could pass
unhindered. Nor was it necessary to slow down (let alone
stop) in small towns, even if the traffic signals were at red.
In Custer the convoy swept past French Creek (where the
gold was found), past a crude stockade (replica of the one
erected by the first illegal prospectors), past the Bank Coffee
House and Gaming Parlor, past restaurants, past a preserved pioneer cabin, past a courthouse, and past a junction
or two, where local cops held back the cross-traffic, thereby
guaranteeing the Governor's priority and safety, as well as
that of unwitting travellers who in law had right of way.

Peppercorn was even more impressed when he discovered that the Governor's fiat did not end at roads, but
extended to mountain peaks, including that of Mount Thunderhead. Whereas hoi polloi were only permitted to view its
glories from ground level, the Governor's charmed circle

were led up a dirt track to the very top. What Peppercorn
saw when he stepped from the vehicle (not without trepidation, being fearful of heights) was a head nine stories high.
It belonged to Crazy Horse, and was carved by a Polish-born
sculptor named Korczak Ziolkowski. Back in 1948 he had
somehow acquired one of the largest chunks of granite in
the entire Black Hills, intending to turn the whole thing into
a Red Indian Mount Rushmore. Would Crazy Horse have
appreciated such a memorial? Unlikely, thought Peppercorn.
All his brief life he had refused – unlike Red Cloud, Sitting
Bull and even the fierce Apache Geronimo – to sit for a portrait of any kind. There were no photographs, paintings or
even sketches of him in existence; no likenesses at all. Ignoring this injunction, Korczak laboured at his Sisyphean task

until his death in 1982.
Accepting a posthumous
award on his behalf his
widow, Ruth, recalled her
late husband's philosophy:
'Never forget your dreams.'
It took her and their children – who inherited both
the dream and the burden
– a further sixteen years
to complete the head that
towered above Peppercorn's.
He felt awe for sure, but
no sense of Crazy Horse's
presence. Korczak's was
another matter. The man
clearly had an ego the size

of Mount Thunderhead, an ego that had condemned gener-
ations of Ziolkowskis as yet unborn to labour at a mission
none would see to completion. The head had required half a
century. The broad promontory on which Peppercorn stood
was destined to be an outstretched arm. That would probably take a dozen more years. And then there was Crazy
Horse's steed, with its flaring nostrils, flowing mane and
flashing hooves. Who knew how long that would take to
finish? Centuries, probably. Long enough for the toilers to
have forgotten the mountain god's immediate origins, and
remember only that they must serve him and obey the commandments of his one prophet.

Back on terra firma Peppercorn entered the Visitors
Center and lingered beside a table piled high with various
lives of Crazy Horse, all by the same author. 'These are the
only books about him written by a member of the Sioux
nation,' said the youthful enthusiast selling them. 'You have
my guarantee on that. I know the author personally. He's
my father.' A woman interrupted and asked him to recommend the best. 'My answer depends upon your needs,'
explained the bookseller. 'My father has written a straightforward narrative like you'd find in a school textbook. But
he has also produced a biography that's more in keeping
with our way of thinking. It tells the story of his spirit, not
his body.' 'That's the one for me,' she said. 'From what I've
heard Crazy Horse is your people's Jesus.' Peppercorn
didn't buy that for a minute. Didn't Christ famously advise
his followers to turn the other cheek? Didn't he also instruct
them to love their enemies? Correct me if I'm wrong,
thought Peppercorn, but didn't Crazy Horse prefer to kill
his? 'Both men were inspirational leaders,' continued the

woman, 'and both in the end were betrayed and killed by their own people.' 'Not so,' responded Peppercorn out loud, 'the Romans killed Christ.' Ignoring his presumption the woman paid for the book, and walked away. 'I'm with you, Peppercorn,' said the author's son. How did he know my name, thought Peppercorn, astonished? It remained a mystery, until he recalled that he was wearing a name-tag.

The Governor's convoy moved north to Hill City, where Peppercorn and others quit the SUVs and boarded an 1880 Baldwin locomotive, with its red cow-catcher and tall silver smokestack. As it steamed out of the station Peppercorn found himself temporarily companionless, Mercy Sweetbriar having abandoned him for consultations with her boss. Not that he minded. The wooded valleys of the Black Hills were good enough company. But even better was en route. Governor Bill Janklow was ambling his way down the aisle. 'Is this seat taken?' he asked Peppercorn. 'Please,' Peppercorn replied, 'be my guest.' 'You British are so polite,' said the Governor, lowering himself. 'And brave. Loyal, too. Makes me kinda wish it was the French we had to lick back in '76. I hope you come to like us half so well.' 'Mr Governor,' said Peppercorn, 'I've been in love with cowboys ever since I was a little boy. At my fifth birthday party I wore a tie decorated with one. He was astride a horse, of course. At full gallop, naturally. A dog loped alongside. Below the little group was the legend: "Riders of the Range". The cowboy was about to swing his lasso. It did not miss. It snagged my boyish heart. Later that same year, when Elizabeth was crowned, we had a fancy-dress party at my kindergarten, in Queen's Road as it happened. I went as a cowboy. My hat was flat-topped. A neckerchief had been knotted at my throat. The rest of my costume consisted of waistcoat, holster, six-gun and chaps. It was not hired from some fancy-dress outfitters. I owned it. I've been prepared for a life of adventure ever since. It's been a long wait.' 'You have my word that your wait will not have been in vain,' said Governor Janklow, clapping Peppercorn on the shoulder. The train, meantime, concluded its journey at Keystone, just around the corner from Mount Rushmore.

The climax of the day was a banquet advertised as Dinner with the Presidents, on account of the fact that the windows of the venue – the Buffalo Dining Room – looked out upon the chiselled features of George Washington, Thomas Jefferson, Abraham Lincoln and Teddy Roosevelt. Peppercorn found himself at a table with Mercy Sweetbriar. Opposite them was a blonde woman. 'Peppercorn,' said Mercy, 'meet Marin, Marin Droz. My boss.' They shook hands. 'You're nurturing a treasure,' he said, causing Mercy to blush. Also at the table were three or four volunteer wranglers not unlike Peppercorn. As they sipped their Zinfandel night descended, and (having briefly disappeared) the faces of the four Presidents sprang suddenly from the darkness as spotlights were turned upon them.

'If any of you guys have seen *North by Northwest*,' said Maureen, 'you'll recognize the location of that movie's grand finale.' It was agreed that Cary Grant was a Hitchcockian hero sans pareil, but none among them could picture him in a Western. They began to call out the names of those they could. Then someone asked – maybe it was even Peppercorn – which cowboy stars they would nominate to replace the old boys on Mount Rushmore. John Wayne was the first nomination. Nobody chose to disagree with that. 'You remember that scene in *The Searchers*, when he's in the foreground and Monument Valley's in the background? I'll swear he looked as durable as those buttes. My God, that man *was* the American West.' Henry Fonda was rejected, not because his performances in *My Darling Clementine* and *Fort Apache* weren't up to the mark, but because he was too versatile, fitted too well into non-Westerns. Clint Eastwood was accepted (much to the delight of Mercy and Maureen) for the opposite reason. 'He's a cowboy, or he's nothing,' was the general consensus. That left two spots to fill. 'Gary Cooper!' yelled someone. 'You betcha,' said someone else. All loved his sensitive but manly face, which so beautifully registered the pain he experienced when visiting violence upon others. *High Noon* and *Man of the West* were cited. So Cooper was in. Someone suggested Alan Ladd. All expressed admiration for his work in *Shane*, but most felt his filmography incommensurate with the proposed honour. Ladd was shown the door in a gentlemanly fashion.

Only when Peppercorn recommended Randolph Scott did the discussion become heated. 'I've heard he was queer,' said one of the would-be wranglers. 'Now you mention it,' said another, 'I don't recollect him havin a woman in any movie, even when he's playin a married man. In *Ride Lonesome* the wife is long dead, and in *Comanche Station* she's been kidnapped irretrievably by hostiles. What relationships he forms are usually with young men, who tend to get shot – luckily for them – before they can ride off together into the sunset.' 'What about *Seventh Cavalry*, you bunch of bigots?' said Peppercorn. 'Has it slipped your narrow minds that Scott gets hitched in that?' 'That movie sucks,' said a wrangler. 'The hell it does,' said Peppercorn. 'If any of you don't know it, here's the pitch. Having played Cupid for his favourite officer, Custer leads the rest to the Little Bighorn, where the arrows are more hostile. Returning from his honeymoon Scott finds himself accused of cowardice. To prove he's anything but, he crosses enemy lines in order to retrieve Custer's body.' 'We ain't accusin him of cowardice,' chorused the wranglers, 'we're accusin him of bein queer.' 'Morons!' cried Peppercorn. 'You have permitted your prejudice to blind you to Scott's greatness as an actor. Take the movies he made with Budd Boetticher. Scott was always the upright man, whose unbreakable code of honour was generally challenged by a chancer with easy charm, and easier morals. But his charm was lost on Scott, whose morality was bred in the bone, not the mind. "I don't do much thinking, Judge," he said in one such movie, when on trial for murder. It took a genius like Sam Peckinpah to force him to do some.

The upshot was *Ride the High Country*, in which Joel McCrea was given the part that once would have been Scott's while Scott himself was appointed to the devil's party. The two old-timers are hired to guard a shipment of gold. Recognizing at last that years of probity have won him neither profit nor respect, Scott decides to steal it. What follows is Scott's conscience made visible. In the end – thanks to McCrea's sacrifice – he learns that he was right in the first place: life ain't worth a shit if you can't enter your house justified.' 'I'll second that,' said Governor Janklow, who had arrived at the table unnoticed (perhaps because he was still wearing sweatshirt, jeans and Nike loafers). 'Are there any dissenters?' There were none. 'Motion carried,' said Governor Janklow, moving on. 'Did he know what we were talkin about?' wondered one of the wranglers. 'It doesn't matter,' said Peppercorn, 'the Governor's decision is final.' 'My daddy's a big fan of Randolph Scott,' whispered Mercy Sweetbriar in his ear.

Having concluded his intervention, the Governor proceeded on his way to the podium that commanded the vast dining arena. 'Before we enjoy the great food that has been prepared for us,' he announced, 'I'd like to invite my dear and valued friend, Webster Two Hawk, to say grace. For those of you who do not know him, he is not only an Episcopal priest, but also Chairman of the South Dakota Commission on Tribal Relations. As such he has been participating in the inquiry I initiated at USD, to find out how fairly Indians are treated in our adversarial court system. Not very, according to his experience with lawbreakers. Mine too, if we go back to when I was a young lawyer on the Rosebud Reservation. I cared, but others didn't, and I saw at first hand how too many Indians were going to jail thanks to prejudice and the want of funds to hire a decent lawyer. Being a good Christian, Webster thinks we need more than a few pro-bono lawyers to alter the balance. He believes that we should move away from a system hell-bent on punishing people, towards one more interested in rehabilitation. Come, Webster, come say a few words on our behalf in honour of the man who lived and died by such ideals.' Unlike his friend, Webster Two Hawk was wearing a suit. He prayed in Lakota, his native tongue. Peppercorn understood but two words: Jesus Christus.

'Just one more item before you finally get to eat your prime ribs,' said the Governor. 'I'd like to ask Mike Pflaum, Acting Superintendent of this incomparable site, to share a few memories of the President's recent visit with you all.' 'As I recollect,' said Acting Superintendent Pflaum, reading from a sheet of American quarto, 'he called Bill over there "a piece of work". Actually what he said was, "I appreciate so very much your Governor, Bill Janklow, for being here. Bill has been a friend of mine for a long period of time. He might have invented the word 'piece of work.' But he's a good piece of work." Most of all, the President appreciated the special meaning this beacon of democracy had acquired since 9/11. "But what a magnificent place on such a beautiful day to talk about America and the challenges we face," he said. "I mean, after all, standing here at Mount Rushmore reminds us that a lot of folks came before us to make sure that we were free. A lot of pioneers came to this part of the world to make sure that enterprise could flourish. A lot of our predecessors faced hardship and overcame those hardships, because we're Americans. And that's what's going to happen in this era too. We've got problems. We've got challenges. This generation has got challenges to meet, and we're going to meet those challenges head on . . . I'm glad to come to share that optimism with you in this historic spot." Eloquent as they are, the President's words do not fully capture the impact of his presence here. You had to be in the audience that day to feel the force of it. But you'll understand well enough when I say that folks seem to make a real patriotic connection with America and all it stands for right here in its geographical centre and spiritual heart.'

After the banquet was over Governor Janklow's guests were ushered outdoors, and led to a large amphitheatre fringed by shadowy pines. Once seated they were treated to a slide-show called Great Places, Great Faces. The faces on display were their own. They were projected on to a gigantic screen that completely eclipsed Washington, Jefferson, Lincoln and Roosevelt. For a few moments Peppercorn saw himself apparently shining down from the summit of Mount Rushmore. It was very seductive, as was the gift he found on his bed in the hotel. It was a black neckerchief with a buffalo printed upon it. Beside it was a card which read: 'Sweet dreams. Then tie on your bandanna, and get ready for the ride of your life tomorrow. Bill.' Peppercorn began to fear what he might permit if Governor Janklow were to knock on his door right now with a Clintonesque gleam in his eye.

Arising at 4.30 the following morning, the last Monday in September, Peppercorn telephoned his wife. 'The inner cowboy is ready to mount,' he said. 'Is the purpose of this call to inform me that you're about to fuck the rhinestone cowgirl?' she said. 'You are confusing my inner cowboy with my penis,' he said. 'What I'm saying is that the Buffalo Roundup is about to begin.' 'Don't tell me you'll be riding a horse like Billy Crystal in *City Slickers*,' she said. 'My inner cowboy is just taking his first tentative steps,' he said, 'riding will come later. Today I'll be in a Jeep of some sort.' 'Good luck,' she said.

In fact his first mode of transport was another SUV that took him (as well as Mercy Sweetbriar and several of the homophobic wranglers) deep into the untamed interior of Custer State Park. 'Jimmy Stewart,' exclaimed one of them suddenly, 'we forgot about Jimmy Stewart last night.' Peppercorn agreed that it was a shameful omission, and they were all fast friends again. Reaching the road's summit they were granted the vision of a fair pavilion in the valley below. It could have belonged to Saladin, but was actually functioning as Governor Janklow's alfresco mansion. Inside it smelt of coffee, maple syrup and hay. With their brown Buffalo Roundup jackets and their peaked brown caps, the gathering congregation looked like members of a private army awaiting final orders. Those orders came when the Governor himself assigned each to one of several open-backed Jeeps lined up outside the tent. Having clambered aboard, Peppercorn and his fellow passengers (three, including Mercy) were advised by their driver to cling for dear life to the racks that looped above their heads once the convoy started to roll. The terrain may look level, he explained, but it wasn't, being full of fissures, depressions, buffalo wallows and all sorts. At first the convoy moved in single file, a formation that remained intact until it had penetrated even deeper into the back country, whereupon all its component parts broke rank, each vehicle seeking its own vantage point.

Peppercorn's sped over prairie grass until it found a perch high on a ridge overlooking a long valley. It must have been a good spot because Governor Janklow's own vehicle appeared a few yards to the right of Peppercorn's. The slopes of the valley were spotted with dark-green trees, while rows of yellowing cottonwoods lined its floor. The remainder was filled with buffalo, hundreds and hundreds of them, who, for the moment, seemed unconcerned by the barrier of cowboys and jeeps blocking their exit.

Peppercorn had not felt such a thrill of anticipation since his father and uncle had promised to take him and his cousin (with whom he regularly played Cowboys and Indians) to a Wild West show at Wembley. Had the show lived up to expectations? Peppercorn no longer remembered. But what he did remember was his behaviour when taken backstage to meet the Redskins. Were they the real thing? Peppercorn had no idea. But they had certainly looked the part, with eagle feathers in their hair and warpaint on their cheeks, and otherwise bare coppery chests. Some grasped tomahawks or bows. One of them held out his hand to greet the young Paleface. Instead of taking it, Peppercorn cringed with fear. Just as he had done when presented with a saddled horse the day before yesterday. Now he had a chance to redeem himself, both in his own eyes and in those of Mercy Sweetbriar. He would bring the buffalo home. Peppercorn looked towards the Governor and waved. The Governor waved back.

Both watched from the heights as the herd was gradually driven towards the open end of the valley. Or at least the bulk of it was. A small remnant had broken away, and was heading uphill in Peppercorn's direction. 'Hold on!' shouted the driver, as he fired the ignition. Swinging round he added, 'Don't forget a full-grown bull can turn on a dime, and has the power to knock us all to kingdom come.' With that he hit the gas pedal, and the Jeep was suddenly bouncing along. Its mission: to head off and redirect the absconding beasts. Peppercorn could hear the drumming of their hoof-beats before he saw them. And then they appeared. About a dozen, cresting the rise, running steadily in single file, their dark and dripping tongues hanging from their pink mouths, their breathing loud. Whooping after them came a bunch of cowboys (and a few cowgirls), led inevitably by Bob Lantis. 'Yea, Bob!' shouted Mercy. Lantis touched his hat in acknowledgement and galloped on. To keep up with them the Jeep's driver was maintaining a speed in excess of thirty miles an hour. Peppercorn was pressing his camera to his eye with one hand while clinging on to the rail with the other. He focused on the bull's curly mane, its in-growing horns, and its brown eye looking angrily back at him. Daring to release his grip on the rail for a moment he squeezed the shutter, and definitely felt his inner cowboy stir as he captured the fleeing creature's likeness. The Peppercorn Kid stirred even more when Mercy Sweetbriar voluntarily elected to act as his anchor, wrapping her right arm tightly around his middle. 'Can't have you bouncing out of the truck!' she shouted against the wind.

Harried by horsemen and vehicle alike the buffalo did indeed turn, and the wranglers turned with them, forcing the mighty quadrupeds down the long slope of the hill. The Jeep was travelling faster than ever now, though never as fast as the leader of the charge, the silver Cadillac Escalade driven by Governor Janklow. Peppercorn tracked the vehicle through his viewfinder, trying to take a photograph as the Escalade helter-skeltered crazily over the corrugated ground. Eventually he managed to freeze his quarry with all four of its wheels airborne, his Illingworth moment.

When the Jeep hit the valley floor it barely slowed, but continued instead its hot pursuit through dry washes (where Peppercorn and the others had to duck and dodge branches to avoid decapitation) and across bumpy grassland until its task was fulfilled and the runaways amalgamated with the main herd, a million and more pounds of living flesh and blood, now funnelling through the open end of the valley in a whirl of dust. Eventually all fifteen hundred were brought in and secured in the stockades. The Roundup was done. The flag-bearer (a veteran in cavalry blue), who had been watching the proceedings from the back of his horse, furled Old Glory and slowly trotted away. Last to leave the field was Miss Rodeo South Dakota. She galloped across hill and dale, her white-as-snow Stetson blindingly bright, and her tight bodice of shimmering turquoise and silver chevrons radiating spangles of light.

Afterwards, steaks were barbecued. Peppercorn lined up for his, satisfied with his morning's labour, both as wrangler and photographer. Meanwhile, the real cowboys got down to business in the stockade, sorting out the bulls, the cows and the yearlings. It was necessary work. Winters were harsh in South Dakota, and every fall it was essential to reduce the herd to a sustainable level, which meant cutting out about five hundred head. Those surplus to requirements were sold off quickly at an auction in the Park; from there some unfortunates went straight to the slaughterhouse, but most were transferred to other herds, including some on Sioux land. Those not selected for life elsewhere – or death – were returned immediately to the Black Hills, except for the yearlings: before being released all two hundred had to be vaccinated and branded.

Spectators were invited to observe the operation, but only from walkways which overlooked the corrals. Peppercorn, however, persuaded the cowboys to let him stand among them. They toiled in silence, speaking neither to him nor to each other. The skittish yearlings were kept in a pen whose only exit was a narrow passage. One by one they were driven into it. Once within, the anxious creature's instinct prompted it to run. But the passage along which it ran led only to a blind wall of steel. Realizing that it was trapped, the terrified animal (whose brown eyes rolled until the whites were showing) tried to backtrack, only to hear a gate drop at its rear like the blade of a guillotine. It was, in effect, caged. Hands grabbed the struggling animal, and wrestled it to submission, whereupon prophylactic drugs were pumped into its flanks. Finally, a red-hot branding iron was pressed against its right shoulder, causing the surrounding fur to ignite, and the flesh beneath to burn. The smell of singed hair and roast flesh lingered long after the last of the yearlings had fled back to the hills.

What will remain of me in Mercy Sweetbriar's thoughts? Peppercorn wondered, as he took off from Rapid City. As a photographer he strove to produce red-hot images that would leave indelible scars upon the memory, but suspected that his true forte was the smell of fear. 'How's my little boy,' said his wife, when he reached home, 'did he enjoy his game of Cowboys and Indians?' Peppercorn joined the first two fingers of his right hand and pointed them at his wife. 'Bang, you're dead,' he said.

Mercy Sweetbriar was seated at her desk in Pierre on a merry morning in May when she unexpectedly received an email from her old pal Peppercorn, whom she had not quite forgotten. 'I must have done something right,' he wrote, 'because the editor of *Terra Incognita* just asked if I would consider a sequel to the Buffalo Roundup. Quick as a flash I suggested the Re-enactment of Custer's Last Stand. The editor was enthusiastic. As you know, the real thing happened on 25 June 1876. The next re-enactment is scheduled for 21 June 2003. Is there any chance of arranging a visit to Wounded Knee immediately thereafter?' 'Every chance,' replied Mercy, a sucker for men who considered 'thereafter' a part of everyday discourse. 'Ride em, cowboy,' said Peppercorn's wife, as she kissed her husband farewell.

'I swear you look more like my daddy every time I see you,' said Mercy Sweetbriar, at the other end of the journey. 'Is that good or bad?' asked Peppercorn. 'Oh, good,' said Mercy, 'I love my daddy.' She stooped to pick up one of Peppercorn's bags, but he would not permit it, and portered both to the rental that awaited him in the airport's parking lot. From where he trailed Mercy to the Alex Johnson. 'Welcome back, Mr Peppercorn,' said Cindy Olson, the hotel's tour coordinator and Mercy Sweetbriar's new best friend.

South Dakota seemed unchanging, but Peppercorn knew there was one big difference. November's mid-terms had seen the election of Governor Janklow to the House of Representatives in Washington, where he was now serving as the state's only Republican Congressman. 'What's it like having a new alpha male in the Governor's mansion?' he asked. 'To tell you the truth,' said Mercy, 'we were all so crazy about Governor Janklow that we can't quite believe he's not still there.'

'Bill Janklow isn't the only one to have risen in the world,' interjected Cindy. 'Even as we speak they are painting Mercy's name on an office door in the Department of Tourism.' 'I'm only the assistant to Marin's assistant,' said Mercy, 'but when both are away – as both are at present – I become the beneficiary of the trickle-down effect.' So saying, she handed Peppercorn a folded card. Depicted on the obverse was a mounted warrior cast in bronze. Astride a rearing horse, he was plunging a spear deep into the shoulder of a buffalo. Within were the words: 'Mr Kevin Costner cordially invites you to the Grand Opening of Tatanka.'

The date was 20 June. The time: 3.00 p.m. The location: Deadwood Hill, about a mile outside the notorious city. 'Since you are going to Deadwood tomorrow,' said Mercy, 'I thought you might like to be my beau.' Like he was going to say no.

'Some people have all the luck,' said Cindy. 'When it comes to Kevin Costner it's my destiny to always be the bridesmaid, never the bride. Even when he shot part of *Dances with Wolves* on my husband's ranch, I didn't get to meet him, because someone else was playing Mrs Olson back then. I'm told that Costner and Co. stuck around for three months. First they built a new Fort Hays – unimpressed by the real one in Kansas – next they filmed Lieutenant John Dunbar's arrival there. He doesn't stay long, you'll recall. Scarred by duty in the Civil War, he wants to be alone on the Frontier. The fort's commanding officer wishes him luck, watches him ride off, then blows his brains out. Finito. My husband wasn't bothered by all the comings and goings, he was being paid well enough. He just thought it odd – even a bit excessive – to pour so much real time and money into a scene that didn't take up but seven minutes of screen time. The abandoned fort was of no use to him, so he sold it to some folks who set it up elsewhere as a roadside attraction. You'll find it on Highway 16 between Rapid City and Mount Rushmore, alongside Marine Life, Reptile Gardens and Bear Country.'

Thirty minutes later Peppercorn and Mercy Sweetbriar were standing inside the office of the self-destructive officer. It was a room of substance. The golden breath of the evening sun vitalized the floaters of dust and caused the wooden floor to gleam. Sounds of carpenters at work – staccato conversation and sawing – came from above. All the sash windows were shut, but the resinous scent of newly cut pine seeped between the cracks and suffused the air, as though the men were not fixing the roof but preparing a funeral pyre for the fort's fallen commander.

Fort Hays was Dunbar's last encounter with civilization. The next people he met were the supposedly uncivilized Sioux. Mutual suspicion gave way to curiosity. Each tried to learn the other's language. Dunbar's tentative first steps came back to Peppercorn with such forceful clarity that he felt compelled to re-enact them. Dropping to his knees he began to scrabble around, using his index fingers to improvise horns. Mercy, an aficionado, recognized the scene instantly. 'Ah, tatanka,' she said. 'Tatanka,' echoed Peppercorn, before offering its translation: 'Buffalo.'

An afternoon of roaring heat had been forecast, but the wind that combed the prairie grass around Deadwood Hill (as well as the fair coiffures of Mercy Sweetbriar and Kevin Costner) kept the air cool. 'Are you going to speak to him?' asked Peppercorn. 'Only if I can think of something worth saying,' replied Mercy. In the meantime, they took the newly laid path that led to the world's third biggest assemblage of bronze sculptures. They saw it first from the distance, silhouetted against the blue sky: a trio of mounted braves in pursuit of ten or more larger-than-life buffalo. Observed in close-up it was clear that the fleeing buffalo were doomed. Ahead of them was a red gash in the prairie, down which three of the beasts were already tumbling. Those nearest reared and stumbled in terror. But even to pause was to invite the arrow or the spear, as another of the beasts had already discovered. Having some expertise in the matter himself, Peppercorn appreciated the courage of the hunters who were forcing their mounts into the heart of the maelstrom. Mercy Sweetbriar, however, was more taken with their bodies. All were naked, their loin-cloths leaving only their privates to the imagination. 'Sioux warriors sure had great asses,' she said, pointing to what the flying back flaps accidentally revealed. It was true that the warriors were classically proportioned, and had the look of immortals, but in reality they were as doomed as their prey. The sculpture did not celebrate a way of life. It was a memorial to its passing. Turning away, Peppercorn looked down upon the evergreen forest far below, and glimpsed a band of Sioux ghosting through the pines.

By contrast, the Sioux who mingled with the other guests on top of Deadwood Hill were all so solidly Sioux they looked as if they had come straight from central casting: wrinkled men in battered toppers and faded jackets jingling with campaign medals, unlined youths who resembled exotic rock stars, and shapely maidens modelling the latest line in Sioux chic. As the sun began to descend silence was requested, and the two hundred guests positioned themselves around a little podium. A tribal elder, blessed with long hair that shimmered like a trout's belly, stepped forward to offer a prayer. 'Every so often a man will receive a vision,' he began. 'This is not so unusual. What is unusual is to have the courage and determination to see it through to reality. Kevin Costner dreamed of telling the story of the buffalo, and through that the story of my people, for the Buffalo nation and the Sioux nation have been entwined since the first days, when the holy man, Tatanka, came to our aid in the guise of a great, shaggy beast. His message was one of peace and unity. Alas, it is a long time since my people have known either. But this place, which is a place of great spiritual energy, reminds us of what we may have forgotten. For that gift I offer a song for my brother Kevin, for his strength, his courage, his persistence, and for his love.' The chant that followed seemed more authentic to Peppercorn than Webster Two Hawk's, if only because it lacked the words, 'Jesus Christus'.

The sculptor, when summoned, was not some bushy-browed Hephaestus, but a dead ringer for Miss Norway. A naturalist from Custer State Park turned artist, Peggy Detmers spoke of a dream that had completely changed her life. Unlike Korczak Ziolkowski, she was using the word literally: while asleep a disembodied hand and voice had directed her to observe the creation of a buffalo from blueprint, via sculpture, to living thing. She understood that she was being directed to dedicate her talent to the depiction of the buffalo, though to what end was far from clear. Trusting the voice (which she later identified as Kevin Costner's) she complied and awaited further instructions. The Sioux –

inventors of the dream-catcher – took such a story in their stride. Peppercorn, however, had to work hard to suspend his disbelief.

Costner then arose to tell his side of the story. He was wearing cowboy boots, jeans, black polo neck, shades. He recalled his first visit to the Black Hills, some thirty years before. Newly graduated, he was on the road looking for adventure. A fellow adventurer, whose name he never knew, gave him a copy of *Bury My Heart at Wounded Knee*. Costner read it every night in the back of his truck, and every night he cried. 'I will always think of that stranger as an angel,' he said. The fate of the Sioux began to haunt him. 'Though I hoped for it,' he said, 'I knew there would be no happy ending. It seemed to cast a spell upon me, that book. Through it the history of this great region took a hold over me, and I would never be the same.' Never be the same as what? wondered Peppercorn. As the all-American boy who hitherto had unthinkingly sided with the cavalry?

In any event the conversion was made manifest in *Dances with Wolves*. 'This was a movie people in my community were not interested in making,' Costner pointed out. 'I soon realized that if this story was ever going to make it to the screen, it was something I would have to finance myself.' The end product was his contribution towards reversing the national amnesia over what had been done to the rightful landlords of the Black Hills. 'A crime was committed,' he said, 'and our fingerprints were everywhere.' His movie proved that the criminal act was not inevitable, that a pacific modus vivendi could have been established with the Sioux. The centrepiece of the movie – as of their culture – was a great buffalo hunt. Shooting it provided the spark for

Tatanka. Thus inspired, Costner made the call that Peggy Detmers had been expecting for years.

They met in Deadwood, and (over drinks) made preliminary sketches on the back of a napkin. 'The result,' said Costner, 'is a sculpture that cannot be repeated anywhere else in the world, a sculpture that will certainly outlive everyone here, giving silent testimony to the beauty and skill of a culture that once reigned here supreme.' By now Peggy Detmers was red-eyed with weeping. Mercy's eyes, Peppercorn noted, were also looking unusually bloodshot. 'For these reasons,' concluded Costner, 'what would logically seem like an end stands clearly as a beginning. Tatanka is meant as a meeting place for two civilizations, where both can begin to appreciate the heroic qualities of the other. For me – and for Peggy – it is a way of saluting the courage of the Lakota people in hanging on to their language and their spirituality. We are in awe of the fact that, despite everything we have thrown at you, you are still standing.' As soon as the applause subsided Mercy leapt forward to give her idol a hug. Peppercorn noted that there was a brief exchange. 'What did you say to him?' he asked. 'I said that *Dances with Wolves* had completely changed my attitude towards the Native Americans,' said Mercy, 'and he said that he felt very gratified. He also told me not to miss *Open Range*, which premiers in August.'

The Midnight Star, on Main Street, was Kevin Costner's other contribution to Deadwood's cultural milieu. The brick building was large enough to contain numerous bars, a couple of casinos, and a classy restaurant with a jazz pianist. Peppercorn suggested dinner, but Mercy insisted she only had time for a Diet Pepsi. 'I promised to spend the evening with Cindy in Rapid City, and I want to get there before the Friday-night DUIs begin their killing spree,' she said. Seeing Peppercorn's expression she added, 'No need to look so crestfallen. We'll meet again on Monday, when you return to South Dakota. Besides, I'll be leaving you in good company.' A hostess in black beachwear, topped with a jelly-mould bra (into which her breasts fitted as best they could), was leaning over him to take their order.

After Mercy's departure Peppercorn downed a second Maker's Mark, and wandered aimlessly from floor to floor. As he ascended the stairs he passed the costumes Costner had worn in various Westerns, which hung framed on the walls. Among them were Wyatt Earp's empty suit and Lieutenant Dunbar's vacant uniform. Peppercorn recognized them for what they were: promiscuous garments, for hire to anybody. As such they symbolized the democratic nature of American history, or at least that part of it that was played out on the frontier. Any actor or re-enactor could try them for size, declare them a perfect fit, and then behave as if they were as one possessed, with unique insight into the thoughts, words and deeds of the born-again hero. The same went for historians. Nor were the men he was going to see fight to the death on a battlefield in Montana any different. Custer, Crazy Horse, Sitting Bull: nothing now but empty outfits awaiting reanimation.

Early next morning, as the re-enactors awoke in Montana, Peppercorn crossed the state line north-west of Spearfish and entered Wyoming. Until the middle of the nineteenth century the Sioux had Wyoming more or less to themselves. Outsiders called it the Great American Desert. It was said to be baking in summer, forty below in winter, and fit only for nomads and the innumerable buffalo they hunted. Its desirability changed in the 1860s, however, when gold was discovered near Bannock in Montana, and the Bozeman Trail opened. Thereafter the freedom of the paleface to wander at will began to clash with that of the Sioux.

Although the Sioux were a single nation, they were divided into several tribes. Sitting Bull was a Hunkpapa. Crazy Horse's mother was a Brule, though he chose to live with the Oglala (his father's people). Red Cloud was also an Oglala (the most sagacious and long-lived of them all). Throughout the 1860s his was the voice that spoke with greatest authority. Having learned from precedents set elsewhere, he knew that the new immigrants, if not immediately chastised, would quickly threaten his people's way of life. So he called upon the Big Bellies, as the elders were known, and upon the Shirt Wearers, a quartet of leaner and younger men chosen for their courage, selflessness and leadership potential. His aim was to put a spoke in the wheels of manifest destiny. The Big Bellies and the Shirt Wearers nodded their approval. Attacks upon the interlopers commenced at once.

Washington, still dazed and confused by the Civil War and the assassination of Lincoln, was not ready for more hostilities, and so invited Red Cloud to a peace conference at Fort Laramie. Red Cloud refused the first overture, but in 1866 agreed to attend. At the same time, General William Tecumseh Sherman, the army supremo, sent Colonel Henry Carrington into the area with orders to construct a line of forts along the Bozeman Trail. When news of this two-faced negotiating technique reached Red Cloud he stormed out of the conference and prepared to renew his bloody campaign.

Carrington meanwhile had picked a pleasant spot for his headquarters, or so Peppercorn thought, when he found its remains at the fork of Big and Little Piney Creeks. More than four thousand logs had been used to construct the stockade, known as Fort Phil Kearney, which was 8 feet high and 1496 feet around. Despite the army's presence, attacks on the prospectors increased. Carrington made efforts to protect them, but he had no experience of fighting Indians (or anyone else, for that matter), and seemed in no hurry to alter that state of affairs. Then, late in 1866, Captain William Fetterman was visited upon him. Cocky, blooded, and a confirmed Indian-hater, he was determined to become an Indian-fighter too. He taunted Carrington for his caution (which he hinted was lack of backbone), and boasted that with eighty good men he could subdue the entire Sioux nation.

When the first snows fell, it became apparent that Fort Phil Kearney would require a never-ending supply of wood to sustain life. The wagons sent to gather it were constantly harassed, though the attackers were often merely decoys. On one occasion Carrington chased them off, only to find himself face to face with a huge war party. He turned tail, but not quickly enough: two men died. Thereafter he forbade any pursuit. On December 21 another party of woodcutters was attacked. Fetterman was so insistent that he be allowed to reinforce them that Carrington gave in, with the proviso that he was on no account to follow the Indians over Lodge Trail Ridge. In every fairy story – especially the grim ones – the reader knows with absolute certainty that such prohibitions will inevitably be ignored.

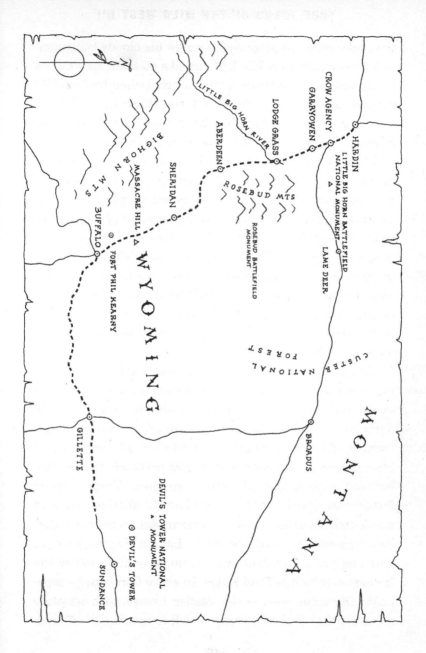

Perhaps Carrington knew it too, because he let Fetterman have his eighty men.

It is said that Crazy Horse (one of the aforementioned Shirt Wearers) was a brilliant decoy that day, the one who led Captain Fetterman's men the merriest of dances. Before long – and despite the better judgement of most of them – they had transgressed: they had been lured over Lodge Trail Ridge. They had time for one last look around them. Deep snow covered the ground, from hilltop to horizon, affording them a sneak preview of eternity. Then they peered down. Immediately, they recognized the wisdom of their commanding officer's injunction. The coulee they were looking into must have contained a thousand Sioux and Cheyenne. Waiting just for them. Nor could they regain the ridge. As many Indians had amassed to their rear. The trap closed. They could hold out for no more than twenty minutes. By then each soldier's ration of blood was bordered by snow, so that in death all resembled Santa Claus. Some say that Fetterman saved his last bullet for himself, others that he and his second in command shot each other in the head simultaneously. American Horse later claimed that both versions were lies, and that he and none other had clubbed Fetterman to the ground and slit his throat. Red Cloud, when asked, replied that he did not remember American Horse's presence at the battle.

Poor Fetterman. No posthumous glory for him. No re-enactment of his embarrassment. Unlike Custer, he was all but forgotten, his only memorial a tall stone cairn which Peppercorn found at the summit of Massacre Hill. Attached was a brass plaque. It read: 'On this field on the 21st day of December, 1866, three commissioned officers and seventy-six privates of the 18th US Infantry, and of the 2nd US Cavalry, and four civilians, under the command of Captain Brevet Lieutenant Colonel William Fetterman were killed by an overwhelming force of Sioux under the command of Red Cloud. There were no survivors.' More recently a second memorial tablet had been added, which was in effect a critique of the first. 'Today this monument still honors the battlefield dead,' it began, 'but it should be remembered that members of two cultures died here, both fighting for their nations . . . "There were no survivors" obviously refers only to US military casualties, since approximately fifteen hundred Sioux and Cheyenne did survive.' It concluded that the language of the original marker reflected 'racial feelings of the times', the clear implication being that times had changed for the better. Certainly the bloodied snows of yesteryear were long gone. In their place Peppercorn looked down upon summer meadows sparkling with yellow pea. And rather than dark and bellicose smoke signals, white puffball clouds hovered above the distant Bighorn Mountains, as if each peak were smoking the pipe of peace. Was it really true? Did the two peoples live in harmony at last?

Peace came for the first time in 1868, when Washington effectively surrendered to Red Cloud at Fort Laramie. The Bozeman Trail was closed, as Red Cloud had demanded, and all the forts that protected it abandoned. Fort Phil Kearney was immediately torched by the local Cheyenne. The month was August, the wood was dry. It burned in next to no time. For a few years it seemed that those flames were a symbol of hope, that Red Cloud's vision had indeed saved his people from the common fate. It was their *Dances with Wolves* moment. But Peppercorn knew, as well as Kevin Costner, that there was to be no happy ending. Custer's 1874 Black Hills Expedition saw to that.

After the presence of gold became public knowledge, the pressure on the Sioux was relentless. Prospectors were no longer required to suffer on exposed trails as they had in 1868; now they had trains. They took full advantage, and arrived in their thousands. In order to legitimize the anticipated theft, Washington offered to buy the Black Hills for six million dollars. Neither Sitting Bull nor Crazy Horse were prepared to sell so much as a handful of dust, but Red Cloud had grown realistic and was ready to negotiate. Much good it did him, thought Peppercorn. The talks failed. An ultimatum was issued by President Grant: any Sioux still living in the traditional way after 31 January 1876 would be treated as hostile. In other words, it was life on a reservation or death. Sitting Bull and Crazy Horse obviously failed to understand they had no choice but choose. So Custer and the 7th were dispatched to teach them a lesson. Peppercorn drove directly from the site of the Fetterman Massacre to the place where the lesson was learnt, the place known as Greasy Grass to the victors, and Little Bighorn to the vanquished.

The first thing Peppercorn saw was Last Stand Hill, where Custer and his closest associates (including his brother Tom) had sought sanctuary. They probably thought they could see for miles from their vantage point. They may even have thought they were safe. But the terrain was deceptive, being criss-crossed with blind coulees, out of which hundreds of Sioux and Cheyenne unexpectedly emerged to disabuse them. Lingering on its summit under a bright sky, Peppercorn could hear the wind breathing through acres of wild grasses and see the pale yucca bells sway. Only the white markers, bearing the legend 'US Soldier 7th Cavalry Fell Here June 25, 1876', failed to respond. Peppercorn understood that there were 249 in total.

In reality, there was no Randolph Scott to ensure that the fallen were given a decent burial. On the contrary, the dead and nearly dead were stripped to the buff and mutilated. According to one version, two Cheyenne women found Custer's corpse, and perforated his eardrums with an awl, to punish him for not listening when their chiefs spoke words of peace. After those unwelcome attentions, the dead were left unattended for three further days, until soldiers came to bury them in shallow troughs more or less where they fell. A year later the remains of Custer and the other officers were reinterred in grander plots elsewhere. The enlisted men were stacked neatly in a mass grave.

What had brought them to such an undignified end was a series of catastrophic errors made by their leader, the worst of which occurred at a place called the Crow's Nest. It was from there that Custer's scouts had first witnessed the overwhelming strength of the new Indian alliance, pulled together by the power of Sitting Bull's charisma. But Custer wasn't bothered by the unprecedented number of lodges. He was more worried by the possibility that he had forfeited the element of surprise, his signature tactic. This explains why he made the elementary mistake of dividing his command. First he ordered Captain Frederick Benteen south with 125 men to scout the bluffs and report all comings and goings. Then he sent Major Marcus Reno and a further 140 men in hot pursuit of a small band of warriors that suddenly showed itself, and equally suddenly turned

45

tail. Reno will fall upon the village, he thought, like a wolf upon the fold. And he would be waiting for the panic-stricken heathens. Instead of safety they would find only a mighty fist awaiting. He turned his horse and led his men to the north-west at a gallop.

Back in the twenty-first century, Peppercorn considered an alternative proposition: that Custer's decision to divide his forces was no error, but a calculated gamble. The risk was big, but then the stakes were higher than ever. And if Custer's luck held, as it always had in the past, the honour of defeating Sitting Bull, Crazy Horse and God knew who else would belong to him alone. He could already picture his triumphal entry and progress at the Centennial Exhibit in Philadelphia on 4 July, little more than a week away. Or perhaps his imagination had taken him beyond even that, to the not-too-distant day when his accumulated glory would sweep him to the presidency. This was an ambition not entirely thwarted by his death, for his reputation proved immortal, and just kept marching on: in the fullness of time it graduated from dime novels to Hollywood, where General George Armstrong Custer featured in numerous epics, and was impersonated not only by Errol Flynn but also by Ronald Reagan. So you could say that Custer's gamble paid off in the long run, concluded Peppercorn, that he made it to the White House after all – if only by proxy.

Last Stand Hill was connected to the Crow's Nest by Battlefield Road, enabling Peppercorn to retrace the 7th's path to destruction. What Custer didn't know, as he rode boldly along it, was that Reno had been suckered, just as Fetterman had been ten years before. Both had chased decoys and paid the price. The few who survived the ambush (including Reno) scrambled to the bluffs, where Benteen and his shattered battalion soon joined them. There they remained until well into the next day, pinned down by deadly fire from Sharpshooter Ridge (on which Peppercorn now stood). It was at Medicine Tail Coulee (where Custer first grasped the true extent of the opposition's strength) that the word 'ignominious' first began to vie with 'glorious' in his vocabulary – to such a nagging degree that he scribbled a useless message ordering Benteen to abandon the scouting mission and rejoin the main body: 'Come on, big village. Be quick. Bring packs. Hurry.' At Medicine Tail Ford, where Custer's diminished command launched an unsuccessful raid on the great encampment's ragged edge, Peppercorn was given a fright, for he really could see men of the 7th Cavalry skirmishing with mounted warriors in the shallow waters of the Little Bighorn. Shots were fired and stricken men tumbled from their mounts into the stream. Others, already soaked, were engaged in fierce hand-to-hand combat. A makeshift stadium on the far bank, packed with spectators, gave the game away.

The road curved sharply, then ascended to Greasy Grass Ridge, where waiting snipers cut Custer's boys to pieces. Those still able made it to Calhoun Hill, at which point it became every man for himself. A cluster of markers was all that remained of Captain Myles Keogh's company, brought low by Crazy Horse's unstoppable charge. All bar one shot their horses, and used what protection their corpses afforded. The exception was Myles himself. According to some eye-witness accounts he crouched between his mount's legs, not letting go of the reins, even after he was killed. Respecting this bond, the Sioux left the horse where it stood. Next came Deep Ravine, through which, according to latest research, a few desperate troopers tried to flee from the inevitable. Some now reckon that they were actually the last to die.

'Tell me,' asked Peppercorn of a park ranger in the Visitor Center, 'I've got a ticket for the re-enactment in Hardin. Did I pick the wrong re-enactment?' 'That's for you to decide,' he replied. 'The one up in Hardin's the official one, but the one you maybe saw from Battlefield Road is clearly much closer to the actual site. Could be that makes it more authentic.' 'Is one Custer superior to the other?' asked Peppercorn. 'Can't tell you that either,' replied the ranger. 'They've got a new man in Hardin. Don't recall his name. Steve Alexander did it eight times in a row, but this year he switched loyalties. Don't ask me why. Folks say he's as close to the real thing as you're likely to get. I do know that he purchased Custer's property over in Monroe, Michigan, and even sleeps in the old devil's bed.'

The site for the official re-enactment of Custer's Last Stand was a dusty field six miles beyond Hardin's city limits, which placed it plumb in the middle of nowhere. Because there was rain on the wind and thunder in the air, the powers that be had elected to postpone its start, hoping for clearer skies. It amused Peppercorn to learn that their chairman was a certain John Dahl, owner of Dahl's Funeral Chapels, a state-wide chain. Wandering around, he felt he was among circus folk, even though he could see no elephants. A woman in sweatshirt and jeans was chatting to a medicine man who had a bear's head augmenting his own. Red Indians and 7th Cavalry squaddies snacked, but at separate tables. A woman in pioneer-style bonnet and skirts purchased a tamale. Two types of drink were also on sale: cola and water. Peppercorn requested the latter, but the vendor just looked at him as though he were speaking Chinese. 'What's he want?' he asked of the pioneer. 'Wtr,' she replied. Although cloudbursts were visible everywhere none occurred overhead. Lightning also remained a distant phenomenon, save for one flash which forked up and down like a stairway to heaven. It was followed by a crack of nuclear proportions, loud enough to startle the horses. One reared so high on its hind legs that a back somersault seemed inevitable. Its rider, caught unawares, slipped out of the saddle and straight over the horse's rump. The terrified creature balanced for a moment longer on two legs, but its momentum was unstoppable, and down it went. How could its erstwhile rider not be crushed? But both arose, the one kicking the other furiously.

Peppercorn spotted an army wife chatting to a couple more men from the 7th. She was wearing her cap (with its badge of crossed sabres) at a jaunty angle. Her cavalry tunic was tight and buttoned to the throat. She was unmistakably Libbie Custer. Peppercorn told her she looked very fetching, and asked if he might take her picture. 'Are you flirting with me?' she enquired. He told her he was a photographer by profession. She told him that she taught business studies at a college in Hardin, and knew just enough about the economics of photography to be pretty certain that the majority of its practitioners would do well to attend her course. 'How long have you been Mrs Custer?' he asked. 'This is my third year,' she replied. 'Have you learned much about her?' he asked. 'Mainly that she was a loyal wife,' she replied, 'as am I to Mr O'Dell. In fact she was more than loyal, she was absolutely crazy about her Autie (which is what she called Custer), and he was no less enamoured of her. Libbie liked to accompany him in the field, and he was happy to oblige, so long as there was no real danger. After his death she was an equally devoted widow, outliving him by nearly sixty years, and never remarrying. D'you have a wife, Mr . . .?' Before Peppercorn could answer there was an announcement calling the re-enactors to their stations, and the spectators to their seats in the bleachers.

When they had settled, the director stepped forward to crave their indulgence. He wanted to remind them that while no performer was likely to get killed, the re-enactment was not risk-free. Horses were sometimes unpredictable, and the bullets – though all blanks – could do considerable harm if misused. By way of demonstration he levelled a loaded pistol at a can and fired. The impact ripped it open. 'Kids,' he said, 'if that's what a blank does, imagine what a real bullet could do. So never never go near a gun unless you're in the company of a responsible adult.' (Peppercorn wondered what sort of responsible adult would let a child anywhere near a gun, but he was probably in a minority of one.) 'Don't you go thinkin I'm some namby-pamby type who believes guns should be taken away from the people,' added the director. 'I'm shoulder to shoulder with Charlton Heston on that. What did he say? "You can have my gun . . . When my fingers are stiff and cold."' It got him a cheer.

'The director's name was Richard Sobek, though he preferred to be known as Bear. He was a big man, with a grey beard and long grey hair, and wore a black suit with a buttoned-up waistcoat that made him look more like a card sharp than a man of the theatre. He laid great emphasis upon the fact that his scriptwriter was an Indian. 'For once,' he said, 'the famous story will be told from an Indian point of view.' That made it sound as if there were only one Indian point of view, whereas Peppercorn knew different. For example, the scouts who found Sitting Bull's encampment for Custer were Crow. The Crow were happy to scout for Custer because they hated the Sioux even worse than they hated the paleface. One of their number was known as White Man Runs Him; his step-grandson, Joe Medicine Crow, was the author of Sobek's script. There was no denying that a Crow point of view was an Indian point of view, but it was obviously never going to speak for the Sioux – especially as the Crow liked the Sioux no better now than they did then. This led to a big problem when it came to casting, since the re-enactment of Custer's Last Stand took place on Crow land, where the Sioux remained unwelcome. The only solution was for the descendants of Custer's allies to play his (and their) mortal enemies. 'Let history and legend begin!' cried Sobek confusingly.

So how did this revisionist pageant commence? With a parade led by Custer, wearing buckskin and a bright red neckerchief. The audience applauded him like crazy. At his side rode another officer, and behind them came two sergeants holding aloft the Stars and Stripes and the pennant of the 7th Cavalry. They were followed by the troopers, the dog soldiers. As they circulated around the field, loud country music filled the air: 'And I'm proud to be an American, / where at least I know I'm free. / And I won't forget the men who died, / who gave that right to me. / And I gladly stand up, / next to you and defend her still today. / 'Cause there ain't no doubt I love this land. / God bless the USA.' Peppercorn reluctantly followed the example of his neighbours and stood, though he could not bring himself to place a fist upon his heart. He didn't dare not doff his hat, however.

Then Sitting Bull appeared, also carrying the Stars and Stripes, trailed by Crazy Horse doing likewise. So much for the Indian point of view . . . The woman beside Peppercorn could barely contain her patriotism, singing words she clearly intended for God's ear. Maybe she has a son or nephew in Iraq, thought Peppercorn, some of these people surely must. In which case why are they so enthused by the sight of a reckless leader whose bad end they are about to witness? A bugler, sent by Custer's descendants in Michigan, walked out into the centre of the field and played taps for the dead soldiers. On cue the spectators rose again, like they had springs up their backsides.

The seat into which Peppercorn descended for the umpteenth time was located directly above the performers' entrance. It turned out, however, that the performers were not actually required to speak: instead, their parts were voiced by high-school students, who observed proceedings from a glass booth. This is not Custer's Last Stand exactly, Peppercorn thought, more an illustrated guide to the philosophy and execution of Westward Ho-ism. While the dumbshow continued, he observed the growing restlessness of the eager young bucks waiting for action, especially when they caught sight of a wagon train on the immigrant trail. The pioneer woman who got Peppercorn his wtr was walking alongside one of the horse-drawn wagons. He felt a strange obligation to warn her of impending danger. Meanwhile, the restlessness was increasing as more and more Indians nudged their ponies into the confined space. Most of them were naked to the waist, their chests and faces streaked with warpaint. Their mounts, sensing that something was up, sniffed the air and got a blast of testosterone and adrenaline, which did nothing to calm them. The more experienced performers tried to curb this overexuberance, which was edging close to violence, reminding them that the safety of all depended upon them awaiting their cue. These old pros were resplendently attired, especially in the hat department, with gorgeous warbonnets, buffalo heads, and wolf pelts. But they cut no ice with the unruly young. Soon everyone was jostling for position, and when the call finally came the riders lit out as if in a race. 'Indian attack!' screeched the loudspeaker. Alerted, the wagons began to form a circle, around which the attackers spun. When all seemed lost the distant sound of a bugle was heard, and the cavalry pitched in, slashing and shooting until the Indians were put to flight.

But not for long. The story marched on to 1874, and Custer's Black Hills Expedition. The bloody climax was approaching. The event Peppercorn had travelled many miles to see. Significant events began to speed by. Sitting Bull recounted his sun-induced vision of the upside-down soldiers falling lifeless from their upside-down horses into the Sioux lodges, a sure premonition of victory. Equally confident, Custer led the 7th Cavalry out of Fort Abraham Lincoln, near Bismark, for what turned out to be the last time. Libbie rode part of the way with him in a buggy, then husband and wife kissed, also for the last time. At which Peppercorn found himself unexpectedly moved.

When the scene shifted to the Little Bighorn he recognized certain key moments. There was Custer with White Man Runs Him at the Crow's Nest. And that must be Reno's ill-advised charge. The equestrian skills on display were extraordinary. Riders from both sides weaved in and out of the struggle without any apparent misjudgements or entanglements. The trouble was that the horses kicked up a lot of dust, thereby hampering visibility to a considerable degree. As the battle progressed Peppercorn became increasingly uncertain as to what he was photographing. Eventually he hadn't a clue, for whatever was happening was happening within a cloud. The dramatic impact and pathos of the final act was further reduced by the decision to stage it on the remote rise, so that it was rendered almost invisible by both dust and distance. The first indication that Custer had fallen came when the victorious Indians emerged from the fog of war bearing their spoils.

After the dust had settled, Peppercorn entered the field of battle hoping to get a word with Custer himself. Although the friendly Crow were only pretending to be Sioux, Peppercorn could not help but notice signs of tension along the racial fault-line. The hot spot was a dispute between a cavalryman and a brave, both still mounted. Peppercorn gathered the latter had done something unscripted and probably dangerous during the final melee, which had caused the officer to lose his temper and say something he now felt it necessary to apologize for. At the same time he felt obliged to berate the young brave for his foolhardiness, and expect some expression of contrition in return. Nothing doing. The Crow wouldn't give an inch. Whereupon the officer did a stupid thing: he got on his high horse and, like a power-drunk referee with a red card or an Indian agent of yesteryear, tried to dismiss the headstrong and unrepentant youth. Far from leaving, the Crow insinuated himself among a larger group of warriors. Meanwhile, other soldiers had ridden across in a show of support for their own. Peppercorn had been to enough football matches to recognize a punch-up in the making when he saw one. At the last moment, however, the officer attempted to mitigate his overbearing behaviour by nominating Crazy Horse for the role of ombudsman. Crazy Horse trotted over, looking thoroughly regal in his warbonnet and silver bracelets. The officer wrapped his arm around the great chief's shoulder and said, 'This man is my best friend, I'd trust him with my life.' Without further ado Crazy Horse evoked the universal solution to all sporting conflict, and ordered the potential combatants to shake hands.

Custer on his horse with the descending sun behind him cut quite a figure. Seeing Peppercorn sneaking a portrait he wondered if he might have a copy. His real name, he said, was Tony Austin, born not in the saddle but in Brighton. His family had emigrated to British Columbia in 1967, where he still lived and worked as a letter-carrier, when not pursuing his alternative career as General Custer. His life as someone else had begun in 1988, when he started dressing as the General. His first public appearance was at the Little Bighorn Association a year later. Since then he had represented his hero and better half at museums, country fairs, and Captain Jack's Wild West show. He had also stood in for Custer at the behest of many American artists, including Don Spaulding, whose *Thoughts of Libbie* had won an award at the American Cowboy Artists show in El Paso, Texas. 'That's all very well,' Peppercorn said, 'but he keeps dying on you. How do you feel about that?' 'Very moved,' Custer's alter ego replied. 'Every time I go down I try to think how he must have felt, watching his two brothers die, and knowing that he would never see his beloved Libbie again. Not to

mention all the unrealized ambitions of a half-spent life.'
Peppercorn remembered the Crow's Nest, the crossroads of
Custer's life, and wondered if he had considered the possi-
bility that a wrong turn might cost him everything.

Not that the victors fared much better. Theirs was a truly
pyrrhic victory. The great confederation quickly broke into
its various components, each one of which was hunted down
and mercilessly subdued by Washington's long arm. Even
the great Sitting Bull and Crazy Horse were starved into
submission. In the event, Crazy Horse outlived Custer by no
more than a year. Sitting Bull did better, surviving until
1890, but in the end he too was murdered by a co-tribalist
(albeit one co-opted as an agency cop). However, sagacious
Red Cloud experienced a more peaceful old age, having
declined to join Sitting Bull's defiant coalition, and retired
to what was now the Pine Ridge Reservation.

It was to the Cultural Center named in Red Cloud's
honour that Peppercorn headed on the Monday for his
reunion with Mercy Sweetbriar. Leaving Hardin long before
dawn, he drove south through Montana, Wyoming and
South Dakota, and reached the rendezvous at noon precisely
(as arranged). Upon seeing him again Mercy issued her
familiar whoop of joy – as did his inner cowboy in response.
'Hello, Sweetbriar,' said he. 'Hello, Peppercorn,' said she.
The Cultural Center encompassed a school, church, museum
and art gallery, and resembled a small university campus.
The school published an information booklet for visitors,
from which Peppercorn learned that the population of the
Pine Ridge Reservation was approximately thirty-six thousand; that its land was conducive to neither farming nor
industry, that unemployment stood at 85 per cent; that the

average per capita income was $4,000; that life expectancy
was fifty-five for men and sixty for women; that the infant
mortality rate was twice the national average, as was the
suicide rate; that diabetes affected 37 per cent of the population; and that alcohol was an even bigger problem. No
figures were quoted, but a child's prayer printed in another
of the school's leaflets ('If You Could See What They See')
gave a clue as to its prevalence and damaging effects: 'Dear
God, thanks for life. But, can you tell me somehow how you
thought of human people? Thank you for my body parts so
that I can move. Thank you for my family, even though they
like to drink. Thanks for school; without school, some of us
would probably be in jail.'

The Cultural Center was run by the 'Blackrobes' (as Red
Cloud called the Jesuits). One of their leading lights was
called Brother Simon. 'The Christianity we preach is carefully crafted to meet the needs of the Sioux,' he explained.
'But why do the Sioux need it in the first place, don't they
have an adequate religion of their own?' asked Peppercorn.
Brother Simon was not a Jesuit for nothing. 'Their time-
honoured traditions served the requirements of a nomadic
people,' he replied. 'But the Sioux are no longer a nomadic
people. So they need something more. Not instead of, but in
addition to. That something is Christianity. It places the
church at the centre of the community, and therefore roots
its worshippers to the spot.'

Brother Simon's church had recently hung several paintings depicting the stations of the cross. He called upon Ron
Kills Warrior, an alumnus turned teacher, to show them to
the visitors in order to prove his point. Although only
twenty-six, Ron Kills Warrior already had gravitas and girth

58

enough to be one of Red Cloud's Big Bellies. He led the pair
– whom he took to be father and daughter – through the
Holy Rosary's wooden doors. In the paintings within, Jesus
was unambiguously Sioux. 'Nor are the Romans Romans,'
said Ron Kills Warrior, 'but either men of the 7th Cavalry
or Crow.' 'What marks them out as Crow?' asked Peppercorn. 'Look again at their headdresses,' said Ron Kills
Warrior. 'Maybe now you can see they are shaped like birds?
A Sioux will register that detail instinctively.' 'Why Crow?'
asked Peppercorn (as if he didn't know). 'They were our pri-
mary enemies,' said Ron Kills Warrior, 'even before the
Europeans.' 'Are they still?' asked Peppercorn. Ron Kills
Warrior smiled, then shrugged. It was of course un-Christ-
ian not to forgive your enemies. 'They aren't supposed to
be,' he said. The last in the series showed Christ being
nailed to the cross by his own people. 'It is the greatest
humiliation in our culture when our own people – our own
family – turns against us,' explained Ron Kills Warrior.

Before Peppercorn could remind him that John XXIII
had let the Jews off the hook, seven middle-aged women
burst into the church. Wearing shorts or jeans they looked
like a bunch of sassy academics on a field trip. 'Shall we
invite them to join us?' asked Ron Kills Warrior. 'Libby
Bernardin,' said their leader, extending her hand. She added
that she taught creative writing at the University of South
Carolina, and that she had published poetry and a novel
called *The Stealing*, based upon the life of her Choctaw
grandmother. Her companions also hailed from South Carolina. All belonged to the same workshop, in which they
were able to freely reveal and discuss their most intimate
dreams without fear of embarrassment or ridicule. They had

travelled to the Pine Ridge Reservation to learn ancient techniques of divination from the Sioux. 'You are right to have come,' said Ron Kills Warrior. 'Dreams are important to my people. It is good to meet outsiders who understand that. When most outsiders say, "He's a dreamer," they mean it as a put-down. Such an attitude does much damage. For example, a boy dreams that one day he will become an important figure like a medicine man. He tells this to a counsellor from the Bureau of Indian Affairs, who says that it is foolishness best forgotten. This distresses and confuses the boy, so that his spirit leaves him, and he becomes lost. He begins to smoke, to drink, to say and do inappropriate things. Many on the Reservation still take this path. We endeavour to save as many as we can. It is not easy. As you know, prospects are very limited. One of the few available choices for young men is the military. It may astonish you to learn that forty-eight from Pine Ridge participated in Operation Iraqi Freedom.' 'Can you show us how to make our own dream-catchers?' asked Libby Bernardin. 'I am surprised that you have heard of our dream-catchers,' said Ron Kills Warrior, 'but I will be happy to give you a demonstration.' He led the group outside and into the sunlight. They followed him up a grassy bank, until he stopped beside a reddish tree trunk. 'You will need a bough from a cherry tree,' he said, breaking off one. 'Pick it carefully; it must be young and pliable. Bend it slowly. Bind it when you have formed a hoop. Build a web like a spider's within its centre. Place it above your bed.'

Pinned to the cherry tree was a wooden arrow pointing to the grave of Red Cloud. Peppercorn asked if it would be possible to pay their respects. Ron Kills Warrior said by all means. He herded them to the top of the slope, which opened upon a sparsely populated meadow. Red Cloud's handsome tomb was at its far end, flush against the barbed-wire fence. Its marble marker was festooned with prayer scarves in the traditional colours of white, yellow, red, green and blue, as well as flowers, and a swatch of tan suede that turned out to be a tobacco pouch. Red Cloud was buried alongside his wife Mary (who merited only a wooden cross). Born in 1835, she lived to the extraordinary age of a hundred and five. The couple had a daughter named Elizabeth (known to all as Libby). She married Slow Bear. 'Libby and Slow Bear were my great-grandparents,' said Ron Kills Warrior.

His great-great-grandfather was not as private as Crazy Horse and sat for several portraits. Most showed a man with features as strong as Mr Punch, and hair as long as Samson, but neither feature could disguise the fact that his strength was gone. His eyes did not meet the camera, and his mouth was clamped shut against the truth. No wonder. In September 1876, just three months after the great Sioux victory at Little Bighorn, and eight years after his own military and diplomatic triumphs, the fierce and far-seeing warrior was forced to sign a new document that reversed the Treaty of Fort Laramie and delivered the Black Hills, the sacred Paha Sapa, to the palefaces. When he finally spoke, it was with a bitter irony that must have tasted like poison: 'They made us many promises, more than I can remember, but they never kept but one. They promised to take our land, and they took it.' They did worse than that.

By 1890 the Sioux were broken and starving. Crazy Horse was but a memory. Their reservation had been divided into seven separate lots, and the better land between

sold to settlers. Hope was as scarce as food. This was all fertile soil for a false messiah. His coming was foretold by a
Paiute holy man named Wovoka, who claimed to have
entered the spirit world and been told that resurrection day
was any day now. Not only would the Indians' dead return,
but the buffalo too. As if that weren't enough, a great flood
would sweep the palefaces to oblivion. And Christ, when he
showed, would be no white man, but an Indian. While waiting for these miracles the Indians were to perform a dance,
which involved shuffling counter-clockwise with ever
increasing speed. At the same time they were to chant songs
of welcome for the returning dead. This is why it became
known as the Ghost Dance.

The cult spread from tribe to tribe. When it reached the
Sioux their dancers added shirts which, some claimed, were
impervious to bullets. The famous Ghost Shirts. The
authorities immediately asked themselves why the Sioux
needed bullet-proof vests. Ignoring the fact that followers of
this false messiah preached non-violence – were merely
repeating and adapting the good news they had heard often
enough from missionaries – they sent for more soldiers.
Their presence, in turn, made the Sioux jumpy. Then General Miles (in overall command, though stationed in
Chicago) ordered the arrest of Sitting Bull, thought to be
one of the new cult's ringleaders. Instead of arresting him,
the Indian policemen sent to do the job shot him. This
killing made the Indians even more excitable – though
scared might be a better word. Many of the Hunkpapa, now
leaderless, sought sanctuary with a band of Miniconjou
Sioux led by Big Foot. The army intercepted their flight and
ordered them all – Hunkpapa, Oglala and Miniconjou alike

– to make camp beside an ice-bound creek. There are many versions of what happened at Wounded Knee on the morning of 29 December 1890. The first – the army's – spoke of a great victory. Twenty Congressional Medals of Honor were issued with unseemly speed. The same Congress commissioned a report on the incident from General E. D. Scott. Its conclusion was unambiguous: 'There is nothing to conceal or apologize for in the Wounded Knee Battle – beyond the killing of a wounded buck by a hysterical recruit. The firing was begun by the Indians and continued until they stopped – with the one exception noted above . . . That women and children were casualties was unfortunate but unavoidable, and most must have been [killed] from Indian bullets . . . The Indians at Wounded Knee brought their own destruction as surely as any people ever did. Their attack on the troops was as treacherous as any in the history of Indian warfare, and that they were under a strange religious hallucination is only an explanation, not an excuse.'

But even among the army there was disquiet. General Miles, in particular, was appalled at what his officers in the field had done. Writing to the Commissioner of Indian Affairs in Washington (on behalf of the survivors), some twenty-seven years after the event, he repeated his unfavourable opinion: 'During the night Colonel Forsyth joined the command with reinforcements of several troops of the 7th Cavalry. The next morning he deployed his troops around the camp, placed two pieces of artillery in position, and demanded the surrender of the arms from the warriors. This was complied with by the warriors going out from camp and placing the arms on the ground where they were directed. Chief Big Foot, an old man, sick at the time and unable to walk, was taken out of a wagon and laid on the ground.

'While this was being done a detachment of soldiers was sent into the camp to search for any arms remaining there, and it was reported that their rudeness frightened the women and children. It is also reported that a remark was made by some one of the soldiers that "when we get the arms away from them we can do as we please with them," indicating that they were to be destroyed. Some of the Indians could understand English. This and other things alarmed the Indians and scuffles occurred between one warrior who had a rifle in his hand and two soldiers. The rifle was discharged and a massacre occurred, not only the warriors but the sick Chief Big Foot, and a large number of women and children who tried to escape by running and scattering over the prairie were hunted down and killed. The official reports make the number killed ninety warriors and approximately two hundred women and children. The action of the Commanding Officer, in my judgment at the time, and I so reported, was most reprehensible. The disposition of his troops was such that in firing upon the warriors they fired directly towards their own lines and also into the camp of the women and children, and I have regarded the whole affair as most unjustifiable and worthy of the severest condemnation. In my opinion, the least the Government can do is to make a suitable recompense to the survivors who are still living for the great injustice that was done them and the serious loss of their relatives and property – and I earnestly recommend that this may be favorably considered by the Department and by Congress and a suitable appropriation be made.'

To the Sioux it seemed the 7th Cavalry had taken belated but bloody revenge for Custer's humbling. It was an action best exemplified by the infamous photograph of Big Foot's frozen body, his head wrapped in a scarf, his unbelieving eyes open, his arm raised in supplication.

Mercy Sweetbriar had no qualms about showing Peppercorn the mass grave of the victims, located in a small cemetery at Wounded Knee, about half a mile from the scene of the crime. The cemetery stood at the summit of a low, lonely hill. At its base was an unpaved car park and an explanatory marker in some disrepair. It was headed 'Massacre of Wounded Knee', but the word 'Massacre' had clearly been tacked over the original 'Battle' in belated deference to local feeling. The path to the top was dusty. The walkway within was narrow. No flowers were growing, not even weeds. There were a couple of trees in the graveyard, and a few lines of them in the distance. Otherwise the short, undernourished grass rolled undisturbed to the horizon. The memorial itself was a tall, four-sided pedestal of stone supporting an urn. It was grey like a silver-fish. It said: 'This Monument is erected by surviving relatives and other Oglala and Cheyenne River Sioux Indians in memory of the Chief Big Foot Massacre. Dec. 29, 1890. Col. Forsyth in command of U.S. Troops. Big Foot was a great chief of the Sioux Indians. He often said "I will stand in peace till my last day comes." He did many good and brave deeds for the white man and the red man. Many innocent women and children who knew no wrong died here.' In addition to Chief Big Foot they were: 'Mr High Hawk, Mr Shading Bear, Long Bull, White American, Black Coyote, Ghost Horse, Living Bear, Afraid Of Bear, Young Afraid Of Bear, Yellow Robe, Wounded

Hand, Red Eagle, Pretty Hawk, Wm. Horn Cloud, Sherman Horn Cloud, Scatters Them, Red Fish, Swift Bird, He Crow, Little Water, Strong Fox . . .' The names continued, covering all four faces of the monument. Its modesty seemed hardly commensurate with the enormity of the deed it commemorated.

On the further side of the hill Peppercorn noticed a circular structure that looked like a pillbox built with nuclear conflict in mind. 'What's that?' he asked. 'You don't need to go there,' said Mercy Sweetbriar. 'Has it anything to do with the Massacre?' he asked. 'It's an exhibit of sorts,' she replied, 'organized by the American Indian Movement. How shall I put it? They have their own particular way of looking at things. Very one-sided. Very confrontational. To the point of hostility. Anyway, not very helpful.' 'Would you mind if I took a look,' he asked, 'just out of curiosity?' Despite her misgivings Mercy Sweetbriar gamely insisted upon accompanying Peppercorn down the hill. The building was mainly grey on the outside, and even gloomier within. A few females sat at trestle tables reading or talking. They took no notice of the newcomers. Hand-written manifestos and mini-histories, each illustrated with appropriate scenes, surrounded them. The image of Chief Big Foot's icy corpse was ubiquitous. The guiding principles of AIM were spelled out for all to see. If only they didn't sound as if they came from the desk of Stan Lee, thought Peppercorn. 'Pledged to fight white man's injustice to Indians, his oppression, persecution, discrimination and malfeasance in the handling of Indian affairs. No area in North America is too far or too remote when trouble impends for Indians. AIM shall be there – to help the native people regain human rights and achieve restitution and restoration.' Dated, Dec. 1973.

The significance of the date was explained a few steps on: 'During the 1970s terror once again filled the Pine Ridge Indian Reservation. The traditional Lakota people were being terrorized and murdered. The corrupt Tribal Chairman and his goons along with the FBI carried out the reign of terror. The Chiefs and Headsmen had meetings and called AIM to come and assist. On February 27, 1973 the siege began here, and the War was on for 71 days. Two Lakotas were killed in action, Buddy Lamont and Frank Clearwater, who gave the ultimate sacrifice. Lakota war leader Pedro Bissonette was gunned down by the BIA [Bureau of Indian Affairs] police 6 months after the takeover. The American Indian Movement was instrumental in a lot of the positive changes that affect us today. Indian pride was revived and the resurgence of our spirituality.'

Their chief antagonist was an ambitious assistant prosecutor in the State Attorney General's office. Guess who? 'Did you know that?' said Peppercorn. 'No,' said Mercy Sweetbriar. All she knew of the matter was that Bill Janklow had once been an idealistic young attorney, working for peanuts on behalf of poor Indian clients, and that he had numbered at least two of AIM's founders among his best friends. She understood he had been so well liked that he'd ended up more or less running the Rosebud Reservation's legal services programme. What she didn't know was that one of the responsibilities he had assumed was the guardianship of a schoolgirl named Jancita Eagle Deer. In fact, Mercy Sweetbriar had never heard of Jancita Eagle Deer. Amicable relations between Janlow and his clients (potential and actual) lasted until 14 January 1967, when

Jancita Eagle Deer sought a meeting with her school principal, and declared that her guardian had raped her. Mercy Sweetbriar didn't know that either. The case never came to court. Some say Janklow used his position to block it. Others that he didn't need to, because there was no case to answer. Either way, Janklow resigned his position and left the Rosebud Reservation, as did Jancita Eagle Deer. She remained a missing person for six years, until Douglass Durham, an AIM associate, traced her to Des Moins, Iowa, and brought her back to the Rosebud Reservation. Standing before the Tribal Court in late '73 she repeated her allegations. Janklow had ignored the summons, and was charged in absentia with, 'assault . . . intent to commit rape . . . carnal knowledge of a female under 16'. He received the maximum sentence: 'being disbarred from further legal practice on the Rosebud Reservation'. This handicap did not prevent him from becoming the state's new Attorney General in November 1974. If anything, it helped.

Jancita Eagle Deer and Douglass Durham, lovers by then, vanished from sight. The next thing anyone knew of Jancita Eagle Deer was in March 1975, when her body was found beside a road in Nebraska. Shortly before that Douglass Durham had been exposed as a long-time FBI informant. No connection was ever established – or even sought – between Durham and Jancita Eagle Deer's unexplained death, leading some to wonder at this judicial indifference. But not for long. The mystery of how the poor girl ended up as road-kill was soon forgotten when a far more spectacular event occurred on the Pine Ridge Reservation.

On 25 June 1975, two FBI agents had raided a cabin on

the property of Harry Jumping Bull, located midway between Wounded Knee and Manderson. Did they know the significance of the date, wondered Peppercorn, ninety-nine years to the day since the defeat of Custer? The agents had failed to find the fugitive they were seeking, but their suspicions were not allayed. The following morning the same two – Williams and Coler – returned to the Jumping Bull property. By noon both men were dead. Somehow they had become trapped in an exposed bowl, pinned down by continuous sniper fire from hidden gunmen on the surrounding ridges. However, that was not the actual cause of death in either case. Both were finished off by close-range shots to the head. In other words, they had been executed in cold blood. Three men were arrested and charged with first-degree murder. The first two were acquitted, because of the unreliability of the evidence offered. The third, however, was found guilty on the same tainted evidence. He was sentenced to life imprisonment. His name was Leonard Peltier.

One of the furies at the trestle table, registering the interest of the two strangers, approached them with a clipboard. 'Would you be willing to add your names to a petition calling on the government to free Leonard Peltier?' she inquired. Both Peppercorn and Mercy Sweetbriar hesitated. 'Nelson Mandela has already signed it,' added the woman, 'also Desmond Tutu and the Dalai Lama. But if you're still in need of convincing, read *In the Spirit of Crazy Horse* by Peter Matthiessen, which details what he calls, "the story of Leonard Peltier and the FBI's war on the American Indian Movement".' She explained that the war had initially been fought by proxy, through the corrupt running dogs who ran the Pine Ridge Reservation. As in any puppet Latin American dictatorship, opponents were beaten or murdered with the connivance of the greater power. When AIM elected to meet fire with fire, the involvement of the FBI became less covert. Matthiessen fearlessly exposed their habit of bearing false witness, and intimidating others until they did the same. However, the book's chief villain was none other than Bill Janklow. Among many things, Matthiessen discovered that poor Jancita Eagle Deer was not the first woman to accuse him of sexual assault. Janklow responded to its 1983 publication with a libel suit. He alleged that the book portrayed him as 'morally decadent, a drunkard . . . a racist and bigot'. He accused Matthiessen of peddling AIM lies, either 'with a reckless disregard for the truth or with actual malice for plaintiff'. He named the author, the publisher and three South Dakota bookstores as co-defendants. He sought damages of $24 million. Judge Gene Kean found in the defendants' favour. However, the Supreme Court of South Dakota reversed his decision, and requested reappraisal. Judge Kean saw no reason to change his mind. Nonetheless, Janklow pursued his claim with such zeal that no one was able to sell the book for seven long years, until once again the case came before Judge Kean, who dismissed it for a third time. On this occasion the Supreme Court of South Dakota backed him up. Despite vowing to do so, Janklow never pursued the matter as far as the United States Supreme Court. The book was republished in 1991. When the reality instruction was complete, not only Peppercorn but also Mercy Sweetbriar signed her petition. Free Leonard Peltier.

Mercy Sweetbriar walked back to her car without saying a word. Peppercorn followed her along the empty road from

Wounded Knee (pop. 328) towards Manderson (pop. 626). At
the crossroads just before Manderson she turned left down
a dirt road cut deep into the fields. Looking up, Peppercorn
could see the legs and hairy bulk of a small buffalo herd. The
viable track ended at a house of some substance. Mercy
Sweetbriar knocked at the front door and a little girl made
a reluctant appearance. It seemed that her father had gone
to the dentist. 'Pity,' said Mercy Sweetbriar, 'you would have
found his views of interest. He's not a member of AIM –
thinks they are too fond of guns – but is sympathetic to their
four principles of sovereignty, spirituality, sobriety, and support.' They were about to depart when Alex White Plum
himself emerged from the back of the house. He smiled. And
it became immediately apparent why a visit to the dentist
had been deemed more important than meeting Peppercorn.
His front teeth were missing. 'Appointment cancelled at the
last minute,' he said, 'so I won't be entering any beauty con-
tests for a week or two.' He was wearing work clothes and
a baseball cap. Uncombed hair sprang from either side. He
invited his visitors to sit on folding chairs in the backyard.
His dog (some sort of collie) sought affection, but was
brushed aside. 'I'm afraid that dogs are at the bottom end
of my totem pole,' he said. 'Top are my buffalo, which you
probably saw as you entered. Then come my horses, which
I breed. Mostly "medicine hats", greys with brown ears,
which are supposed to be able to hear the spirit world.' As
if summoned by some sympathetic magic a group of a dozen
suddenly galloped around his low fence, exciting the dog to
a frenzy of barking, followed by a brave riding bareback in
naught but shorts. 'Come Wednesday there will be a big race
around my land,' explained Alex White Plum. 'Unfortu-

nately, it is for young men only. In my day I was a champion racer. If the rules allowed it I'm sure I could still give the new generation a run for its money.' 'I just saw some excellent horsemanship up in Montana,' said Peppercorn, 'at the re-enactment of Custer's Last Stand. Have you ever been?' Alex White Plum snorted. 'Why would I travel hundreds of miles to see Crow apeing their betters? The enmity between our tribes is eternal. Because the Crow are not natural. They are intruders from somewhere else. Maybe across the Missouri.'

Not that Alex White Plum was always so proud to be a Sioux. At school he had been humiliated by his nationality. When he and his friends played Cowboys and Indians, they all wanted to be cowboys. His favoured heroes were John Wayne and Paladin from *Have Gun, Will Travel*. Tonto was a no-no. After high school he joined the army and was in Berlin for five years, during which time he ignored the order not to fraternize with the locals lest they be communists, and discovered that he would rather be a German than anything else. He also realized for the first time that the continent of Europe was divided into separate peoples, each with its own nation. He began to reconsider his position as an American, and concluded that he wasn't one. He wanted to be a Sioux in a nation run by Sioux. As a result he felt that recent military adventures had nothing to do with him. Indeed, he heard an echo of the Bureau of Indian Affairs in the new BIA, the Bureau of Iraqi Affairs.

Returning from Berlin he started to take being a Sioux seriously, began to follow the rituals, and to converse in Lakota. Eventually he had become leader of his family clan. As such he was determined to impose traditional values and rules upon all its members. Without exception. He especially abhorred violence against women. Not long ago he had to banish his own nephew from the Reservation for striking a woman. 'And because my nephew had to go,' said Alex White Plum, 'so did my second son when he did a very bad thing against a woman. I loved him dearly, but I had no choice. And it still breaks my heart when I hear him ask me, "When can I come back?" He is begging to come back. But what can I do? He asks. I tell him, "First you must make a name for yourself, so that you can regain respect in your own home."' 'Where is he now?' asked Peppercorn. 'When I last heard from him he was in Denver,' replied Alex White Plum.

'Look around you,' he said. 'As far as the eye can see my word is law, and yet if I need to sign a document I must still seek the approval of the BIA.' To him the Bureau was a colonial institution, which existed because the government continued to hold the attitude that Indians were like children in need of good governance and civilizing. He showed Peppercorn and Mercy Sweetbriar his identity card issued by the BIA. Among other things it quantified the purity of his blood. He was 4/4, meaning that all his grandparents were Indian. His contempt for the Bureau was endless. However, his real bête noire was not unexpected, at least not to Peppercorn. 'Have you ever seen that man's website?' he asked. 'You should take a look. It's a real education. He actually boasts that he's an "Indian Fighter" of the old school just like George Armstrong Custer. He proved that as far back as '73 when he declared, "The only way to deal with the Indian problem in South Dakota is to put a gun to the AIM leaders' heads and pull the trigger." Janklow is one leopard who never changed his spots.'

Peppercorn asked Alex White Plum what he thought of the Red Cloud Cultural Center, expecting an equally damning response. Instead, he replied that over the years he'd had many enjoyable religious disputes with Brother Simon, which invariably remained unresolved. He added that other faiths were of great interest to him also. Only a few days before he'd seen a bunch of PhDs from New York on some TV show put together a very convincing case that Moses received the Ten Commandments from the pilots of a flying saucer. The proof had something to do with a number of otherwise inexplicable circles in the ancient texts. 'I sometimes wish my people were more like the Jews,' sighed Alex White Plum, 'and had the determination to take back and rebuild our lost homeland, as the Jews have done in Israel. Somehow they managed to make the whole world weep for them. Because they lost five thousand of their people to the Nazis. But no one sheds a tear for the Native Americans, who lost tens of millions. Why is that?' His collie was snoozing in the sun. Peppercorn thought it better to let sleeping dogs lie.

'Have you been to our ground zero?' asked Alex White Plum. 'Have you been to Wounded Knee? My own ancestors were killed there. There's no one hereabouts who was not touched by the killing – I prefer that word to massacre. Even though I knew all about it as a child, I didn't learn to grieve properly until after I came home from Berlin. Our grandparents were always telling us stories they had heard from people who were there. They were all at slightly different locations, and they were all terrified, so that no two stories match up or are exactly the same. It doesn't mean they are lying or making them up. Not that anyone could doubt who

did the killing. For some reason the 7th Cavalry recently
arrived here unannounced wishing to make amends. They
had brought thousands of tons of horse manure as a peace
offering. To fertilize our soil, they said. I had them shown
off the Reservation. Somehow horse shit and repentance did
not seem an appropriate combination.' There was, it
seemed, a continuing argument about what to do with the
site of the massacre. Should there be a new memorial? If so,
what? Alex White Plum would rather the whole area be left
alone, allowing nature to transform it into a place for quiet
meditation. A place where this Theodore Herzl of Manderson could dream his dream of rebuilding the Sioux nation,
of reclaiming Wyoming, Montana, Nebraska and the Dakotas, of recreating the nomadic lifestyle.

Mercy Sweetbriar led Peppercorn to the crossroads, and
stopped. Both drivers got out of their automobiles. To the
left was Pierre, to the right was the strange-sounding lodg-
ing where Peppercorn had been assigned a room for the
night. 'From here,' said Mercy, 'you must go back to
Wounded Knee, then shadow the Nebraska border as far as
the junction with 391, where you take a right. Immediately
thereafter you will find two dirt roads on your left. You need
the second. Travel along this for exactly three miles, looking out for an Indian war cemetery. One more swing to the
left and you'll be at the Bar-O-Bar Farm, also known as
Wakpamni Bed and Breakfast. Despite its name it is not
owned by the Sioux, but by the Swicks.' She paused. 'Would
you like me to come with you?' 'Do you mean what I think
you mean?' said he. 'I mean what you think I mean,' said
she. What should he do? Mercy Sweetbriar was lovely in his
eyes. If he were judging Miss Rodeo South Dakota she would

be it. 'What are you waiting for?' said his inner cowboy. But Peppercorn told him to shut up, and let the trail boss do some thinking. He stood at the crossroads and asked himself a simple question: what would Randolph Scott have done? 'You know the answer to that already,' said Scott. 'If I didn't lay a finger on Mrs Lane in *Ride Lonesome*, despite her havin such stupendous breasts, and bein a widow, and me bein a widower, then surely you can find it in yourself to show Mercy some mercy. The man she hero-worshipped has just been exposed as less than perfect. She is lookin to you as a father-figure. Act like one.' Peppercorn knew that to do otherwise would be to expose his inner cowboy as a dickhead. But still he hesitated. In the end, he couldn't say what settled it for sure, but he felt there was something in himself, and in the landscape he had adored since childhood, that was better than that. He had seen it in Bob Lantis, and could see it now in Mercy Sweetbriar (and by implication in the parents who had raised her so well). To betray that indefinable something (not to mention his wife) would be an abomination. He held Mercy's face in his hands and kissed her goodnight. It wasn't easy.

An hour later he was beginning to wonder whether Mercy Sweetbriar might have led him astray in a different way, until he saw the tall flagpole flying the Stars and Stripes across the black fields, and maybe a score of white crosses enclosed by a white picket fence. Betty Swick was in the main house, but that was not where Peppercorn would be staying. He was to be the only sleep-over in the original farmhouse, boyhood residence of Betty's spouse, Larry. A large barn separated it from the main house. 'I don't provide dinner,' said Mrs Swick, in the kitchen of the farmhouse, 'but the previous guests left some pizza in the fridge. You're welcome to that.' Peppercorn followed her from the kitchen to the living room, which was dominated by a portrait of Larry Swick's grandparents, a grim-faced pair of settlers from Germany. Grandpa Swick gave him the willies. He had greased-down hair and a large but carefully trimmed moustache. He also had the unforgiving stare of a witch-burner. 'One word of warning,' said Mrs Swick. 'If you go out on the porch after dark, make sure the house lights are off, otherwise it will quickly fill with moths.' Miller's moths, he thought she called them.

While it was still light he stood on the porch and watched tern-like birds with switch-blade wings climb and dive through the limitless sky, its pearly opalescence dramatizing the whiteness of the gulls. Their cries were long and rasping, like chalk on a blackboard. After dark Peppercorn noticed that the 360-degree horizon was alive with lightning. He moved the net curtain on the french windows to get a better view and accidentally scrambled an unfeasible number of moths. Large brown things. They circled the lights, spiralled to the floor, roosted on walls and pictures. Old Mr Swick glared at him with more than necessary malice. Lightning, accompanied by the tremendous percussion of thunder, was moving closer. It flickered in the near distance like a failing neon bulb. Then it was directly overhead, bringing perfect enlightenment, if only for a few seconds. Long enough to expose blue trees flailing and bending in the wind. The spaces between seemed empty, but any experienced moviegoer would have known that somewhere out there were zombies risen from the Indian boneyard. Not that the interior was any more comforting. Old Mr Swick looked ready to step from the confines of the frame, brush the moths from his black suit, and do ghoulish things to Peppercorn. Meanwhile, the lightning continued to flash and the moths to circle the bulbs. And the rain had begun to fall, torrents of the stuff, rattling on the windows like the bony fingers of the long dead. Would Peppercorn survive the night? He retired to the bedroom, only to discover the Visitors' Book with its unsettling narrative. It began conventionally enough, with thanks to Betty and Larry for an unforgettable visit. Betty's famous breakfasts received extravagant praise. Larry's expert knowledge of the land was noted. Then Larry slipped into the background. There were casual references to his absence. And hints as to the reason. Hope he's on his feet again soon, that sort of thing. Gradually it became apparent that whatever ailed Larry was more serious than the common cold. Finally, there were prayers for him. By now Peppercorn was seriously worried about Larry. He turned on the bedside radio, tuned in to NPR, and listened to Indian chants until he fell asleep.

On Tuesday morning, mist hung heavy over the land as he made his way to the main house. 'We haven't had a storm like that in years,' said Mrs Swick, greeting him at the door. He followed her into the kitchen. The table was laid for one, though there were several chairs around it, including a motorized wheelchair. 'Do you eat bacon?' asked Mrs Swick. 'No,' replied Peppercorn. 'I didn't think you would,' she commented dryly. Talk was of local flora and fauna. Pelicans lived on the nearby lake. Her sons, when they were home, hunted pheasants for the pot. Onions, carrots and turnips all grew wild. Turnips clung to a central root stem, and resembled wooden grapes. A local man ground them very fine to make flour for fry bread. Mr Swick was recovering from a very serious spinal infection, Peppercorn learned, but still needed the wheelchair to get around. His arms still functioned, however. Were he to see a wolf near his livestock he would shoot it without a second thought.

Back in his own bathroom after the long flight, Peppercorn unzipped his Homer Simpson toilet bag and reached inside for his toothbrush and toothpaste, only to disturb a stowaway. Tickling his hand, a solitary Miller's moth flew out. Switching off the light, he opened the window, and watched as it absconded into the alien night, with its whispered tales of the distant west. Mrs Peppercorn was waiting for him in the marital bed. He entered it justified.

At 4.29 on the afternoon of 16 August 2003 Congressman Bill Janklow was travelling south on Highway 13 from Flandreau, where he was born, to his present home in Brandon, both of course in South Dakota.

The road ran north to south in the straightest of lines. It was a journey Janklow had made countless times. He was speeding, of course. 'Bill Janklow speeds when he drives,' he had once boasted, 'shouldn't, but he does.' As a result he had collected at least a dozen tickets while Governor, all of which he had paid without demur. You did the crime, you paid the fine. End of story. Things were going well for him in Washington. There was even talk of the Senate. But now he was back on home territory, and his biggest decision was whether to stop at the approaching junction, as the red octagon demanded. Not stopping had become almost second nature, being one of the perks of high office. Though there were no police watching out for him today. So perhaps he should stop.

But where was the danger of not? The land was flat, visibility excellent. He could see if there were any cross-traffic. On the other hand, he hadn't noticed the car driven by Jennifer Walters, which he had missed by a whisker at exactly the same junction last December. He could hardly blame her for reporting the incident to the cops. Nor was it her fault that he was later pulled over by an alert deputy who had clocked him at 92 in a 55 mph zone. But, all things considered, there had been no consequences. And what were the chances of lightning striking twice in the same spot? His foot needed instruction: gas pedal or brake? So what clinched it? What made him jump that junction at 70 mph (the lowest estimate)? Peppercorn liked to think that Bill Janklow asked himself, as he rapidly approached the point of no return, What would Custer have done? The question answered itself: advance blindly and trust to Custer's Luck. Janklow had always been blessed as a politician. Why not do the same, and trust as ever to Janklow's Luck? So at 4.30 that Saturday afternoon, he ignored the stop sign, and . . . and his luck ran out, just as Custer's had done at Little Bighorn.

Though at least he survived the crash, unlike the unfortunate motorcyclist who – unhelmeted – helplessly hit the white Cadillac which suddenly appeared in his path, and was flung into a soybean field where he died. He was fifty-five. His name was Randolph Scott, in honour of the great cowboy star. He was a Vietnam vet, a volunteer firefighter and a farmer. He rode a Harley. 'He was always there for you,' said one friend. 'He liked hamburger steaks,' remembered another.

Janklow sustained minor injuries to head and arm. However dazed he was, he must have understood he was facing something worse than a fine, that this time there would be consequences. His first excuse, that he had swerved to avoid a white car and careered across the junction, lasted as long as it took for a forensics team to arrive at the scene. There was no option but to charge him with second-degree manslaughter, with a maximum prison term of ten years. He made his first court appearance on 2 September. A *Washington Post* staff writer filed an 'eyewitness' account of his arrival at the courthouse in Flandreau, 'a dot on the vast prairie where the highest structure is the grain elevator and the most popular shop is the town bakery, with fresh doughnuts priced at 28 cents'. (Brandon is described as being 'even smaller'. In fact, Flandreau, with a population of 2,376, is rather large by the standards of South Dakota, and Brandon is more than twice its size.)

Janklow, innocent till proven guilty, obstinately declined to resign his seat in the House of Representatives. His trial began in December. He must have drawn some comfort from the knowledge that it was being held in the community that greeted visitors with the sign: 'Flandreau – hometown of US Representative William J. Janklow.' By now he had a new defence. He was innocent. His diabetes was the guilty party. He claimed he had missed the stop sign on account of hypoglycaemia or low blood sugar. The doctor who had examined Janklow at the scene of the crash remained unconvinced. He had detected no sign of the condition, and had even asked his accidental patient about his blood sugar. 'He said it was okay,' testified Dr Jacobs. Despite this, Janklow stuck to his guns. He insisted that the hypoglycaemia was occasioned by his failure to eat anything since bedtime the previous night. Various witnesses were called to swear that they had seen nothing pass his lips throughout the day. These testimonies were greeted by the prosecution with raised eyebrows, but Janklow wouldn't budge. He answered all questions about the fatal collision with answers such as, 'Sir, I don't recall the automobile trip,' and, 'I don't, sir, have any independent recollection.' At the same time he needed to win the jury's sympathy, by demonstrating that he was the pile-up's second victim. But how could he be stricken by something he couldn't remember?

Thank God for nightmares. 'You can't imagine what it is like,' he murmured from the witness box, while holding back the tears, 'I wake up every night, just sweating. Every time I woke up for weeks after the accident, there were cars.'

In the end it came down to this: would justice prevail, or would the jury turn a blind eye to the evidence and acquit the local boy who had put their town on the map? Peppercorn wasn't entirely convinced he would have done the right thing. Fortunately, the jurors were made of sterner stuff. Perhaps they were shocked, like a lot of Janklow's constituents, by their hero's refusal to own up and take his medicine like a man. Anyway, on Monday, 8 December, he was found guilty on all charges, including second-degree manslaughter. An hour after hearing the verdict Congressman Bill Janklow wrote the following to the leader of the House of Representatives: 'I wish to inform you that because of present circumstances, I will be unable to perform the duties incumbent on me in representing the people of South Dakota as their US Representative. Therefore I wish to inform you that I will resign from the House of Representatives effective Jan. 20, 2004. Please let me know if there are any further formalities which I must perform or accomplish to effectuate this resignation.'

On 22 January 2004 Circuit Judge Rodney Steele sentenced Janklow to one hundred days in jail, three years of probation and a fine of $5,400. He was further ordered to reimburse the county $50 for every day of incarceration. Finally, Janklow was banned from driving for three years. He was required to report to the Minnehaha County Jail in Sioux Falls on 7 February. He ended up serving just thirty days behind bars, the remainder of the time being spent performing community service.

Hearing of Janklow's conviction, Leonard Peltier issued an open letter from his cell in Leavenworth, Kansas: 'This is the same man who said – "the way to stop AIM is to put a bullet through their head". This decision is from a state that historically practiced a program of polarization and racism toward Native People. A place where the native people still own the Black Hills, yet are forcibly denied access to their own land; a place where previously the cries of a young native girl went unheard by South Dakota officials, when she cried rape by Janklow; where her death by a supposedly unknown hit-and-run driver was quickly forgotten . . . I could go on and on but alas, it took the death of one white man to make a difference, or for someone to care. I heard Janklow cried on the stand. I truly wonder where his remorse started. Was it for his behavior or was it because he got caught? It will be interesting to see what his sentence will be. I suppose he'll get a fine that he won't have much trouble paying; a suspended sentence, maybe lose his driving privilege for a time, and get a couple years probation. I wish somehow someone could read the statements he made to Bill Clinton about my clemency back to the judge, substituting his name for mine. Oh well, I guess that level of poetic justice won't come around for a while.'

'Hear, hear,' said Mrs Peppercorn. And that seemed to be the last word on the subject, at least until the story took another unexpected turn.

Among the more attractive characters who had attached themselves to AIM in its struggle at Pine Ridge was a young Micmac woman from Nova Scotia named Anna Mae Pictou Aquash. Buffy Sainte-Marie referred to her in that stirring chant, 'Bury My Heart at Wounded Knee'. Right after the verse about Leonard Peltier, comes this angry squib: 'My girlfriend Annie Mae talked about uranium / Her head was filled with bullets / and her body dumped / The FBI cut off her hands and told us / she'd died of exposure . . .' Her body was found on 24 February 1976 (eight months after the murder of the agents), curled up in a ditch near the road to Wanblee. For some reason, no one recognized the corpse. It was buried in an unmarked grave. Cause of death was recorded as 'exposure'. Buffy Sainte-Marie was right about the hands, too: they were retained, so it was said, to assist any future enquiries. When Anna Mae was subsequently identified, her suspicious family demanded a second post-mortem, during the course of which a fatal bullet wound was found in her head. But it seemed that no one would ever be charged with the crime until, in March 2003, two members of AIM were named as the killers. The trial of one, Arlo Looking Cloud, began in Rapid City on 3 February 2004, and ended four days later with his conviction.

The evidence the jurors heard was not pleasant. Anna Mae was snatched from a supposedly safe house in Denver, Colorado, by the accused, together with a second man and an older woman named Thelma Clark. The three drove their prisoner to the South Dakota Badlands. Anna Mae's hands were bound throughout the journey. On the edge of the cleft where her body was found she was made to kneel, or else knelt voluntarily to pray. Maybe she pleaded for a lifting of the evil decree. She must have asked why they were doing this to her. What could they reply? That they were only obeying orders? Executing someone who deserved no better, who had been fingered as an informer, a spy for the FBI. Perhaps her prayers were heeded, but her more immediate pleas fell upon stony ground. One of her abductors shot her in the back of the head, then kicked her unprotesting body over the edge. Giving evidence, Ka-Mook Banks – ex-wife of Dennis Banks, one of the founders of AIM – told how her ex-husband had called to inform her of Anna Mae's death on 25 February, even though she was still listed as a Jane Doe, and would remain so for another week or more. Ka-Mook Banks also told the court that Leonard Peltier had once boasted to her, in the presence of Anna Mae and others, about shooting the two Feds. Peltier had even re-enacted the killing, making a gun with his fingers, adding that one agent 'begged for his life, but I shot him anyway'. Ka-Mook Banks held a white feather throughout her testimony, as if to draw strength from it. Paul DeMain, editor of *News from Indian Country*, went so far as to suggest that this forbidden and dangerous knowledge was the real reason for Anna Mae's bad end. Not best pleased by these accusations, Peltier sued DeMain for libel. Perhaps he had justification, and Ka-Mook was another false witness. Or just maybe she was telling the truth. Either way, Paul DeMain thought it wise to issue a statement declaring that Leonard Peltier had no involvement in the death of Anna Mae Aquash.

Innocent or guilty, Peltier was more like his nemesis than either of them knew. 'When I met him in '74,' recalled one of his admirers, 'I thought, Gee, this is a crazy guy! *Crazy* guy! But fun, *good* crazy, not nuts, really fun to be around with. We took a trip one time to Rapid, we were going down these back roads, and I mean they're barely cut out. And there're potholes and they're dirt and they're rugged. And Leonard took us at about eighty miles an hour through that road. That guy really knows how to drive!'

Peppercorn drove fast too, but not so recklessly. He never jumped red lights. He stopped at junctions. He had an abiding fear of speed cameras. Years before, when Mrs Peppercorn still accompanied her husband on his assignments, they had been pulled over by a state trooper somewhere in Wyoming. Peppercorn had rolled down the driver's window. 'I just clocked you going at 84,' said the cop. 'I apologize unreservedly,' said Peppercorn, trying to sound as English as possible. 'Where you folks heading for?' asked the cop. 'Cheyenne,' said Peppercorn, 'then through Colorado, Kansas and Oklahoma, right down to Texas. We're getting to know the real West.' 'Do you like what you've seen so far?' asked the cop. 'There ain't nowhere else on God's earth to match it,' said Peppercorn. The cop's face relaxed. 'I'm not issuing a ticket this time,' he said, 'but try to keep within the limit.' With those words he sealed Peppercorn's fate: he was, and always would be, a man who kept within the limit. That was why he would never rise as high as a hero, but then he would never fall as far as either Bill Janklow or Leonard Peltier. Peppercorn had discovered his inner cowboy, but he knew that it was destined to remain trapped within his body, like a roll of undeveloped film in a camera.

True Tales of the
WILD WEST Nº2

Calamity Jane
Turns the Tables

Although citizens of St Albans were called Albanians, its
university was known as the USA. Like its namesake it was
a federation, though its constituent parts were schools
rather than states. Among the weakest was SAS, or the
School of American Studies. This was an irony not lost upon
the post-modernists, post-colonialists, deconstructionists,
feminists and queers who populated it. One of the po-mos
looked around the near-empty lecture theatre and wondered
what the hell he was doing there. The room could accommodate a hundred and fifty students, and he was about to
address a tenth of that number. He placed his notes on the
lectern and forced himself to begin.

'No one ever said "fuck" in a John Ford movie . . .' he
said, then paused. That 'fuck' got their attention right
enough, and may even have held it, if only they had known

87

who John Ford was. Pearls before swine, he thought, then pressed ahead: 'No one ever said "fuck" in a John Ford movie, whereas in HBO's *Deadwood* every other word is an expletive undeleted. David Milch, the show's progenitor, justifies the blazing tongues of his creations by evoking the goatish vocabulary of working folk through the ages. But I intend to convince you that he's also attempting something more original, is taking up a theme only hinted at by the man who introduced the cowboy to literate readers. This theme has to do with bad language, sexual arousal, and alcohol-induced carousel, the town of Deadwood's unholy trinity. Do any of you know to whom I am referring?' As if any of them gave a shit. Needless to say, there was no response.

'In the early 1880s Owen Wister, of whom you will be hearing more, penned an autobiographical novel called *A Wise Man's Son*,' he continued, 'which demonstrated surprising knowledge of the aforementioned vices. He unwisely showed the manuscript to William Dean Howells, mentor of both Mark Twain and Henry James, who deemed it dangerously revealing, and advised against publication. Wister bowed to the sagacious counsel, and promptly suffered facial paralysis and a nervous collapse. Wyoming, with its wide-open spaces and healthy pursuits, was prescribed as a cure for the guilt-stricken Easterner.

'Wister lit out for the territory in 1885. It was the first of many such excursions. From the start he kept a journal. His entries form the basis of the Western stories he began to publish in the 1890s, and of *The Virginian* (which first saw light of day in 1902). In his note "To the Reader", Wister calls the latter an historical novel, meaning that the world it depicts is no more. The period it covers runs from 1874 – when Custer was still alive, the Sioux still a great nation, and the cattle barons in their pomp – to 1890 – the eve of the Johnson County War, when the hitherto all-powerful ranchers organized an invasion to overthrow their democratically elected opponents, and thereby precipitated what they had fought to prevent. Wister, always a supporter of "the quality" over "the equality" regarded this defeat as the end of an era, a fall from grace.

'The novel proper opens with the tenderfoot narrator (Wister in all but name) disembarking from a train at the meagre settlement of Medicine Bow, Wyoming. Here he meets the Virginian, sent by his host, Judge Henry, to escort him on the last leg of his journey. Since it is too late in the day to set off for the Judge's ranch, the narrator and his guide are compelled to spend the night in each other's company. The Virginian has many friends in Medicine Bow. One of whom, with a grin, calls the Virginian "a son of a—" (the chastened Wister can't even allow himself to write the word "bitch"). The narrator is astonished at this overfamiliarity, and expects the speaker to be struck down instantly. Not so. "Evidently . . . no offence had been taken," he concludes. "Used thus, this language was plainly complimentary." Later, however, during a tense game of poker, the book's villain uses exactly the same epithet. This time the Virginian is not amused. This time he draws a pistol, and speaks the immortal line, "When you call me that, *smile*!" Thus the narrator learns an old lesson; it ain't what you say, it's the way that you say it.

'Needless to add, the Virginian is as proper in his dealings with women as he is with the Queen's English. At least, he is in the portrait Wister allows. For (as I have intimated) there are hints throughout of behaviour (and its attendant speech) he has chosen to suppress. This is already apparent in the narrator's description of Medicine Bow. Of its twenty-nine buildings, he declines to identify a dozen, "for one reason or another". Nor does he reveal what precisely the Virginian utters while delirious with fever ("the language of the round-up", he calls it). Finally, the narrator reports a conversation during which the Virginian "fell into the elemental talk of sex", talk so natural it was without offence. "But," he concludes, "it would be offence should I repeat it."

'These are the dark interstices that *Deadwood* cheerfully illuminates in its three dozen episodes of counter-history, flaunting those devilish delights Wister never dared embrace, offending with relish. The first (directed by Walter Hill, no less) was set in the summer of 1876, in the immediate aftermath of Custer's defeat at Little Bighorn (or, if you prefer, Crazy Horse's victory at Greasy Grass). Much good it did the Sioux. Illegal camps continued to measle the Dakotas, as prospectors despoiled the Black Hills in search of the gold Custer had unearthed there. Some of these misbegotten camps took root, Deadwood being the most notorious.

'Regardless of their differences, a point comes where the divergent visions of Wister and Milch converge. They are as one on the subject of leadership, both recognizing that in lawless societies only the dictate of a Mussolini clone can provide order. To Wister, Judge Henry and his ilk are empowered by divine right, and therefore unimpeachable and impeccable. But God has no place in Milch's Deadwood (its one preacher succumbing to a brain tumour at the end of the first series, after experiencing Wister-like paralysis), so his strong-arm men rise by reason of might alone. Initially he offers three candidates for supremacy.

'First is foul-mouthed Al Swearengen (played with satanic glee by Ian McShane). Of him William Dean Howells would find nothing good to say. Yet he is Deadwood's role model. Thanks to his example the lingua franca of Deadwood is profanity. There are no "sons of a bitch" in Deadwood, there are only "cocksuckers" and "cunts" (words issued without a smile).

'This is not to say that Swearengen's speech is as flat as an English footballer's. On the contrary, his rhetoric is not only vulgar but also stately, a rich mix of over-elaboration and shocking directness. The verbal equivalent of the iron fist in the velvet glove. Swearengen's business is supplying human needs and weaknesses, which he does in his saloon-cum-whorehouse. He is often shown looking down upon the town he hopes to control from the elevation of his balcony.

'Second is his business rival Cy Tolliver, who looks uncannily like Gregory Peck (though he is actually played by Powers Boothe). But don't be fooled by appearances; his methods may be less blatant than Swearengen's, but they are no less brutal.

'Al's only other opponent is Seth Bullock, a former lawman from Montana. As it happens there really was a Seth Bullock, who became sheriff of Deadwood and survived to found an eponymous hotel, which still stands (and is reported to be haunted by his ghost). Timothy Olyphant (his re-enactor) mimics McShane's black hair and moustache. But he is the younger man, and his face has yet to decide whether to fix itself as saturnine or angelic. Either way, he is Deadwood's superego, in opposition to Swearengen's id.

'It is with Bullock's arrival that the series begins, the camera lingering upon those businesses Wister was too prim to name. However, his presence is immediately overshadowed by the appearance of a much more famous duo: Wild Bill Hickok and Calamity Jane. Keith Carradine has been slowly preparing for his role as the former over a number of decades. Back in 1971 he played a wet-behind-the-ears cowboy in Robert Altman's *McCabe and Mrs Miller*, which (with its Marxist view of history) may well have set the tone for *Deadwood*. By 1980 he had aged sufficiently to play the outlaw Jim Younger in *The Long Riders*. Directed, as it happens, by Walter Hill. Carradine must have made an impression upon the latter, because Hill offered him a part in the 1995 bio-pic *Wild Bill*, playing Buffalo Bill to Jeff Bridges' Hickok. It was a romantic movie; Jeff Bridges was impetuous, and Ellen Barkin (as Calamity Jane) sexy. No such romance the second time around. Keith Carradine (switching from Buffalo Bill to Wild Bill) is far more world-weary, and Robin Weigert almost devoid of femininity. This is a revisionist Jane, with no trace of Doris Dayism. Nevertheless, the shining eyes of Weigert's Jane manage to convey how much she worships Wild Bill, while always knowing that (being so plain) she can never have him.

'Now the Western is essentially a crescendo progressing towards a violent climax. As long as Wild Bill is around we know that the climax will be his murder at the hands of a punk named Jack McCall. But once he is dead and buried Milch and his co-writers are faced with the problem of dramatizing a confined community in statis, a problem that was brilliantly solved by the introduction of George Hearst, the ubercapitalist, who shares Swearengen's habit of looking down upon Deadwood from a great height. Except that he opens no door to reach his vantage point. He simply knocks a hole in the wall and walks through it, as if to announce that there's a new id in town, one as big and as hairy as King Kong.

'Sure enough, Hearst's ruthless pursuit of monopoly makes his rivals seem like provincials (and Bullock impotent). Offended by the town's only newspaper he sends thugs to intimidate its ace reporter, thus initiating his family's interest in the communications industry. Don't forget that Hearst's son was the even more notorious William Randolph, inventor of the gutter press and architect of the eponymous castle. By the end of the series we realize that Deadwood is not only a place, but is also the crucible of contemporary America, its Bethlehem.'

When the lecture ended the students made straight for the door, their minds already elsewhere. None stopped to ask questions or express appreciation. The course in which they had so little interest was named 'Deconstructing the West'. Lectures were delivered on Monday mornings. Follow-up seminars were timetabled for Wednesday afternoons. About a dozen showed up for the first of them. When they were all sitting comfortably their prof cleared his throat and introduced the subject for discussion.

'David Milch is not alone in highlighting his country's dark and dirty secrets,' he said. 'Another kindred spirit is the artist Kent Monkman. Seen from a safe distance his canvases could be mistaken for examples of the Hudson River School. There are characteristic crags of lavender and grey, waterfalls, luminous pools, and forests in which every leaf is particular. Barely visible are a few human figures. Closer inspection, however, delivers a few shocks.'

So saying, he plucked a large volume from his briefcase, and held it aloft. Called *The American West*, it appeared to have been designed for the coffee table but was in fact the catalogue of an exhibition recently mounted at Compton Verney, near Stratford-upon-Avon. Its curators were Jimmy Durham, a Cherokee, and Richard William Hill, a Cree. From their point of view cowboys were the bad guys, the whole lot of them, from Buffalo Bill to John Wayne, 100 per cent unauthentic, and the duo took pleasure in debagging and mocking them from their custom-made boots up. Though never as much or as perversely as Kent Monkman, one of whose works featured on the book's jacket (half on its obverse, the remainder on its reverse).

'The painting you are looking at is titled *Artist and Model*,' said the prof. 'I assure you that you are presently regarding the former, even though her outfit suggests otherwise.' Her naked back was presented to the viewer. A long feather headdress ran the full length of her spine, stopping at her ankles. Otherwise, her only items of clothing were rosy pumps with the highest of heels, and a pink creation that could easily have been designed for Cher (which was more flesh than dress, and didn't even begin to cover her genitalia). Gradually his students were beginning to notice that these were of the wrong sort, that there was a pair of balls between her legs.

'Allow me to introduce Miss Chief Share Eagle Testickle,' he said. 'It may interest you to learn that many tribes accommodated at least one transvestite, or berdache (the Crow called them bote), who were venerated as seers. In any event our mischievous heroine is bathed in yellow light. The land-scape is Arcadian (bearing a passing resemblance to Joshua Shaw's *On the Susquehanna*). Tree and shadow combine to form the shape of an eye. Miss Chief stands at its pupil. On her easel (made of sticks) is a sheet of birch bark, upon which is the figure of a man drawn Indian-style. The artist holds the charcoal in her right hand. In her left is a loaded bow. A quiver full of arrows hangs usefully from the easel. Miss Chief is drawing from life (or perhaps death). Her model fills the remainder of the painting, as you shall see . . .'

Whereupon the speaker flipped the book to reveal its darker side. What the students saw was a man bound to a tree. He was naked but for a cowboy hat and boots (plus jeans that were rolled around his ankles). His pose and ecstatic expression closely resembled that of St Sebastian. Like that saint he was pierced by arrows. Unlike the saint he had an erection. There was a collective gasp when the students recognized what they were looking at.

'It seems that the martyr did not begin the day expecting to be a model,' remarked their professor, 'for his plate camera is on the ground before him, broken open and exposed to the light, allowing the imprisoned souls to flee. Have the tables been turned? Has the vanishing Indian returned to finally vanquish the Yankee? What do you think?' Silence. 'Okay,' the professor asked, 'if the cowboy is so obviously aroused by his captor and his fate, what of the viewer? Perhaps the captive's role is not so passive after all. Why do you think Monkman has transformed him into an object of homoerotic desire?' 'To cause maximum embarrassment,' said a student. 'Good,' said her professor. 'Because Monkman wants us to recognize that our enduring attraction to the cowboy isn't entirely a function of masculinity,' volunteered another. 'Clever boy,' said his professor. 'That's why the hat and boots remain; to remind us that he's not just a naked man, but a naked cowboy. Perhaps what Monkman is suggesting is that we – by we I mean the males among us – may be facing our inner cowboy, our secret desire made manifest.'

After the students had vacated the room their professor wondered whether he had gone too far, had exposed too much of himself, so to speak. That last pronouncement had popped into his mind unscripted, and he had uttered it without thinking. As he slipped *The American West* back into his briefcase, he reflected upon the sentences he considered to be the most honest in the entire volume. They were written by Richard William Hill, and described an exhibit he had seen at the Autry Museum of Western Heritage in Los Angeles: 'There is a boy's bedroom that is done up entirely in cowboy products: bedding, curtains, toys; the entire environment is cowboy with no relief. It is a kind of nightmare of indoctrination, yet in my heart I know I would have loved a room like this when I was a kid.' It seemed that if all men were closet queers, then all Indians longed to be Gene Autry or Roy Rogers.

He remembered his own bedroom, decorated upon similar lines, and that of his cousin and near-contemporary, with whom he used to play endless games of Cowboys and Indians. Both would have shot the other to acquire the room that had so captivated Hill. In fact, an unspoken rivalry was born in those days that time had not extinguished. It had revisited him unexpectedly in one of the galleries at Compton Verney, the one that looked out upon the stately home's green acres. The space was large but empty, save for a small blurred photograph of buffalo in motion. Beneath it was a name – Alan Michaelson – and a title – *He(a)rd*. He had duly listened and sure enough had heard the thrumming of distant hoofbeats, as though buffalo were on the move in an English country garden. The sound had grown in intensity as the beasts stampeded towards the french windows (or so his ears had led him to believe), and then had diminished again as the ghostly creatures had vanished into history. How he had envied his cousin who had seen such a herd in the flesh, and not just as a passive witness either; he had actually been a participant in South Dakota's Buffalo Roundup.

When the professor left his seminar room the following

week he was accosted by three men in black suits. He immediately assumed that one of the girls – or, God forbid, one of
the boys – had accused him of sexual harassment, citing the
display of an erect penis as proof positive. But it was worse
than that. 'HEFCE has ordered another RAE,' said his Head
of Department, 'and unless one among us can come up with
the goods we're fucked.' 'You're the nearest thing our school
has to a star,' said its Director of Research, 'in that you alone
have published anything of quality in the last three years.
For God's sake try and think of something new. Good if it
catches the eyes of our peers, better if it's a money-spinner.'
'No students, no publications,' said the Pro-Vice-Chancellor,
twisting the knife, 'no department.'

It didn't take him more than an afternoon to compose his
proposal. That's what I call grace under pressure, he
thought. The Director of Research was no less congratula-
tory: any project that had 'deconstructing' in its title was all
right by him; he nodded vigorously as his colleague spoke of
'deconstructing *Deadwood*', of comparing the fake city at
Gene Autry's Melody Ranch in Santa Clarita, California,
where most of the series had been filmed, with the real thing
in South Dakota, and proving that the former was more
"real" than the latter; he rubbed his hands as the names
Barthes, Baudrillard and Umberto Eco were dropped. 'I suspect Deadwood, South Dakota, is less a place, more an act
of collective will,' explained the professor. 'It is a sort of
Brigadoon, a ghost town sustained by a civic pact of self-
delusion, which forces all its citizens to be complicit in the
charade until they shuffle off the motley. I started out thinking of them as exiles from the world of spontaneous gesture,
but soon saw them as axiomatic, as Mr and Mrs America.'

'You'll be poking fun at them then?' asked the Director of Research. 'Not since Bedlam closed its doors will such fun have been poked,' replied the department's saviour.

That very night he telephoned his cousin. 'Peppercorn,' he said, 'it's Saltzman.' 'Pity,' said Peppercorn, 'I was expecting John Wayne.' 'My department is sending me to South Dakota as well as California for a spot of R&D,' said the caller, 'and I'd be obliged if you could give me the name of your contact there.' 'Maureen Droz,' replied Peppercorn. 'Thanks, coz,' said Saltzman. 'By the way,' said Peppercorn, 'she has an assistant named Mercy Sweetbriar, a girl so apple pie she makes Anne of Green Gables seem like the Whore of Babylon. Exactly the sort to appeal to a priapic old bastard like you. I'd take it kindly if you curbed your libido for once, and kept your hands off her. In fact, if I hear any whisper to the contrary you'll be guest of honour at a neck-tie party on your return.'

Saltzman's departure date was determined by the fact that Melody Ranch was hosting the Santa Clarita Cowboy Poetry and Music Festival at the end of March. His fare and expenses for one week were to be paid out of an obscure bequest controlled by the Pro-Vice-Chancellor. The plan was for Saltzman to start at Santa Clarita, an easy drive from LAX, and fly back to St Albans by way of Deadwood, South Dakota. Once home he would immediately commence work on the post-modern classic that would not only bring glory to the USA, but also be a best-seller. For the first time in months (if not years) Saltzman felt genuine enthusiasm for his job. The sun-dried waitress who served him dinner at Santa Clarita's Garden Inn sounded like the ghost of his former self. 'I come to work to get away from home,' he heard her say to a colleague. 'My tragedy is that work's shit too.' Bright and early the next morning Saltzman took the shuttle and was bussed via Antelope Valley and Placerita Canyon to the gated community of Newhall, wherein was his starting point.

At the Melody Ranch Museum, housed near the entrance in a converted three-bedroom hacienda, Saltzman learned something of its history, which began in 1915, when Monogram Pictures reconstructed an entire frontier settlement on grazing land in Placerita Canyon to provide a convincing location for their numerous Westerns. Between shoots they hired the set out to other studios. For John Ford it became Lordsburg, end of the line for the Overland Stage, and for Luke Plummer, gunned down in its streets by the Ringo Kid. Later it served as Hadleyville, whose forsaken marshall had a noon rendezvous with Frank Miller and his gang. In 1952 the founder of Monogram Pictures died, and Gene Autry bought the old place for a song. At the time he was hosting a radio show called *Melody Ranch*, supposedly recorded around a campfire on the imaginary spread. Autry promptly renamed his new acquisition Melody Ranch, thereby redeeming the fib.

Filming continued under Autry's watch, which happened to coincide with the apogee of both the TV Western and Saltzman's impressionable years. The production that impressed young Saltzman the most was *The Life and Legend of Wyatt Earp*, closely followed by *Gunsmoke*. He watched them both on the stylish Ultra Bermuda acquired by his father to keep one step ahead of the Peppercorns. Pretty soon he felt he knew the streets of Tombstone and Dodge City as well as he knew the suburban avenues and crescents of his native Hendon. Indeed, the one became the other on Sunday afternoons, when Saltzman and Peppercorn patrolled them (and the badlands of Sunnyhill Park) on their two-wheelers – though they were usually so busy arguing over who should be the sheriff and who the deputy that the outlaws held up stages and banks uninterrupted.

The ranch's golden years came to an abrupt end on a windy day in August 1962 (the year of Saltzman's bar mitzvah). As the breeze grew into a blast Autry's mount Champion (star of *Champion the Wonder Horse*) began to whinny, and the eyes of his minders began to smart. Smuts were blowing down from the San Gabriel Mountains. Smoke soon made the wind visible. A firestorm followed, destroying all in its path. Autry didn't have the heart to rebuild. And after Champion (the third and last with that name) gave up the ghost in 1990, he put the place up for sale. Enter the Veluzat brothers. Relying upon the memories and memorabilia of aficionados they set about replicating the lost replica. In pursuit of authenticity they acquired seventy-four truckloads of frontier-style windows, furniture, bars and swinging saloon doors, tossed out by another studio that saw no future in Westerns. And their efforts were rewarded. Walter Hill, liking what he saw, turned the sappy set into Deadwood for his movie about the life and rough times of Wild Bill Hickok. If it was good enough for Walter Hill, it was good enough for David Milch. But was it good enough for Saltzman? How could he continue to justify his veneration of the unauthentic, when the belated revelation that the Tombstone and Dodge City of his childhood were fakes had occasioned the same stab of betrayal as his ex-wife's infidelities?

Perplexed by the persistence of these unironic feelings, Saltzman explored the rest of the museum as if expecting to find a guide who would explain them away. And – what do you know? – he saw John Wayne. The great man was sitting cross-legged on a wooden chair, placed on a low stage. He was wearing an old hat biased toward the left eye, and a pale neckerchief knotted at the back like a lobster-bib. And he was breathing. More than that, he was eating cake. Behind him was a painted backdrop reproducing the dramatic landscape of the south-west: desert, red mesas and the prickly tridents of saguaro cacti. On his face was the far-away expression of a cowboy scanning the horizon for strays, although the piles of books at his feet suggested that he was actually looking out for readers, that John Wayne had (of all things) been reincarnated as a novelist. A large promotional card disclosed both the book's title – *Across the Brazos* – and the name of its author – Ermal Walden Williamson. A photograph of a man on horseback, who also looked a lot like John Wayne, made it pretty obvious that the book was a Western. Saltzman purchased a copy from the great man's assistant, and was invited on stage to have his photograph taken with its scribe, who rose majestically from his seat. The two men shook hands, while the same assistant took a polaroid, thereby creating the illusion that Saltzman had joined forces with John Wayne on a lonesome trail in old Arizona.

'Has anyone ever told you that you're a dead ringer for the Duke?' said Saltzman. 'As a matter of fact,' said Ermal Walden Williamson, 'I was just honoured with a Cloney for the "Most Outstanding Impersonation of a Male Legend" from the International Guild of Celebrity Impersonators and Tribute Artists.' 'Congratulations,' said Saltzman. 'Did you ever meet your role model?' 'Nope,' said Williamson. 'Don't you ever worry that the gap between your personality and his will become so narrow that yours will disappear?' said Saltzman. 'Why should I?' said Williamson. 'We have a lot in common.' 'So have you ever felt yourself actually possessed by your subject?' said Saltzman. 'Oftentimes I have felt his presence within,' said Williamson. Mostly he impersonated Wayne at corporate events, trade shows, parties and the like. Harmless stuff. However, there was some queasiness when he elected to go a step further in some commercials for Coors Light. To produce these sixty-second inserts Williamson had acted out scenes from some of Wayne's most famous movies, and then had his own head replaced by that of the Duke in post-production. This was no longer impersonation, this was metamorphosis. Williamson, however, saw nothing improper in passing off counterfeit as real. On the contrary, he was proud to be the rear end of this pantomime creature. 'Thanks, Duke,' he had said, 'for letting me slide my feet into your big shoes.' For the brewers the campaign was a triumph. No longer could Coors Light be dismissed as the choice of wimps. In fact, it sold in record amounts. Saltzman pictured a darkened den filled with brain-washed hoi polloi growing more thirsty by the moment and not knowing why.

'Mr Williamson,' he said, 'are you familiar with Plato's allegory of the cave?' 'I am an educated man,' said Williamson. 'I have a master's and a doctorate.' 'Then,' said Saltzman, 'you'll certainly recall the passage in which Socrates asks his students to imagine a subterranean cavern full of prisoners, all of whom have been chained at the neck since childhood, so that they can only look at one thing. That thing is a low wall upon which the shadows of men and objects play. Socrates compares it to the "screen that marionette players have in front of them" when they manipulate their puppets. Of what does it remind you, Mr Williamson? What else but a movie theatre? Or perhaps a darkened room in which a television is the dominant object. In either case, the images that captivate the viewers are clearly descendants of those shadows that represented reality to the philosopher's captive audience.

'You remember what happens next, of course. Socrates asks his students to suppose that one of the prisoners is released, and permitted to ascend to the world of solid things. Naturally, he will be dazzled by the sun at first, but gradually his eyes will become accustomed to the light and he will realize that the images on the wall of the cave are nothing but shades, the shadows of reality. Now, says Socrates, imagine that the man is returned whence he came. Naturally, he informs his unenlightened companions of their ignorance. But his eyes, having adjusted to the light, can no longer cope with the darkness below, and his movements resemble those of a halfwit. Alas, his new ideas are accorded the same respect. No doubt a similar fate would await any latter-day heretic bold enough to announce that the images being projected of – let's say, John Wayne drinking Coors Light – are no more than glitter from a dead star. Instead of considering their circumstances the ignorant masses will simply tell him to piss off, order more beer and popcorn from their captors, and continue to watch the commercial. How quaint, how old-fashioned, it was of Fred Astaire's daughter to take offence when she unexpectedly spotted her late father partnering a Dust Devil vacuum cleaner on prime-time TV. Didn't she know that morality and mortality were things of the past? For tuned-in po-mos like you and me, Mr Williamson, there's no real life, and therefore no death either.'

'I don't know what a po-mo is,' said Williamson, 'but I can go along with your second proposition, being a Southern Baptist Minister, ordained at the Fuller Theological Seminary in Pasadena, California. We Christians are pretty confident that the sting has been plucked from death. But I have to take issue with your belief that men enslaved to false gods are necessarily hostile to those of us who bring the good news. So long as it is presented in the right way. What true man of the West could turn his back on a minister who looks and sounds exactly like John Wayne?' Be he selling beer or Jesus. Clutching his new purchase Saltzman did precisely that, any doubts concerning his thesis now banished. Indeed, he was willing to bet that the real Tombstone, the real Dodge City, and the real Deadwood had tailored their historic cities to meet the expectations of the troglodytes.

Like the ancient philosopher's cave-dweller, Saltzman was blinded by the unfiltered sunlight when he exited his dark retreat. He was dimly aware of mounted men, one of whom wore a sombrero so large it looked as though a UFO had touched down on his head, and women dressed like Dale Evans. In the distance beneath a stand of cottonwoods, he could just make out a trio led by a Patsy Cline look-alike, whose yodels galloped straight from her epiglottis to his ear. By the time he finally reached much-filmed Main Street his vision was more or less restored. But instead of witnessing some greater reality, instead of seeing free individuals

engaged in spontaneous expression, he saw clones throng-
ing the thoroughfare. Men and women alike were all dressed
in the same fashion: sharply creased jeans and well-ironed
shirts, with the same bat-wing pleats at the back, and the
same pearl-faced buttons down the front. On top they all
sported Stetsons, and below tooled boots of Spanish leather.
To assist them to resemble ever more closely the actors and
actresses they modelled their appearance upon, Main
Street's vacant stores had been occupied by peripatetic boot-
makers, milliners, tailors and haberdashers. There was the
Rocky Mountain Hat Co. from Bozeman, Montana, whose
dream-provoking products gave Saltzman some insight into
why Jeff Bridges' Wild Bill was ready to kill anyone foolish
enough to molest his headgear. Then there was William
Shanor, a quietly spoken bootmaker from Ashland, Oregon,
whose soft touch had seduced many feet – including those
belonging to one of Saltzman's idols. So delighted had he
been with his new cowboy boots that he had written a letter
in praise of their manufacture and appearance, and ordered
another pair of the same. It was now on display for all to see.
The way the famous playwright had described the boots
made them sound as desirable and delicious as ice cream on
a hot day, what with their chocolate uppers and their vanilla
shins. Saltzman almost found himself coveting them, until
irony stepped in. Am I the only one round here who hasn't
put away childish things, he thought? He pointed the first
two fingers of his right hand at the framed testimonial and
slowly pulled the trigger. And another of his heroes bit the
dust. As he blew the smoke from his fingertips he whispered,
'Et tu, Mamet?'

Being a fan of Kinky Friedman and the Texas Jewboys,

Saltzman had acquired a ticket to see a performance by the band that had inspired them, Bob Wills and his Texas Playboys.

When he entered the theatre (a barn in all but name) the emcee (who sported moustaches thick enough to holster a pair of derringers) was already introducing the support act. He explained that the Hot Club of Cowtown (out of Austin, Texas) liked to mix European jazz with Western swing, 'to make music that fits into no conventional genre'. Whereupon a member of the audience yelled, 'No French in here, if you please!' The rest of the audience whooped its approval. The master of ceremonies smiled wryly and voiced a pious tribute to 'our boys' fighting to preserve the American way in Eye-raq. 'Though I'm pretty sure,' he concluded, 'that they wouldn't want to stop us enjoying ourselves.' Another whoop. At which point the Hot Club of Cowtown launched into 'Ida Red' with such ferocity and virtuosity that if the audience had been a schooner it would have been blown halfway to Hawaii. The Hot Club had three members: Elana Fremerman, violin, lead vocals; Whit Smith, guitar, lead vocals; Jake Erwin, upright bass, vocals. Erwin jived with his instrument, Smith was having a thing with the microphone, while Fremerman looked like she was trying to saw off her left arm at the shoulder. What made her so appealing (apart from the fact that she was wearing something tight) was the impression she gave of being no one but herself. Saltzman was unable to take his eyes off her. He even managed to convince himself that the words of the torch songs she crooned were directed at him. 'Take it easy,' whispered his neighbour, 'that beauty is my baby, and those boobs are shaking just for me.' Saltzman glanced at the speaker, a man as time-worn as himself, and wondered if he were delusional. 'I consider myself a bit of a pugilist,' the man continued, 'and if you don't take that disbelieving look off your face, I may well decide to remove it myself.' He stared as Saltzman attempted to look credulous. 'I'm sure I've seen that ugly mug of yours before,' drawled the stranger. 'Were you ever in Elko, Nevada? You kinda resemble the guy I had to chase out of the Stockmen's Casino, on account of the way he kept butting into a private conversation I was enjoying with Annie Proulx. You probably remember it. About bronco-busting, and how the cowboy's short ride is a metaphor for life itself.' 'Must have been my double,' said Saltzman, 'I was back in the USA – the University of St Albans – teaching a course called Western Writers. Are you one of them, by any chance?' 'In a manner of speaking,' said the man. 'The name's Tom Russell. I write songs.' 'And good ones too,' said Saltzman. 'None more so than the "Ballad of Edward Abbey".' 'On which I was backed by that dreamboat up there,' said Russell. 'Will you two shut the fuck up?' said someone in the row behind. 'We came here to listen to the band, not you.' Tom Russell did not return after the interval. Saltzman stayed to hear Bob Wills and his Texas Playboys, or rather someone pretending to be him, since the real Bob Wills had long ago been called to the Grand Ole Opry in the sky. Today's Bob Wills (like the late maestro) clutched a long cigar. Except that his wasn't the real thing, wasn't even lit; it lacked the smouldering tip that signified life. Truly a man of his time, thought Saltzman.

He expected to find more of the same in Deadwood. Driving there from the airport with Maureen Droz at the wheel he asked: 'What did you make of my cousin, Peppercorn?' 'I thought you looked kinda familiar,' she said. 'He was a funny guy. I liked him a lot. But I don't think I understood more than two words he said.' 'I know what you mean,' said Saltzman, 'he's not exactly a man of the people. But there was one who took a particular shine to him. God knows why. He asked me to look out for her.' 'You must mean Mercy Sweetbriar,' she said. 'She's long gone. Lit out for Wyomin to raise horses.' Saltzman rubbed his Adam's apple. The last thing he saw of Rapid City was a crude sign painted on a tin roof: 'Outer Limits / Cocktails / Nude Girls'. Tempted as he was, he didn't think it prudent to ask Maureen to stop.

The first thing he saw of Deadwood was a casino named Mustang Lee's. Its manager let out a majestic wolf whistle when Maureen (trailed by Saltzman) entered the emporium of blinking lights and elderly gamblers. Seeing the manager, Maureen squealed and leapt several inches vertically. The two hugged. Then he said: 'I've got something for you.' He returned with a portrait of the pair of them, taken at a travel convention in Orlando. The glossy 10 x 8 had been computer-enhanced, whereby his prematurely grey hair had been dyed samsonite black, and his head grafted on to the muscle-bound body of Conan the Barbarian; meanwhile Maureen had been gifted the biceps and uberfeminine cleavage of Red Sonja. What's up with Americans, thought Saltzman? If they aren't acquiring new heads, they're acquiring new bodies.

Over lunch Maureen asked if business was good. 'We had a short-lived little boom a few months back,' the manager said. 'Word got around that we were a homosexual hang-out after that queer Western got released. Had no idea why.

Until someone whispered the name of the guy who made it.'
As if to offer further assurance that Mustang Lee's was
straight, Saltzman's new buddy elected to tell him about
Deadwood's red-light district (known to the locals as the
Badlands), and how he lost his virginity there. 'Marin's a
real lady,' he said, 'but she's also a sport, and won't mind
sitting in on some bar-room talk.' Maureen didn't. 'Well,'
said her friend, 'a lot of young bucks – and I include myself
– had our first experience of the opposite sex behind Pam's
Purple Door, or maybe at the Shasta Rooms. What else were
we supposed to do? Good gals like Marin here were savin
themselves for their weddin nights. And God help them if
they didn't. In the meantime, our blood was boilin, and who
knows what mischief we might have done, if it weren't for
our very own soiled doves. Bless em all. You'd knock, and a
peephole would open long before the door. Provided you
looked clean and well-enough heeled to pay the price, you'd
hear a bolt slide, and you'd be led upstairs and through some
beautiful lace drapes. Inside you'd be offered two cups of
coffee, and the girl of your choice, if not your dreams. Not
only did those darlins let us do what we'd been itchin to do
for years, but they also taught us how to do it better. To my
mind they were on a par with golf pros. It was a sad day
when the state put em all out of work.'

'It wasn't just the whores and their customers who suffered when the brothels were closed,' said Maureen. 'The
whole community did. Believe it or not, prostitution was
second only to gold as a source of municipal income. And the
gold was already runnin out. So there was a lot of resistance
to the move. In the end a public meeting was held in the
dining room of the Franklin Hotel (where you'll be spendin

a night or two). Anyways, Pam Holliday, proprietress of the Purple Door, took on Craig Grotenhouse, the local state's attorney. Also involved were a handful of academics and clerics. Pam spoke first. "The only thing I have control over any more is my body," she said. "The government owns everything else." Asked why she didn't simply call her establishment a massage parlour (thereby sidestepping legal problems), Pam was shocked. "What kind of girl do you think I am?" she cried. "I'm not going to try and change things in Deadwood. Who am I to come in after a hundred years and call them massage parlours? What was good enough for Madam Moustachio and Dirty Em back then, is good enough for me right now." She got a big cheer for that. But Grotenhouse was equally unbending. "Whether we like it or not, it's illegal," he said at the outset (and then emphasized the point). "It's illegal in every sense of the word. As long as I am state's attorney, they will be closed." The audience was not impressed. Many members booed; others wanted to know why the authorities had suddenly decided to act, having turned a blind eye for so long. Grotenhouse merely repeated that brothels were banned by the state constitution, and suggested that the hecklers should get off their backsides if they wanted to keep them so badly. "If you don't like it, change it . . ." he yelled. "Your job, if you want it that much, is to get it legalized." They didn't, and Deadwood fell upon hard times. What saved it was gamblin.'

Naturally, Saltzman was curious to visit what remained of the Badlands, so it was agreed that they would leave the auto at Mustang Lee's and walk the length of Main Street. They left their jackets too, the weather being unusually warm for late March. Hot even. But not in the Badlands.

There it was the Ice Age. Substituting for flesh-and-blood sporting girls were wax mannequins in frilly underwear, mocking provocation with frozen poses. They stood at a chaste distance, behind the uncurtained upstairs windows of Nos. 610, 612, 614 and 616. There was another lifeless (though not entirely bloodless) group of dummies in the basement of a nearby bar, established upon the charred remains of the original Saloon No. 10. This was hallowed ground, a place of pilgrimage; it was the very spot where Wild Bill Hickok was assassinated on 2 August 1876 (a mere five weeks after the death of Custer). As in some ancient crypt or grotto, the crudely cast figures re-enacted the moment of martyrdom.

Being constructed of timber, most of Deadwood – like Saloon No. 10 – had succumbed to the great fire of 1879. It was rebuilt with brick, mainly by Jewish pedlars sick of the itinerant life. One of them, Sol Star, featured in the

TV series as Seth Bullock's business partner. According to
Saltzman's research, 669–71 had formerly housed Sol Bloom's
clothing store, while 670 was Jacob Goldberg's grocery. Max
Fishel sold stationery at 657, while his partner, Ben Baer,
went native and bottled beer. In time Max Fishel was succeeded by Sol Levinson, who preferred marketing jewellery
to paper, pen and ink. The buildings all remained, but their
purposes had changed (as had their owners). Instead of
catering to the urgencies of frontier life, they now serviced
appetites.

The smarter end of Main Street was crowned by the
Franklin Hotel, a neoclassical confection. Its exterior was
enhanced by a wide balcony, supported by eight neoclassical
columns. All were painted virgin white. Its owner was
stretched in a chair on the wooden porch, enjoying the afternoon sun. His pale Stetson shone like a halo. He waved at
Maureen, and beckoned her over. He was long-legged and
lean; broken-nosed but handsome, rather like a Jack
Palance dusted with talc. His style was casual: boots, beige
slacks and a green rollneck (with a shamrock embroidered
on its emerald collar). 'Marin Droz, as I live and breathe,'
he said, rising from his basket-weave seat, 'what brings you
to my neck of the woods?' 'Professor Saltzman,' she replied.
'He's writing an important article about Deadwood. And
you – or someone speaking on your behalf – agreed to host
him while he was in town.' 'Terrific,' said the man, holding
out his hand. 'Bill Walsh,' he said. Saltzman took it, notic-
ing that his head was on a level with his host's collarbone.
'Let's hunker down for a while,' said Walsh. Maureen and
Saltzman pulled up a couple more wicker chairs. A waiter
brought them iced tea. 'This,' said Maureen, 'is the man

who saved Deadwood.' 'Come on with you,' said Walsh, 'I was just one among many.' 'But you were the one who counted,' said Maureen, 'it was your blarney that turned the "Deadwood You Bet" campaign into a vote-winner.' 'People understood that it was a matter of survival,' he said. 'The alternative was to become another ghost town, the fate reserved for all such out-of-the-way places when the mother lode runs out, which it was about to do.' And so rather than succumbing to dilapidation and other ravages of time, the citizens of Deadwood voted to legalize gambling, and ensured that their city received a facelift. The manifest price for loving restoration – at the Franklin as elsewhere – was lobbies full of blackjack tables, roulette wheels and psychedelic gaming machines.

'Saltzman,' said Maureen, 'd'you know what this gentleman did before leadin Deadwood into temptation?' Saltzman hadn't a clue. 'He was a priest,' she cried, lifting her glass. 'And not just any priest. This priest shepherded the Kennedys. Some say that Rose Kennedy would confess to no one but him.' 'There you go again, Marin,' said Walsh. 'Did you lose your faith?' asked Saltzman, who lost his long before his virginity. 'No,' said Walsh, 'I found love.' 'Didn't your bishop object?' asked Saltzman. 'Not once he'd met JR,' said Walsh. 'His only advice thereafter was, "Walsh – just have a small wedding." So we did. But he never said anything about the reception. So we invited four hundred folks to that. Turned out there was only one room in all Deadwood big enough to contain the multitude. And that was in the Franklin. I liked it so much I didn't rent it, I bought it.' 'So you're a bit of an outsider,' said Saltzman. 'On the contrary,' said Walsh, 'my great-uncle Tom Callahan – hailing like Wild Bill and the Earps from Troy Grove, Illinois – rode with the former, having crossed his path right here in Deadwood. I doubt there's another soul hereabouts with those historical connections. Make sure you put that in your article, Professor.'

Saltzman was given a choice at the reception desk: the room in which Kevin Costner had slept when directing *Dances With Wolves*, or the room once occupied by John Wayne. By way of an answer he pointed to a neon sign on the far side of the lobby. It burned green. It hung like a lucky star above the entrance to a gaming room. It said: John Wayne. The receptionist handed him the key to Room 206.

He was about to ascend the stairs with his bag, when three kids (two little girls and a bigger boy) ran past. 'Stop right there!' cried someone Saltzman initially mistook for their big sister. Well, she was holding an Instamatic to her eye, which meant that he couldn't see her face properly. But he could see that she had long blonde hair, and that she was wearing haute-couture copies of trailer-trash originals: a white vest (marked Miami Bitch) with deep-pan cleavage, plus sparkles on the exposed mezzalunas, not to mention denim hot pants. 'Keanu,' Miami yelled, 'if you don't keep still, you ain't gonna see a red cent of that hundred-dollar bet!' Saltzman remained at the base of the staircase, so as not to spoil the family group. By then he had realized his error: not their sister, but their mother. Her three children held their pose on the stairs. The click of the shutter released them all, including Saltzman.

'Look,' exclaimed young Keanu, pointing to the name-plate on the door, 'he's going into John Wayne's room.' 'Can we have a peep inside?' enquired the boy's mother. Saltzman was going to say no? 'Did John Wayne really stay here?' asked the kid. 'During the shooting of *Stagecoach*, so they claim,' Saltzman replied. 'Can I look in the bathroom?' asked Miami. 'Be my guest,' he said. 'Oh, look!' she cried. 'A bath with claws. And with brass faucets too.' She backed out. Her britches were cut so high, and dug so deep, that her buttocks were forced apart. She turned and walked towards Saltzman, her chest more Montana than Miami.

Saltzman took a corresponding step backwards. Whatever film John Wayne was shooting when he stayed at the Franklin, the size of the room indicated that it was before he became a living legend. So small was it that after a few further steps Saltzman found his retreat blocked by the radiator.

'Keanu,' said Miami, 'take your sisters and see what other famous names you can find. I want to have a few words alone with this gentleman.' Apart from the blonde, the room now contained a bed, a dressing table, some photographs of John Wayne, and Saltzman (eager to hear what those words might be). 'We drove here all the way from Florida,' she said. 'Do you know how far that is? I'll tell you somethin, I ain't ever doing it again. Before we even started I discovered that my ex had cancelled the insurance on my Merc 500 as soon as he became my ex, which meant that I'd been driving without cover for months. It cost me over four hundred dollars to make that right. And then we've hardly been drivin for an hour when this deer jumps right in front of my car. I really needed that. The deer's by the road dyin, the kids are in the back wailin. But what can I do, except drive and drive? By the end of the day I'm whacked, but we can't find anywhere to stay. So I drive some more, until I'm as good as dead. Then we come upon some hole-in-the-wall place. My kids refuse to stay there, but I tell them they've got no choice. Besides, I can see that they're serving fried chicken gizzards. Oh, God. I haven't seen them any place since I was a girl, but I still love em. So I drag my kids in, and order a plate. They taste as good as I remember. So good that I'm almost cryin. Finally I bite into the last one – the last one – and see that it's green inside. Can you imagine? Green! I spit it out. But what of the others that I swallowed? Great! We're in the middle of nowhere, and I'm about to die of food poisoning. But a miracle occurs, I don't die. I only puke up for half the night. You can imagine how I feel when I eventually reach Deadwood. And then what happens? I get to the forest and start to drive up the unmade road that leads to my mother's house. We're all stayin there, not at the Franklin. But it's full of ruts, and my Merc, which wasn't made for such tracks, gets stuck.'

With barely a pause for breath she explained to Saltzman how she tried to get it fixed under warranty. She's told, no way, even though she's certain-sure that the warranty hasn't expired because she bought the auto on her birthday – June 9, if you want to know – so she warns them that if they don't fix it pronto she's going to find the address of the CEO, and make sure he knows how some of his employees treat their customers. Meanwhile, her mother is telling her that she shouldn't have tried to drive up the mountain in the first place. She's taking charge of everything . . . as usual. But how else is she supposed to have gotten up there? 'You tell me,' she concluded, challengingly. At which point her kids returned. 'Go away,' she said. 'I'm not finished yet.' 'Come on, Mom,' they insisted. She shrugged. 'My mother likes to gamble at the Silverado,' she said, 'I'll be there around six, if you want to get together again.'

Saltzman, shaken, sat on the side of his bed. Although he had been longing for her to shut up, he began to miss Miami almost as soon as she quit the room – or rather he mourned the possibilities that her presence offered. If Peppercorn had been allowed his Mercy Sweetbriar, why shouldn't Saltzman be permitted his Miami Bitch? Perhaps he should have taken a leaf from Ermal Walden Williamson's book and copied the swagger of his room's most famous resident, or at least have asked himself the question: What would John Wayne have done? And acted accordingly. Next time, he promised himself, next time.

In the meantime, Maureen was awaiting him in the lobby. From Main Street they rode a bus (run by a man who called himself Alkali Ike) to the summit of Mount Moriah. Not Mount Moriah, Jerusalem, where Abraham raised the knife to Isaac, but Mount Moriah, South Dakota, where Deadwood buried its illustrious dead. The cemetery proved to be bosky, smelt of pine resin, and afforded a fine view of the city below, emphasizing its location in a narrow gulch between a rock face and a river. Having stopped his bus beneath a stand of evergreens, Alkali Ike led his passengers up a slope to where Wild Bill Hickok and Calamity Jane saw out eternity within spitting distance of one another. The climbers rested beside a picket fence, within which was a bust – cast in bronze – of the deceased gunfighter. 'Ol Wild Bill was a handsome son of a b— in life,' said their leader, 'and it seems he didn't lose his looks in death. Ol Doc Pierce, who laid out his corpse, claimed it was the prettiest he ever saw. His long moustache remained attractive, even in death (he wrote), and his long tapering fingers looked like marble. Needless to say, the funeral was the best Deadwood could provide. Thousands trooped past the crude coffin in which he was stretched out, with nothing but a Sharps for company. Some said that he was smilin, though what he had to smile about I do not know. Anyways, they put him in the ground at Ingleside. So how did he get to Mount Moriah? Well, Deadwood was growin by the minute, and pretty soon Ingleside was required for housin, so they decided to move him up here. Three years had passed, but accordin to eye witnesses, his profile was intact, as were the pleats on his dress shirt. For all I know the ol devil is still grinnin away in his box, as dandified as he ever was.'

Alkali Ike turned his attention to the adjacent plot. 'Accordin to the dime novelists,' he said, 'Wild Bill's dyin was attended by the lady lyin under that headstone yonder. Never mind that he died instantly. Anyways, they had her sobbin, "Don't go away from me, Bill . . . I love you . . . Don't you know that? I love you." Then she had to lean closer to catch Wild Bill's last utterance, which came out little better than a whisper: "My heart has been yours from the first." When it was Calamity Jane's turn to go – also on August 2, though more than a quarter of a century later – her dyin wish (so it was said) was to be buried alongside the love of her life. Of course, modern folks like us no longer fall for stuff like that, but here they both are – James Butler Hickok and Martha Jane Cannary – and here we are.'

Wandering around Mount Moriah's more shadowy groves, Saltzman found congenial company. He especially liked the sound of Sidney Jacob, actor, practical joker, haberdasher; but there was also Blanche Colman, the first woman lawyer in the state; and Harris Franklin, hotelier extraordinaire, who was not born with that monicker. 'Lucky he changed his name,' said Alkali Ike, out rounding up strays, 'else you'd be stayin in the Finkelstine.'

After Maureen had taken her leave (she planned to spend the evening with friends at Mustang Lee's) Saltzman wandered across Main Street and entered the Silverado. He waited there until 6.45, but Miami Bitch didn't show. He ate dinner alone in the Franklin's dining room, and ended the evening downstairs in Durty Nellie's transcribing her conversation from memory.

Early next morning he bumped into Wild Bill Hickok, who was taking the air on Main Street despite being deader than mutton. There was no mistaking him, with his chevalier's silken hair (beneath a bad-boy black hat), Chinese moustaches, fancy waistcoat and studded holsters, from which the butts of two six-guns protruded at acute angles, primed for his trademark cross-draw. 'Have you had breakfast yet?' said Saltzman. 'Nope,' said Wild Bill. 'I'm just about to have mine,' said Saltzman, 'so come with me, sir, and be my guest.' 'That's a very generous invitation,' said Wild Bill, 'which I've a mind to accept.'

Taking their seats in the Franklin's dining room, both ordered sausage, biscuits and fried eggs sunny side up. The waitress also brought them glasses of orange juice and poured large cups of coffee. Saltzman drank his black, but Wild Bill asked for milk. 'Is it true that Custer made a pass at you when you scouted for him over at Fort Hays?' said Saltzman. 'No, sir, it is not,' said Wild Bill. 'Hand on heart?' said Saltzman. 'Judging from his description of you it certainly sounds like he wanted to. How does it go? "Whether on foot or on horseback, he was one of the most perfect types of physical manhood I ever saw." And that's only the half of it. "Wild Bill was a strange character, just the one which a novelist might gloat over," he wrote. "In person he was about six feet one in height, straight as the straightest of the warriors whose implacable foe he was; broad shoulders, well-formed chest and limbs, and a face strikingly handsome; a sharp, clear, blue eye, which stared you straight in the face when in conversation; a finely shaped nose, inclined to be aquiline; a well-turned mouth, with lips only partially concealed by a handsome moustache. His hair and complexion were those of the perfect blond. The former was worn in uncut ringlets falling carelessly over his perfectly formed shoulders. Add to this figure a costume blending the immaculate neatness of the dandy with the extravagant taste and style of the frontiersman, and you have Wild Bill, then as now the most famous scout on the Plains." What do you say to that, Mr Hickok?' 'I always liked to think that it was his wife – Libbie – who penned those words,' said Wild Bill, carefully slicing his egg. 'A good point, Mr Hickok,' said Saltzman. 'But it'll take more than a ready wit to persuade me that you aren't queer. Too many of your biographers feel it necessary to defend your heterosexuality for me to think that there's no smoke without fire. One writes, "Considering that Hickok was involved with women at almost every stage of his career, it is curious, if not inexplicable, that rumours and hints have long been circulating that Hickok was not as manly a chap as he pretended to be." Another is equally insistent: "Hickok was a handsome ladies' man, a flashy dresser and had a fair complexion with possibly some feminine characteristics, but one story for which there is absolutely no foundation was that he was a 'queer', or 'homosexual.' Well, Mr Hickok, were you or weren't you?' Wild Bill Hickok rose to his full height, and pushed back his chair. 'Luckily for you, sir, I am not the real Wild Bill,' he said, 'otherwise you'd be dead by now.' 'Please sit down,' said Saltzman, 'I was merely testing a theory.' Wild Bill relented. 'I've also done some readin on the subject,' he said, 'and recall that one of the gentlemen you quote so freely noted that those most eager to "pin the homosexual label on someone else are often exhibiting tendencies in that direction themselves".' 'Touché, Mr Hickok,' said Saltzman.

'How's about a change of subject?' said Wild Bill. 'Agreed,' said Saltzman. 'So now tell me something about yourself. Is being Wild Bill Hickok a full-time occupation?' 'No, sir,' said Wild Bill, 'it's seasonal. I'm Wild Bill Hickok all through the spring and summer seasons. But during the winter I'll only get in costume if required to open a supermarket or a new casino. As you can see, sir, the spring season is upon us. If you have nothing better to do this afternoon you might like to catch my show across the street at Saloon No. 10. The first is at two.' 'I hope you are a better actor than the original Wild Bill,' said Saltzman, recalling reports of Hickok's brief encounter with theatricals.

In 1873 Wild Bill's good chum Buffalo Bill had summoned him to New York in order to play himself in Ned Buntline's epic, *Scouts of the Prairie*. Unfortunately Hickok, for all his flamboyance, was not a natural performer. Nor did he much care for the conventions of the stage. And he liked Buntline's script even less. "Fear not, fair maid!" it had him declaim. "By heavens, you are safe at last with Wild Bill, who is ever ready to risk his life and die, if need be, in defence of weak and defenceless womanhood!' He felt that such arch twaddle made a complete fool out of him, and a mockery of his achievements. His behaviour on stage became unprofessional to the point of anarchism. And he parted company with Buffalo Bill before long. But he wasn't quite done with the footlights. Leaving New York he happened upon an unauthorized version of *Scouts of the Prairie*. He entered the auditorium anonymously. But the sight of a hammy Wild Bill mouthing nonsense and shooting his way through a Comanche war-party proved too much provocation for his fragile temper. He rushed the stage and attacked the impersonator who had traduced his good name, finally throwing him through the painted backdrop – a stout defence of authenticity, for which Wild Bill was arrested and fined $3 the following morning.

'Marlon Brando's skills ain't required,' said Wild Bill. 'All I need do is play some poker, get shot in the back of the head and fall flat on my face.' 'I look forward to seeing that,' said Saltzman.

Before Maureen lit out for the state capital (via Rapid City) she insisted upon introducing Saltzman to Calamity Jane. 'Calamity has agreed to meet with you while she's preparing for her show in the Old Town Hall,' she said. 'Come, I'll walk you down there.' The Victorian building stood opposite an art deco saloon called the Wooden Nickel. They descended into its vestibule, arriving a few minutes in advance of the leading lady. All of a sudden the patch of sunlight in which they stood was suddenly eclipsed as a bear-like creature filled the door.

'Here she is,' said Maureen (as if there were any doubt). 'Opinion is that she could pass for Calamity Jane at the

Pearly Gates,' she whispered. It became immediately apparent that Calamity's reincarnation was already in character and costume (though it looked likely that she was never out of either). Instead of rouge she had smeared mud upon her cheeks. On her head was a domed cowboy hat, its brim pushed up at the front, as though its wearer had spent a lifetime walking into the wind. Covering her pink and white gingham shirt was an embroidered waistcoat (copied from an original in the Buffalo Bill Museum, Cody, Wyoming). The sleeves of her shirt ended not with dainty cuffs, but with leather gauntlets studded with toadstools of brass. Hanging around her neck, like a shrunken breastplate, was a turtle shell. Holsters girdled her generous waist, hosting a six-gun on either hip. Her pants were tucked into knee-high boots. Finally, there were the spurs, like a pair of exclamation marks. At first sight Saltzman thought, this is a woman who doesn't take prisoners. Then he glanced at her eyes, and saw a kind of vulnerability there. She shook Maureen by the hand, and nodded in Saltzman's direction. 'Don't worry,' she rasped, 'you can leave him here with me. I won't hurt him.'

Calamity Jane parted a curtain and led the way into the auditorium. Every night the little theatre hosted the Trial of Jack McCall (who was acquitted of Hickok's murder, though much good it did him, since he was found guilty at a second trial elsewhere and hanged). Saltzman watched as Calamity transformed the courthouse into a saloon for her matinee. Seen from the stalls she filled the small stage, and seemed even larger than life. She warned Saltzman that her version of Martha Jane Cannary was going to be iconoclastic. 'I hope I don't burst any of your bubbles,' she said, while shifting furniture and exchanging props, 'but I'm going to blow the lid off the traditional picture of Calamity Jane. All the stuff about her being a prostitute, all the stuff about her sayin: "Bury me next to Wild Bill Hickok, he's the only man I ever loved." Sorry, but it's baloney. She never said a word of it. The stories they tell about Wild Bill Hickok are baloney too, if you want to know. He only lasted two weeks in Deadwood, during which time he was either in an opium den or a gambling house. Makes no difference, he was addicted to both. Here's another thing they won't tell you in the official biographies. By the time he arrived in Deadwood he was half blind. He could just about find his way around when there was daylight, but at night he had to be led. His apologists point the finger at some vague condition called ophthalmia, but in truth it was syphilis that ruined his eyesight.

'Nevertheless, the men who ran Deadwood felt he was a threat to their interests, and arranged his assassination. They wanted to keep Wild Bill off his guard, so they hired a nobody to do the job. Jack McCall may have pulled the trigger, but the truth is that Wild Bill was killed by his own reputation. At any rate, Wyatt Earp took the hint. He was on his way to Deadwood at the time in search of easy pickings, but he refused to enter the town once he heard the news, preferring to earn a safer living as a logger in the woods.'

Having set up the bar, it was time to fix the drinks. 'Like Calamity I've always been an outsider in a man's world,' she said, 'and I carry the scars on my back to prove it. I got em because, like Calamity, I was good at what I did. People who dismiss Calamity as nothing but a whore and a drunk have no idea what it takes to drive an oxcart. And Calamity could do it better than most men. You could call her a feminist, I guess, though she probably never uttered the word in her life. I certainly wouldn't object if you called me one, having proved myself the equal of any man in Vietnam. I did two tours of duty over there; the first with the air force, the second with the Department of Defense as a propagandist. At that time I was drinking a quart of whiskey a day. You'd be astonished at how much a person can drink and still be functional. Even so, I'm on the wagon these days, which is why I use Dr Pepper's in my show. When diluted it makes a very convincing substitute.' Neither her feminism, nor her experiences, seemed to have altered her views on foreign policy, which made George W. Bush sound like a peacenik.

Without warning she fixed Saltzman with her innocent eyes. 'Marin told me that you're writin an article about Deadwood,' she said. 'What sort of article? After Vietnam I went to England to clear up a few misunderstandings. Stayed on a base in a place called Suffolk, which is where I learned to throw darts so well that I'm now a world-class player. But I also learned all about the English and their wicked sense of humour, and realize that what I am doing may seem very silly to someone like you, even though I have a degree in anthropology, access to university libraries, and plans to write the definitive biography of Martha Jane Cannary. So I have a question for you. Are you planning to make fun of me?' Saltzman felt like a character assassin caught red-handed. Of course he was planning to make fun of her. What else did she expect, an Oscar? But owning up was hardly an option. For one thing, those guns of hers might be loaded with real ammo. And her bare hands looked lethal. So what choice did he have but fib? 'Heaven forbid,' he said.

As the clock struck noon Calamity Jane picked up a bull-whip and headed for the street. Waiting for her were half a dozen men and women dressed as showgirls, gamblers and gunfighters. 'The first year I played Calamity the City Fathers wouldn't let me carry a gun, let alone shoot any-body,' said her representative on earth. 'It was considered far too unladylike. The second year they actually let me fire the gun, so long as it was not pointed at anyone. The third year I put my foot down. Told them that I could shoot as well as any man, and was itching to prove it. Okay, they con-ceded, kill whoever you like. So I plugged those I liked, then I took care of those I didn't.' She positioned herself like some colossus at the corner of Lee and Main, and cracked her bull-whip. Pretty soon families were lining the side-walks, thereby sandwiching the players. The simple script they acted out reminded Saltzman of the gunfights he used to have with Peppercorn every Sunday afternoon. Calamity Jane was now kneeling, blasting away in the general direc-tion of the bad guys at the far end of Lee. Alongside her was a bearded psychopath, with a black hat and long black coat: the trigger-happy sheriff. The baddies were no match for these warriors of righteousness, and before long were can-didates for Mount Moriah, whereupon Calamity rose to her full height, took a bow, and invited the spectators to join her in the theatre.

A few, including Saltzman, followed her. He was in-structed to sit in the middle of the front row, and cast as Mr Thomson, a reporter from Cheyenne. 'Since there are kids present I'd better give you the afternoon version,' said Calamity, pouring herself a large slug of Dr Pepper's, 'the one without the cussin, which is a pity, because Calamity was world class when it came to cussin. But don't worry; I'm not gonna stint on the truth. So if any of you gentlemen in the audience are scared of the truth – which is that Calamity Jane was a strong and independent woman – best bail out now.' Then she turned her attention to Saltzman. 'Mr Thomson,' she said, 'accordin to your newspaper I have been married umpteen times. Well, I have a surprise for those poor fools who believe what they read in the press. I never married no one, not even once. Though, to be fair, I did sometimes call myself Mrs This or That. Because it was easier – given the morals of the time – to pass myself off as the wife of the man I was livin with. But take holy vows? Never!' The rest of the show followed a similar pattern. Saltzman sat, the silent stooge, while he and his paper were taken to task for consistently falsifying the record. Was Calamity an alcoholic? Certainly she liked to drink – didn't everybody in those days? – but never lost control, at least not until the last few years. Was Calamity a prostitute? On the contrary, she infuriated Madam Moustachio and the other brothel-keepers, since she provided the same service as them, but for free. And so on.

'You didn't mind me picking on you?' asked Calamity, after taking her final bow. 'Not at all,' Saltzman replied, 'it was a privilege.' 'So what do you think? Did I make a fool of myself?' she asked. 'On the contrary,' he said, 'you made a fool of me. But you were great.' 'That being so,' she said, 'I have a proposition for you. Why not become my agent in England, and make yourself a rich man? All you need do is set up a few shows for me, and I'll do the rest. You wouldn't be startin from scratch. I'm already somethin of a star over here, with a run at the Sands in Las Vegas under my belt.

Anyway, it's somethin to think about.' She handed Saltzman her card, which had a photo of herself astride a horse on the obverse, and a list of her accomplishments on the reverse ('World Champion EOT, National Champion Winter Range, etc.'). At the bottom she had printed her own sentiment: 'If you're not an NRA member, shame on you.' She signed the card, Calamity Jane.

At two Saltzman ducked into the eternal night of Saloon No. 10 – not the one with the dummies, but the one that was built as its replacement after the fire – in order to witness Wild Bill Hickok meet his maker. Wild Bill was already at work, press-ganging volunteers to join him in a game of poker. His last, as it turned out. There was some mummery over who was going to sit where, and Wild Bill found himself (contravening precedent and his better judgement) with his back to the door. The cards were dealt and Wild Bill fanned out a pair of black aces, and a pair of black eights, ever after known as the Dead Man's Hand. Meanwhile, nemesis, in the ungainly shape of Jack McCall, circled the card table, and then plugged Wild Bill in the back of the head at point blank range. The assassin said but four words: 'Damn you, take that!' This was the closest he ever came to explaining his motivation.

For the remainder of the afternoon Saltzman sat at the glass-topped table in Room 206 (beneath a photograph of John Wayne) and wrote down his impressions of Wild Bill Hickok and Calamity Jane, including as many of their utterances as he could recollect. At 6.30 he closed his notebook, thought, What the hell, and went back to the Silverado. Miami Bitch was nowhere to be seen: not playing blackjack, not playing roulette, not playing the machines, not staring greedily at the gold-plated Cadillac slowly rotating on its plinth. Saltzman was about to leave when he heard a familiar voice shouting, 'What do I want? I want that muppet taken out back and shot.' It came loud and clear from the distant quarter of the room where food was served. He found her sitting on a stool, surrounded by flustered waitresses. It seemed that one of their number had tripped and accidentally launched a bowl of salad in her direction.

The problem was that it had been overdosed with ranch dressing. The waitresses were still plucking green and red leaves from Miami's shirt, but they could do little about the oily cream that was dribbling between her breasts. 'Thank God you're here at last,' she said to Saltzman. 'I need to soak in that wonderful bath of yours.'

'Where is your mother?' he said, as he stepped out of the casino with his winnings. 'And where are the kids?' 'She's taken them to the movies,' said Miami. 'They won't be back for hours.' Could it be that there is a God after all, thought Saltzman, or at least a Devil? They entered the Franklin and ascended its grand staircase. Saltzman unlocked the door to his room and held it ajar for Miami to enter. She opened the bathroom door herself. 'If you'll excuse me,' she said, shutting it behind her. Saltzman listened to the water run, listened to the last drops hit the surface of the full tub, listened to her step into the steaming bath. He envied King David's view of Bathsheba. He knelt at the keyhole, but the key acted as censor. He wished he were a bar of soap. When she emerged she was wrapped in a towel. 'You'll have to lend me a shirt,' she said. 'I'm not puttin mine back on. The thing's soaked through with grease.' Saltzman turned to open the wardrobe, an action that was entirely in character.

But what use was it being Saltzman in such a situation? So he asked himself: What would John Wayne have done? As if he didn't know. He spun round empty-handed and unhooked the towel with his index finger. It dropped to the floor, and Miami stood before him like Venus rising from the waves. Her breasts stood proud from her chest like figureheads on Spanish galleons. Her pubic hair was shaved. Saltzman didn't know the name of the cut. A Brazilian, maybe? Her skin was the colour of toast. 'Are you gonna stare all night,' she said, 'or are you gonna kiss me?' Saltzman kissed her. When they were on the bed she said: 'Don't go gettin any wrong ideas. I'm not doin this 'cos you're God's gift to women. I'm doin it 'cos of where we are. It's kind of a turn-on gettin laid in John Wayne's old pad.' But Saltzman, having got so far, could get no further. He kept slipping out of character, and when he became himself he couldn't perform. Miami was surprisingly tolerant of his inadequacy, perhaps because he knew how to use his tongue for more things than waxing eloquent. Sitting up afterwards she said: 'Don't worry, I know what turns on brainy guys like you.' She took her perfect body to the bathroom, and returned with a pair of stockings. Saltzman, though protesting, allowed her to bind his wrists to the radiator. And she was right. She knew Saltzman better than he knew himself. 'John Wayne you ain't,' she said between mouthfuls, 'but you taste good.'

Miami turned on the TV, wiped her mouth with a Kleenex, then pulled another from the box, intending to mop up Saltzman. If only the careless fool hadn't left his notebook open beside the tissues. Catching sight of some familiar names inscribed therein, Miami began to read. Saltzman could tell she was reading because her lips were moving. He could see her mouthing 'ham-fisted thespian', 'lesbian lumberjack', 'dancing bear', and 'jumped-up historian'. And then struggling over phrases such as: 'Deadwood is the po-mo capital of the world. It is Plato's allegory of the cave made flesh. It is a place where the real looks even more unreal than the unreal, where re-enactors are as likely a Calamity Jane as Calamity Jane herself. Milch was right. Deadwood is America. Rather let us say that America is Deadwood. A log masquerading as a tree, but long cut off from its living roots. How unlike my beloved USA, where everything is illuminated.' 'It ain't what you say,' said Miami. 'It's the way that you say it. I may be too stupid to know what it means, but I'm smart enough to recognize that it ain't real polite.' Unluckily for Saltzman, Miami's curiosity didn't end with his opinion of Calamity Jane and her home town. She wanted to see if he had written anything about her. 'My God,' she said, 'you've recorded just about every word I ever spoke in your presence. Am I supposed to feel flattered, or a laughin stock?' The next line cleared up that little ambiguity. 'So,' she said, 'in your estimation I'm nothin but tarted-up trailer trash.' She looked at the writer. 'Fuck you,' she said. 'Fuck you, you two-faced bastard.' She took one of his shirts, but left without her stockings, which continued to serve as silken handcuffs.

So Saltzman sprawled there spreadeagled, arms aching, and with nothing to do but watch old episodes of *Bonanza*. As the sky lightened he began to wonder just how big a tip he would have to give the chambermaid to buy her silence. But it was not yet dawn when he heard footfalls in the corridor, and saw the door handle begin to turn. Whoever it was filling the door frame was big, because they blocked out the night light from the hallway. Oh no, thought Saltzman. Oh yes, it was Calamity Jane, and she was carrying a camera. 'Once a propagandist, always a propagandist,' she said. 'You don't unlearn the lessons they teach you in the Department of Defense. This is your reward for not takin me seriously. For lyin barefaced. For callin me what . . . a dancin bear?' She pointed the Nikon at Saltzman, and slowly twisted the lens until the full length of him was in sharp focus. 'This is the very latest in digital technology,' she said, 'with enough pixies to ensure that your privates will be visible all the way from Alaska to Zanzibar.' As if that were not bad enough Saltzman's body, though supine, was no longer passive. Feeling like the Naked Maja he had begun to respond to Calamity Jane's artistic gaze. 'Well, what do you know,' she said, 'the pervert's only gettin a boner.'

The prisoners in Plato's cave may have been excluded from the world of real things, thought Saltzman, but at least they were spared its pains and humiliations. He tried to reason with his penis, but it remained headstrong. Calamity Jane knelt beside its owner, and showed him just what it looked like on the SLR's screen. 'Your colleagues at usa.ac.uk are in for a rare treat,' she said, 'not to mention your students.' Saltzman was in uncharted territory for a po-mo. Hitherto, postmodernism had always been there for him as a deflector shield, an armour plating of irony, but now it had been stripped away and he was naked, exposed both physically and mentally, nothing but a bare forked thing with a hard-on. The truth, when it came, hit him hard; he was no longer the artist, he was the model. Calamity Jane had turned the tables, big time. 'I'm sending up the priest,' she said as she quit Room 206, 'looks to me like you've got a heap of confessin to do.'

The Trail of Tears

After his humiliation Saltzman became a wanderer; not a mendicant or a hobo (he still had an Amex card and a bank account) but certainly a lost soul. He quickly grew into the part, sprouting salt 'n' pepper whiskers and thick sidelocks. But on that first terrible morning of his new life he was still clean-shaven. His big problem then was how to sneak out of Deadwood unnoticed. Freed from bondage by God's retired representative the penitent took to its streets, burdened with his bag as well as his sin, seeking a suitable exit. On Sherman Street he paused to admire a ghost sign high on the wall of an erstwhile showroom. It announced the arrival of the latest Terraplane from the Hudson Motor Company. It was a clever name. If aeroplanes criss-crossed the skies, why shouldn't terraplanes cover the continent? But it hadn't caught on. Probably because "automobile" put the purchaser in the driving seat, made him the author of his own destiny. A role that Saltzman had ceded overnight. Not only don't I have a destiny, he thought, I don't even have a destination.

It was while lamenting his lack of direction that Saltz-man spied a more recent enticement to the open road, posted on the same red-brick wall by a company called All-America Driveaways whose office formed part of the building. Its function was spelled out in an irresistible image, which showed a turquoise and cream shark-finned soft-top cruis-ing across the American desert. For those less familiar with semiotics than Saltzman, the following words had been added: 'You drive. We deliver.' Having nothing left to lose, the ex-professor entered.

Although it was before 9 a.m., the company's small office was already staffed. 'What you after?' said the receptionist. 'A one-way ticket to nowhere,' said Saltzman. 'We've a spe-cial that needs to be in Cody, Wyoming, ASAP,' said the receptionist, 'but we haven't been able to find the right driver. We're lookin for someone old enough to know that a little TLC can pay big dividends.' 'I'm your man,' said Saltz-man. 'I knew it as soon as you walked through that door,' said the receptionist, 'but you still have to prove it with a valid driver's licence, a credit card with some credit and a character reference more good than bad.' There was only one person Saltzman could turn to for that. And Bill Walsh, bless him, obliged. 'As if I could turn away a man so down on his luck,' he said.

The special turned out to be a tomato-red convertible with cow-hide upholstery, a stick-shift on the steering wheel, a Navajo rug on the back seat, and chrome six-guns in place of door handles. 'D'ya know what it is you're lookin at?' said the receptionist. 'Sure,' said Saltzman, 'it's the car Clint Eastwood drove in *Bronco Billy*.' 'Howd'ya know that?' said the receptionist. 'I was over in Santa Clarita the day before yesterday,' said Saltzman, 'and happened to see this car's identical twin at the Melody Ranch Museum.' 'Not quite identical,' said the receptionist. 'The one you saw in California was more distressed, bein the actual performer. This beauty here was its understudy. Anyways, they need it for some fool parade organized by the Buffalo Bill Historical Center.' Saltzman was told the name of his contact there, advised that the distance was 450 miles give or take, and allocated two days in which to cover it. 'Treat her like she's a lady,' said the receptionist (patting the auto's sleek flank), 'and you'll get along just fine.'

On any other day Saltzman would have felt like a million dollars, driving through Spearfish Canyon with the roof down and the radio playing Robert Johnson. 'Mr Highway Man, please don't block the road . . . 'Cause she's reachin a cold one hundred and I'm booked and I got to go.' The voice was as insinuating as spilled molasses, but it had no effect upon Saltzman. Even the sight of a bald eagle gliding over the surface of the river failed to lift his spirits. It was already mid-afternoon in England; by now he would be the laughing stock of the University of St Albans, if not the entire academic world. Having crossed the state line into Wyoming he soon found himself in the vicinity of the Devil's Tower, that singular monolith upon whose flat summit the grand finale of *Close Encounters of the Third Kind* was played out. How Saltzman longed for those spaceships to reappear with an offer of safe passage to . . . well, anywhere but planet earth.

Such was his state of mind when he pulled up outside the Occidental Hotel in Buffalo. He knew from the reading he had done for his new course – Contemporary Western

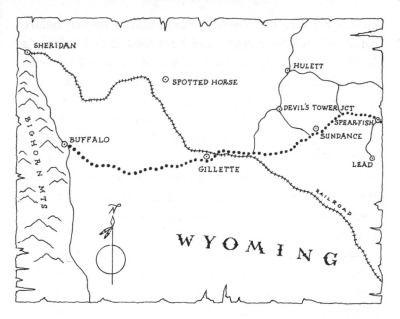

Fiction (now someone else's responsibility) – that old Annie
Proulx wasn't keen on Buffalo, offering its 4 July Parade –
in which the Indians were not Indians, the cowboys not cowboys, the lawmen not lawmen, and the outlaws not outlaws
– as evidence of the West's essential hokeyness. But Saltzman liked the look of the old hotel (which boasted Butch
Cassidy among its erstwhile guests) and besides he was
hungry. The Occidental's restaurant was called the Virginian, after Owen Wister's novel. Could this be a good omen?
Wister, Saltzman recalled, had first visited Wyoming for
therapeutic reasons. Perhaps its bracing air will redeem
even me, Saltzman thought, as he ordered a prime cut. The
waitress, who had the gait of a giraffe, asked him how he
wanted it. Her accent was not only east of the Mississippi,
it was east of the Danube. He said he wanted it rare. Then

137

he asked if Owen Wister had perchance dined here. Unfortunately, Wister was not on the curriculum in Romania or wherever, and she didn't know who he was talking about.

As he was drinking his coffee a woman approached and asked if he had enjoyed his steak. She looked capable, as if she could assemble a house on the prairie out of available timber, and thatch it with peat. Her grey hair was plaited squaw-style. He said that he had. She asked his name. 'Mine is Dawn Waxo,' she said, taking a seat. 'Late of Texas and California, and now joint owner, with Mr Waxo, of this historic hotel. When we first laid eyes upon it, back in 1997, it was about ready for the wrecking ball. But we both felt that it was not a lost cause, that its original splendour, though invisible, was not gone entirely. And we were proven right. Once we had removed all the false ceilings, peeling wallpaper, and rotten carpets, we found ourselves face to face with its glory newborn. It was as if the hotel's former owner, bless her name, had preserved its finest features intact, in hopes they would call out to sympathetic souls at some future date. Now we like to imagine that if Butch Cassidy, or the Sundance Kid, or Calamity Jane or Teddy Roosevelt were to walk through our doors they would chorus: "The old place hasn't changed one bit." You asked about another of our famous guests. Not only was Owen Wister a frequent visitor, he actually wrote a good part of his celebrated novel under our roof. If you like I can show you the very room. It's over in the unrestored wing.'

Yesterday's Saltzman would have jumped at the opportunity. Today's was ready to let it go. 'Most of the other rooms up there were occupied by prostitutes,' added Mrs Waxo. Had they been part of Wister's cure? wondered Saltzman. The possibility of blackening the prissy writer's name persuaded him to take the tour. He paid the check, and followed his hostess into the lobby, which resembled a large Victorian parlour. There he learned that Mrs Waxo pronounced 'cavalry' as 'calvary'. That the hotel's first guests slept in tents. That most of them were travellers along the Bozeman Trail. That one of them was Calamity Jane, who drove a freight wagon as well as any man. That the tents were eventually replaced by a wooden building, which in turn was superseded by the present red-brick structure. That the subject of the full-length portrait above the fireplace was Curley, a Crow who had scouted for Custer at Little Bighorn and lived to tell the tale. That once upon a time the southern boundary of his people's lands had been Clear Creek, which ran alongside the hotel's north side. That Curley's likeness had been captured in the very room in which it hung. That homesick outlaws would check in for comforts not available in their Hole-in-the-Wall hideout. With maternal obstinacy Mrs Waxo tried to convince Saltzman that neither Butch Cassidy nor the Sundance Kid had really passed away in Bolivia. 'They came back from South America. Everyone knows that,' she said. 'Letters from a friend of Butch's sister prove that he was alive and well and living in Oregon long after his supposed demise.' Sundance, it seemed, preferred Wyoming. 'Is there any proof?' said Saltzman. 'You betcha,' said Mrs Waxo. He followed her into the hotel's little bookstore, where an ancient register was on display. She pointed to a particular entry: 'E. E. Lonabaugh & friend'. 'You need to know that the Sundance Kid's real name was Henry Lonabaugh, and that E. E. Lonabaugh, from nearby Lusk, was his cousin,' said Mrs Waxo.

'In order to keep his presence here a secret he signed him in as "friend". Who else would have needed the anonymity?' Was this a mutant form of Christianity, wondered Saltzman, this refusal to believe that America's most notorious were mouldering in their graves? As Mrs Waxo believed that Butch and Sundance had avoided the deaths ascribed to them by history, so others refused to accept that Billy the Kid had died at Fort Sumner, or Jesse James at St Louis. And why did this immunity to death's sting apply only to outlaws? Was it because these believers saw them as Christ-like? After all, Jesus was an outlaw too.

Access to the unrestored wing was via a separate entrance. Out on the sidewalk Saltzman discovered that his automobile had attracted a sizable crowd, among which was Mr Waxo. 'Dawn,' he said, 'dare I hope that Clint Eastwood himself is paying us a visit?' 'Do I look like Clint Eastwood?' said Saltzman brutally. 'Is this your vehicle?' said Mr Waxo. 'Only for the day,' said Saltzman, 'it's a drop-off bound for Cody.' 'But you know its provenance?' said Mr Waxo. 'Sure,' said Saltzman. 'And you're familiar with the movie in which it featured,' said Mr Waxo. 'Depends what you mean by "familiar",' said Saltzman. 'Are you asking whether I've seen it, or whether I was smart enough to appreciate its Fordian notes? Like John Ford, our boy Clint knows that the myths of the Wild West are hokum, but he also knows (as did Ford) that they are necessary hokum. In reality Bronco Billy is nothing more than a shoe salesman from New York living out his dream. But that dream is the American Dream. And his big top a metaphor for America itself, a diverse nation, but bound together by a common mythology. Either way the answer is, yes.' 'Sir,' said Mr Waxo, 'you are a man after my own heart. So please allow me to make you a little proposal. I'll trade a night's accommodation for a ride in this fabulous machine. You're less than two hundred miles from Cody. Make an early start and you'll be there by midday. What do you say?' Saltzman held out his hand. 'It's a deal,' said Mr Waxo, shaking it.

'When we lived in California,' said Mrs Waxo, unlocking the door to the unrestored wing, 'my husband, who was a writer back then, formed many a movie and TV connection.' The spring sunshine had not yet removed winter's chill from the unheated building, and Saltzman shivered as he ascended its wooden staircase. 'I can see that you are sensitive,' said Mrs Waxo, 'so you should know that this section is haunted by at least one very active spirit. A nine-year-old girl, the daughter of a prostitute, who died of cholera. She was first documented ninety years ago. Nowadays she makes her presence felt by tapping visitors on the shoulder. But there are other – angrier – ghosts up here too. Once I saw a gentleman approach one of the rooms as if about to enter it, but instead of going in he jumped back so violently that he knocked his wife over. "There's something in there that doesn't want me near it," he said. "It's not threatening, exactly. It simply doesn't want me to come in." Later he explained that he had become hypersensitive to the spirit world since the death of his father.'

Wister's suite of rooms was at the far end of the corridor. Mrs Waxo pushed open the door. Amid the revealed clutter Saltzman could make out a little table and a fireplace. 'Picture the scene,' said Mrs Waxo. 'Logs are blazing in the fireplace. Owen Wister is sitting at the table trying to choreograph the climax of his novel. At last Molly has agreed to marry its hero. The couple ride into a town – unnamed – to take their vows, but the Virginian's rival for Molly's hand is there already. Ignoring his bride-to-be's ultimatum – it's me or him – the Virginian seeks out the man who would destroy him. He finds him at sundown. They face each other in an encounter only one will survive. Meanwhile, Molly waits heartbroken in a hotel room. Critical consensus is that it was this one.' Mrs Waxo closed the door.

The other doors were wide open. 'Most of these rooms were used for less elevated purposes,' said Mrs Waxo. The names of the women who worked in them are all lost, she explained, with the exception of Red Hills Lil. In order to find out how Lil and her contemporaries went about their business, Mrs Waxo rounded up as many of their surviving customers as she could muster – mostly nonagenarians – and served them tea spiked with whiskey. 'Then I brought them here,' she said, 'and just listened as the memories came flooding back. The first thing I learned was they never went straight to the girls. They always began by getting liquored up in the saloon. When they'd had enough they quit the bar, walked down the alley and used the back stairs for privacy's sake. Once they had been admitted they were required to remove their footwear, boot blackening being part of the service. They also dumped their underwear in the slop sink, where their intimates would be washed and then dried – another part of the service. Next was a visit to the commode, or even to a bath. What happened after that depended upon how much they were prepared to pay.' Saltzman stepped towards one of the rooms to see what remained, only to recoil as he spied a platoon of free-standing ribbed radiators, very like the one to which he had been bound not five hours previously, and saw very starkly the horrid spectre of his folly. Observing his backward motion, the colour drain from his face, and his lips blanch, Mrs Waxo exclaimed: 'Just like before! There's no doubt now! That room definitely has a sitting tenant with a bad attitude.'

When they regained the street Mrs Waxo sought out her husband. 'It turns out that this Saltzman is half a psychic,' she said, 'especially receptive to unquiet spirits.' 'I don't know about that,' said Mr Waxo, 'but he certainly looks like he could do with a shot of 40 per cent proof.' Leading the way into the dimly lit saloon he said, 'From one spirit world to another.' He asked the bartender to pour two shots of Knob Creek, with a Bud for Mrs Waxo. They sat at the centre of the bar, facing the bottles and the glasses, with a good twelve feet either side of them. 'This old place has seen some serious history,' said Mr Waxo. 'Have they heard of the Johnson County War over in England?' 'My students have,' said Saltzman. 'Back in the USA – the University of St Albans – I teach – taught – a seminar on the subject. Since my speciality is not – was not – history, we looked at its representations on page and screen. First we viewed *Shane*, which offers the conflict in microcosm, as a simple dispute between ranchers and sod-busters; then we watched the director's cut of *Heaven's Gate*, which portrays it on a Tolstoyan scale. The way Michael Cimino tells it, the Wyoming Stock Growers' Association was nothing but a bunch of ruthless capitalists (albeit with pretensions to gentility) prepared to murder on a grand scale in order to protect its profits. Its victims – immigrants struggling to hold body and soul together – clearly enjoyed his full sympathy. Your genius loci took the opposite view, of course, both in life and in art. For him the Stock Growers' Association was a cabal of righteous patriarchs, absolutely entitled to defend its God-given empire against rustlers and the small-minded partisans of democracy. But when my students saw their leader, Frank Canton, gun down delicious Isabelle Huppert – playing the real-life figure of Ella Watson – Wister's prejudices didn't stand a chance. My students came down squarely on the side of the little man.'

'A fair number of whom,' said Mr Waxo, 'met in this very saloon and – having availed themselves of what was on offer – made a courageous decision. The year, you'll recall, was 1892. By then the cattlemen were in big trouble. Profits had been in decline since '86, when the worst drought anyone could recall had been followed by the harshest winter in living memory. The range, already ravaged by overgrazing, never properly recovered. But when their European investors asked, "Where are our dividends?" they replied, "In the hands of rustlers." Did they believe their lie? They certainly acted as if they did. Deciding to make an example of someone, they lit upon Cattle Kate, an uncommon whore who let cowboys pay for her cunny with kine. Her real name, incidentally, was Ella Watson, and she was hung, not bushwhacked, as Cimino would have you believe.' ('My husband is a bit of a stickler when it comes to the Johnson Country War,' said Mrs Waxo. 'You see, he's writing his own screenplay about it.') 'Cattle Kate's murder made no difference,' Mr Waxo continued, 'so the ranchers next drew up a list of all those they considered to be rustlers or soft on rustling. There were a hundred twenty-five names in total, including independent ranchers, lawmen and other elected representatives. Slaughter on such a scale required professionals, and so some fifty gunslingers from Texas were hired to do the job properly. Their arrival was nothing less than an invasion. The first men they shot were Nick Ray, and Nate Champion – played in Cimino's movie by Christopher Walken. Then word got around that the invaders were heading for Buffalo. That's when its braver citizens congregated right here, and resolved to take up arms against the killers. How about we follow their trail to the TA Ranch, where the two sides battled it out?' Saltzman and Mrs Waxo drank to the idea. 'Another thing,' said Mr Waxo, 'Frank Canton wasn't the leader of the Wyoming Stock Growers' Association. He was just one of their stock detectives. As a matter of fact, he was beaten to within an inch of his life right where we're standing.'

Mrs Waxo sat in the back of the car, with the Navajo rug over her knees, while her husband sat in the front alongside Saltzman. The TA spread was about twenty miles south of Buffalo, along a country road that ran parallel to the interstate. Bronco Billy's bright-red convertible burned down it like a chariot of fire. 'Ain't this the life?' exulted Mrs Waxo. The ranch house and adjacent outbuildings were surrounded by a circle of old cottonwood trees. Earl and Barbara, the owners, were nowhere in evidence, so Mr Waxo took it upon himself to show Saltzman the wooden barn in which the Texan gunslingers held out for three days straight, against a posse of two hundred concerned citizens armed with repeating rifles. He pointed out the numerous bullet holes. Saltzman said he could see them, but in truth he couldn't tell a bullet hole from a knothole. On the third day the cavalry intervened (though Mr Waxo, like his wife, insisted upon 'calvary'), and the gunslingers were spirited away. Although murders had been committed, none of them was ever charged.

Back in the Occidental the Waxos offered Saltzman the
Cottonwood Suite. During the night he had a vision of
Calamity Jane. She was standing at the foot of the iron bed,
larger than life. Fixing him with a baleful stare she plucked
off the tortoise shell she wore around her neck, then forced
his body into it, so that his head protruded from its front,
and his limbs from its sides. That done she cast him down.
Finally, she cursed him as he crawled in the dust: 'From
today the road will be your university.' He was still shaken
by the dream when he showed up for breakfast. 'Poor Saltzman,' said Mrs Waxo, 'you look like you've seen another of
our ghosts.' 'More like my nemesis,' he said. 'Is it something
you want to tell me about?' she said. 'Why not?' he said. 'I
did a foolish thing in Deadwood, a very, very foolish thing,
that has cost me my career . . .' Just then a stranger entered
the restaurant, and asked if anyone had a light for his cigar.
'Sure,' said Mrs Waxo, approaching him. 'I'll light it, but
you'll have to smoke it outside.' 'Fair enough,' said the man,
exhaling a wisp of fragrant exhaust. 'I do love the smell of
a cigar in the morning,' said Mrs Waxo, linking arms with
the newcomer. Left alone, Saltzman drank his coffee and
departed quietly.

What Mr Waxo failed to mention was that the road out
of Buffalo climbed to nearly ten thousand feet. After crossing the Powder River Pass, Saltzman found himself in the
perma-dusk of Ten Sleep Canyon, whose walls glowered like
the setting sun. At the town of Ten Sleep he took a right,
and headed north-west, crossing the Big Horn River at Manderson. He stopped for a coffee at Tom's Cafe in Basin. Tom
was obviously crazy about singing cowboys. Three guitars
rested on a shelf: memorials to Roy Rogers, king of the cow-

boys, 1911–1998; Hopalong Cassidy, 1895–1972; and Gene Autry, America's favourite, 1907–1998.

Saltzman reached Cody in the early afternoon. Having delivered the auto in good repair and received cash on the nail for a job well done, he thought a tour of the Buffalo Bill Historical Center was in order. If his childhood had been but shadow things, then these were the things that had cast the shadows. Gleaming Colt .45s, with names like Rainmaker, Lightning, Thunderer, Frontier. Their creator – the man who invented the first six-gun a cowboy could depend upon – did not go unsung. A biographical notice concluded thus: 'With a proud and assertive "rampant" colt as his personal and corporate trademark, Sam Colt made his guns an enduring symbol of self-reliant freedom and of the spirit of the American frontier.' Saltzman's first response was: Don't they read Freud in Wyoming? But then he decided that the phallic imagery was probably conscious, that the writer

really did want to suggest it was masculinity (if not actually the penis) that had won the West. He wondered what the writer would make of Kent Monkman's work, whose view, after all, was strangely similar. Not to mention the priapic snaps taken by Calamity Jane that had done for him.

The disgraced professor worked hard to block out the images that were barely old enough to be memories. And Buffalo Bill, a hero since childhood, did his level best to assist. It helped that the reminiscences the museum awakened were entirely benign (even though many included Peppercorn). When Saltzman stopped to pay homage to yet another fondly recalled icon – the Deadwood Stage, no less – they fell upon his tortured soul like balm. The wooden coach in its livery of red was as familiar to him as his late father's metallic-blue Jag. He knew its colourful history thanks to his 1953 *Buffalo Bill Wild West Annual*, could still summon with ease vivid scenes from the comic strip that told it: the Indian attacks, the hold-ups, and then redundancy and dereliction, a state in which it remained until rescued and restored by Buffalo Bill. And then, like a memory come to life, Saltzman spotted the stuttering vitality of an ancient newsreel flickering on a screen. He looked more carefully and witnessed the Deadwood Stage surrounded by hostiles, its passengers inevitably doomed, until the last-minute arrival of Buffalo Bill saved the day. It looked like an outside broadcast from the Wild West, but in reality was shot at one of Buffalo Bill's world-famous shows. At this distance, however, the re-enactment was as historic as the original skirmish (if there ever was one).

The blurring of the borderline between history and make-believe was Buffalo Bill's great legacy. He was hardly the first to make the crossing, but he was the most success-

148

ful. The museum pin-pointed the precise moment when the gates opened for him. 'On July 17 1876, less than a month after Custer's defeat, the 5th Cavalry intercepted a large group of Cheyenne in western Nebraska. The Cheyenne were on their way to join their victorious allies further north. Cody led a squad of soldiers and scouts in a reckless charge on a like squad of Indians. He killed the leader, whose name Yellowhair was mistranslated as Yellowhand, and took "the first scalp for Custer". It was a minor battle but the most important for the future of Buffalo Bill. He was already making a name for himself as an actor. His heroic real-life actions now made the stage drama more believable. He was becoming part of Western myth. There are no modern analogies, but what if John Wayne, after whipping the Japanese on film, had led the charge up Mount Suribachi?'

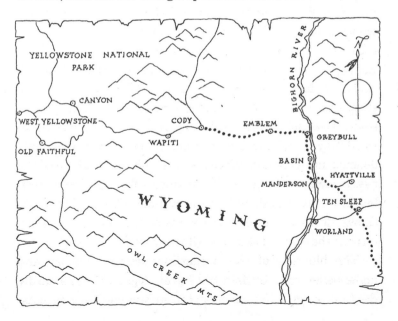

The impresario who eased Buffalo Bill's transition, Ned Buntline, was the same hagiographer who had previously penned the immortal drama *Scouts of the Prairie*. Saltzman had a long familiarity with him thanks to an illustrated biography in the same *Wild West Annual* that had profiled the Deadwood Stage. It began with a full-page picture of Buntline at his desk, cigar in mouth, quill in hand. Around him were the outlines of Buffalo Bill, and an Indian with mayhem on his mind; obviously figments of his imagination. 'The man who really gave Buffalo Bill to the world was known as Ned Buntline,' a caption explained (with surprising frankness). And note the 'known as'. Ned Buntline was not born a Buntline. It was as Edward Judson that he had run away to sea aged ten. He took his nom de plume (Mark Twain-like) from the rope that secured the base of a square sail. A later illustration showed him crouching behind a boulder, alongside his meal ticket. Facing them was a party of hostiles. 'Best use your gun, Ned!' yelled Bill. 'I'll do better with a pencil!' replied Ned, as an arrow took off his hat. 'Ned Buntline always claimed that he was with Buffalo Bill during many of his exciting adventures,' added the caption, 'when he was able to share his hero's dangers.' And that's exactly what young Saltzman had wanted to do when he grew up, having realized early on that he would never be a hero: no, he would share his hero's dangers, and subsequently – like Ned Buntline – broadcast them to an eager public. Then came the second unwelcome revelation; there were no more heroes. And instead of a writer, establishing and burnishing bright reputations, Saltzman became an academic – hell-bent on undermining them. From there he quickly turned into an iconoclast, and gave his students the tools with which to shatter false idols.

Over the years, as was inevitable, cynicism feasted upon his soul. If it existed, thought Saltzman, it must now resemble a piece of mouldy cheese in a rat-trap. The wonder of the museum was that for minutes in a row his soul felt whole again, and he could almost taste the sweet anticipations of childhood. Unfortunately, the feeling did not outlast the journey from exhibit to exhibit, and would certainly have been extinguished altogether if he had not happened upon one of the wonders of the modern age. It was a full-sized foosball table (which looked much like a football table to Saltzman), manufactured by the Triangle Z Ranch Furniture Co. of Wyoming. What made it unmistakably American and unusually desirable were the players. Instead of Manchester United vs Chelsea, it featured (in the blue shirts) the US Cavalry against (in the yellow shirts) the Sioux. The soldiers were evidently the home team, because the table's frame was a miniature stockade. Scenes from Western life decorated its interior. Saltzman had not coveted anything so fiercely since Peppercorn had waved a new gun in his cousin's face (a present for his tenth birthday); Saltzman's palms tingled as he recalled the mustangs embossed upon its faux-ivory handles. Like a real Colt .45 its cylinder revolved every time Peppercorn pulled the trigger. When the cycle was complete the gloating marksman pulled a lever and out fell six likely looking bullets. The fact that Saltzman could still want something so badly offered grounds for optimism. In order to acquire the foosball table he would need a good job. And once he had gotten the thing he would require a house in which to put it. And since it was a game for two players he would also need a wife. He had entered the museum a broken man, but now he strode toward its exit repaired, his gait confident, his eye roving, already auditioning likely candidates for the role of the second Mrs Saltzman. Yes, Buffalo Bill had saved him, as surely as he had saved those passengers on the Deadwood Stage. As Saltzman passed through the lobby a country singer was tuning her guitar. By the time he had retrieved his bag from the cloakroom she was already yodelling the chorus of her first number: 'Whoopi-ty-aye-oh / Rockin to and fro / Back in the saddle again / Whoopi-ty-aye-yay / I go my way / Back in the saddle again . . .' Why not? thought Saltzman. And sought out the nearest All-America Driveaways office.

After just one delivery, it seemed, Salzman was already a byword for reliability, so he was handed a peach. The auto in the parking lot was pinker than a pink flamingo. Its front bumper looked like a chromium brassiere built for a Valkyrie. Its body was longer than Bob Beamon's leap. Its tail fins would not have disgraced a shark. Its wheels were all white-walls, of course. Saltzman recognized it at once: a mythical Cadillac Eldorado, circa 1955. If it had been a chimera or a phoenix, it would not have surprised or thrilled him more. The only other Cadillac Eldorado he had ever set eyes upon was a Dinky toy, previously Peppercorn's, which his cousin had swapped for a set of animal stamps from Tuva (wherever that might be). Peppercorn was welcome to Tuva, and the rest of the world for that matter, save for that part his acquisition represented: as far as the young conquistador was concerned the Eldorado was America, just as America was his Eldorado. So when it came to pass that a counter clerk in Cody, Wyoming, handed Saltzman the keys to one, it felt to him that he was receiving the keys to the Republic. How could he resist crowing to Peppercorn? In return, Peppercorn coolly informed him that his picture had made the Sundays, under the headline, 'Prof in a bind'. 'No disputing that,' said the prof. 'What are you going to do?' asked Peppercorn. 'Hide,' said Saltzman, 'lie low, go on the run, live like the outlaw Jesse James.' 'Don't forget to keep in touch,' said Peppercorn. At about 4.00 in the afternoon Saltzman set off for Cheyenne, where the Cadillac's impatient new owner was awaiting him at the Plains Hotel. The fact that he was being sent to Cheyenne had to be another good omen. The Cheyenne had been big players in the apotheosis of William Cody. Maybe Saltzman was destined to be reborn in the city that bore their name.

He hadn't planned it that way, but Saltzman ended up driving through the night, because he didn't dare leave the fabulous auto unattended in the forecourt of an isolated motel. He did stop a few times to buy gas, and drink dirty coffee, but mainly he drove. First light found him approaching Wheatland, about seventy miles north of his destination. He passed the cut-off for Guernsey and Sunrise, then saw the one for Fort Laramie. Since he had hours to spare he took it. How could he not? His old life was still warm. Fort Laramie was where the Sioux Wars began, back in 1854, after a wet-behind-the-ears officer went to arrest a brave for stealing a cow and got himself massacred. It was also where the hatchet was buried in 1868, only to be exhumed six years later, when Custer's man trumpeted the discovery of gold in the Black Hills. Saltzman, expecting a site haunted by the resentful dead, found himself instead at a place as benign as any English hamlet. The Fort's headquarters reminded him of nothing so much as a cricket pavilion, and its expanse of well-tended grass looked just like a village green. But even in Arcadia discord lurked. As Saltzman walked across the lawns, leaving footprints in the dew, he accidentally disturbed a bird of some sort. It ascended vertically from under his boot, and hovered immediately above his head like a crazed wind-up toy. He couldn't name it, but could see that it had a lavender back, a pale-yellow breast, and dabs of black warpaint on its cheeks. Whatever it was, its song seemed anything but amorous; *whit-ker-whit* it went, *whit-ker-whit*, which Saltzman understood to mean: Fuck off! More familiar and soothing were the plovers flying overhead, with their distinctive wings, their sudden swoops, and their plaintive whistles needling through the golden mist, *queedle, queeeedle*. Before long they were answered by the lonesome toot of a distant train on the other side of the river Platte. It sounded to Saltzman like the ghostly wail of immigrant America, a slow release of pent-up longing for a better life in a new world. How could those courageous pioneers have known that their dreams would destroy those of the people already there?

Saltzman barrelled south, and hit downtown Cheyenne just after the sun. The gilded dome above the State Capitol, which stood at the city's heart, radiated spokes of golden light, as though proselytizing democracy. From there it was a straight run along Central Avenue to the Plains Hotel. Saltzman figured that Mr Mentz would still be abed at that hour, so he decided to breakfast in the hotel's Capitol Grille. Early editions of the *Wyoming Eagle–Tribune* were piled high on a table at its entrance. Saltzman helped himself to one. Upon entry he saw that the dining room was already

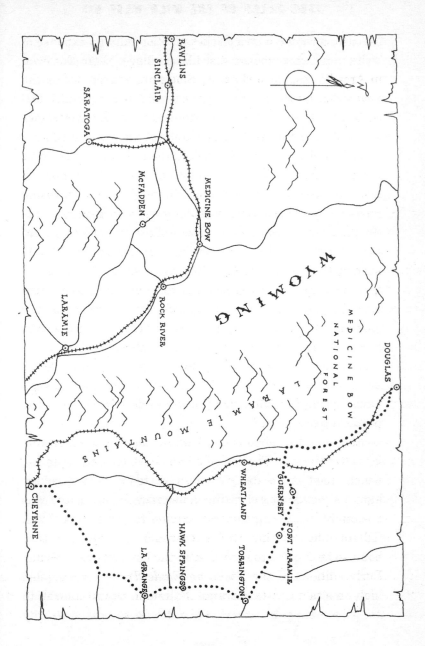

half-full with cowboy types. Polite buckaroos who did not eat with their hats on. Each table had its own surround with hooks and a flat top. Some cowboys chose to hang their Stetsons on the hooks, others to park them horizontally. All the hats, Saltzman noted, were white, and (to his inexperienced eye) identical. He ordered black coffee and a large orange juice from the waitress, then went to the buffet. The eggs, beans and bacon simmering in their silver drums all stirred his appetite, but what really excited his senses was the unexpected view of an imagined world. Made of glazed tiles, the mural depicted cowboys at work and play on the range, at full gallop roping yearlings, on their knees branding them, or sometimes just smoking roll-ups. No, thought Saltzman, it's unfair to call this vision imaginary. For the businessmen in the room in their domesticated cowboy outfits, this was their once and future world, and the city in which they dwelt and worked but a shadowland or purgatory.

The ex-professor returned to his table and began to read the newspaper. Its lead story covered the controversy occasioned by the reintroduction of wolves to Yellowstone. The local ranchers complained bitterly that the newcomers were feasting on their livestock and likely to ruin them. A conservationist patiently explained that losses were actually minimal, and that wolves much preferred to hunt wild game than domesticated stock that had lost the instinct to flee predators. His arguments cut no ice with the *Eagle–Tribune*, whose editorial came down firmly on the side of the ranchers and castigated the Governor for failing to defend their property rights. The fact that the enemy was the wolf this time did not fool Saltzman for a second. He sensed that the paper was still fighting the Johnson County War, still justifying the behaviour of the Stock Growers' Association. Plus ça change, he thought.

Turning the pages he read that Willie Nelson had been booked to headline the entertainment at Cheyenne's summer extravaganza, trademarked as Frontier Days. He also learned that Divinity Love had been elected its Queen. It had been a close call, but she had narrowly pipped Mercy Sweetbriar, who had the consolation of being her Lady-in-Waiting. There were photographs of each in an identical pose. Their outfits were identical too: Stetsons embellished with the insignia of office, ornate blouses and fringed waist-coats. Only with difficulty could Saltzman tell them apart. But when he did he saw that the Lady-in-Waiting far out-shone her Queen. No wonder Peppercorn wanted her all to himself, he thought. And decided, there and then, that what the Lady-in-Waiting was waiting for was him.

Reaching the end of the paper he noted that the Terry Bison Ranch was recruiting drivers for its spring and summer seasons. Testimonials from a delighted Mr Mentz, and All-America Driveaways, ensured his recruitment. His Social Security card, which dated from his days as a teaching assistant at the University of California, meant that no questions were asked about his status. The job required him to drive a pensioned-off school bus from the ranch shop up into the backcountry where the buffalo grazed. It didn't take more than a couple of dry runs to grasp the idiosyncrasies of its stick shift. And a couple more to learn the lay of the land.

On the application form Saltzman had given his address as the Plains Hotel, but he lacked the resources to stay there indefinitely. So he scanned the local papers looking for an apartment to rent. Drawing up a shortlist of six, he checked out the front-runner first because it also happened to be the nearest. It consisted of three rooms above a bookstore on West Lincolnway. The landlady was a tough old cookie who, unlike many he met, did not ask him to thank Tony Blair personally for his support over Iraq. On the contrary, she had a bone to pick with her prospective tenant. Why didn't his Prime Minister use what influence he had to make Bush do something about global warming? 'That cowboy has already wrecked his own country,' she said, 'why are you letting him lay the rest of the world to waste?' Saltzman apologized for his failure to save the planet. 'It's the pot calling the kettle black,' she said. 'I used to look at the State Capitol the way that Muslims still look upon the Dome of the Rock. Not our democracy's holiest shrine, but maybe its third or fourth, after Boston and Philadelphia. Likewise, I regarded our Bill of Rights as holy writ. Now we don't have it any more. Bush snatched it away from us, with Patriot Acts One and Two, just as he stole the presidency from under the nose of Al Gore. When the White House has an illegal occupant – a usurper, you'd call him – the only honourable thing to be is an outlaw. I promise you, Mr Saltzman, if I were any younger I'd change my name to Bonnie and rob banks.' 'And I'd call myself Clyde and come with you,' said Saltzman. He got the apartment.

Next thing he did was kit himself out with a second-hand compact for the short commute to work (Lincolnway joined the interstate, which in turn led to the Terry Bison Ranch). Pretty soon he had the routine off pat. Visitors would exit the shop clutching their bags of buffalo feed (pellets made of alfalfa, corn and molasses), and board the bus. 'That old house to your right,' he would say as they pulled away from the yard, 'is known as the Wyoming White House, on account of the fact that Teddy Roosevelt patronized it. You may be interested to know that it was Owen Wister, President Roosevelt's great friend, who introduced ideas of chivalry to the Wild West. Before him cowpokes regularly rescued damsels in distress, but none ever thought of courting them.' At least he began thus in the early days, until a heckler shouted from one of the rear seats: 'Hey, Prof, where's the beef?' After that he took his passengers in silence to the pastures where sightings were guaranteed. First up was Larry the Texas longhorn. Next came Bob the beefalo, a cross-breed, whose white patches made him look like an unripe conker. Finally, there was Tinkerbell, everyone's favourite buffalo, and her anonymous cronies. At this point Saltzman never failed to remind his charges that buffalo were unpredictable creatures, capable of outrunning the bus, and rolling it too (should they hit it amidships). Then he stopped and permitted his students (whoops) to scatter their feed on the steps of the bus. 'You may be wondering why this vehicle doesn't have a door,' said Saltzman. 'It's because one of my passengers didn't take any heed when I warned her that buffalo don't like to be petted. Well, she goes and does it regardless. The critter wasn't Tinkerbell, and it ripped the door right off its hinges.' In fact, the story was apocryphal, which wasn't to say that it couldn't have happened. For three months straight Saltzman kept up this routine, and then in late July he quit. It was Sweetbriar time.

On 24 July Saltzman locked his apartment and walked the full length of Carey Avenue, passing the State Capitol en route, until he reached Frontier Park, purpose-built to host Cheyenne Frontier Days, also called CFD, and the Daddy of 'em All, in recognition of its longevity and magnitude. Posters on the park's periphery promised 'More Thrills, More Spills, More Broncs, More Bulls, More Foot-Stompin', Heart-Poundin', Bone Rattlin' Action than any other Rodeo on Earth.' Other literature contained the startling claim, 'When cowboys dream, they dream of CFD.' (Were Saltzman still Professor Saltzman he would have subjected that statement to proper scrutiny. For example, he would have wondered how access was gained to the cowpunchers' subconscious. Had every one of their shrinks turned stoolpigeon? Did the dreams include the little 'TM' that always accompanied CFD? And how could anyone be sure that cowboys were dreaming of CFD and not KFC?) But Saltzman was no longer an academic, so he joined the careless throng waltzing through the fair. He saw fathers and sons together, the one the other in miniature, and grasped for the first time the meaning of the suffix Jr. He saw women exchanging hugs, then whispering, and laughing unaffectedly. How pleasant to be mindless, he thought. By this he did not mean to suggest that stupidity was the norm among the merrymakers. No, what he envied was their ability to decouple the mind – to have unfiltered feelings, to behave spontaneously. Had he been at the lectern he would have referred his listeners to those Westerns in which train robbers separate the engine from the rolling stock, and watch as it slips headlessly down the line. What Saltzman longed for was a Jesse James – or, better yet, a Jessica James – to do the same for him. Above all he wanted to be able to enjoy the world's fair, instead of just walk through it. But not today; at least, not yet.

He took his seat in the East Stand just in time to catch the entrance of the Rodeo Dandies. Each Dandy held a banner that fluttered horizontally in the hot summer wind. Round and round the hippodrome they rode. Rather than the colours of robber barons or knights errant, their flags displayed the logos of (among others) Coca-Cola, Bud, McDonald's, Wrangler, Wal-Mart, and Qwest. The hierarchy among these sponsors was as intricate as anything in *Burke's Peerage*. Bud Lite was top of the tree as the CFD's Platinum Arrowhead Sponsor. Just below it were the likes of Qwest, CheapTickets and Community First National Bank, all Gold Boot Sponsors. Below them were the Silver Boot Sponsors: Coca-Cola, Chevy Trucks, State Farm Insurance, Wrangler, McDonald's et al. Each of the main sponsors had its own day. 'Today is not Thursday,' said the announcer, 'today is Coca-Cola Day.' In spite of the logorrhoea the woman seated beside Saltzman wept at the beauty of the spectacle. Even he felt a touch Walter Scottish at the sight of all that trumped-up medievalry.

Having advertised their riding skills as well as the products and services they represented, the Dandies formed an honour guard for the State Governor and his First Lady, who appeared in an open surrey. Like every other male in Wyoming (Saltzman included) the Governor was sporting the full cowboy rig. The landau that followed contained no less a personage than Calvin Jumping Frog, great-grandson of Sitting Bull, and without doubt the most resplendent oxymoron Saltzman had ever set eyes upon: an American Indian cowboy. Trailing the two carriages were Divinity Love and Mercy Sweetbriar, one on a pinto, the other on a sorrel. Now that's more like the stuff of this cowboy's dreams, thought Saltzman. He stood with the other spectators when the first bars of the patriotic medley sounded, even took off his hat, but instead of asking God to bless America, he was begging for Mercy.

'Thank the Lord for the USA,' said the announcer when it was over. 'And thank the Lord for our military. Some of its finest men and women are with us today. Let's give a warm welcome to the crew of the USS *Cheyenne*. The Tomahawk missile it fired in the early hours of March 19 was the starting pistol that set Operation Eye-raki Freedom in motion. That phase of the war is already – in the words of our President – mission accomplished. All our boys – and gals – have to do now is win the peace.' Despite the cheers, thought Saltzman, a man in uniform will never be a true American hero. Okay, he countered, explain Custer. An exception, he conceded, but remember also that his immortality is contingent upon defeat, not victory. More typical is Audie Murphy. He may have been the most decorated soldier of the Second World War, but it took Hollywood to make him really famous. And upon what figure did that fame rest? You didn't need to be a professor to know the answer to that one. Even the announcer knew it. Referring to the competitors now readying themselves for their eight-second ordeal, he said, 'They are eighteen hundred role models, eighteen hundred cowboys with their cowboy honesty and sense of fair play. Always remember: A cowboy says what he means, and means what he says. Learn from him, and you'll all leave with a good feeling about life, and the cowboy way, a way of life that's still very much alive and kicking . . .'

And out of the swinging chute gates shot one of the aforementioned eighteen hundred, riding two thousand pounds of bullish bad temper. The rider used one hand to hang on to a rope knotted around the brute's heaving chest, and the other to maintain his balance as the bull bucked and jumped. He maintained it for five seconds. 'He wasn't going to let go of the bull till the back of his head hit the ground,' remarked the announcer. Clowns distracted the strutting bovine, while horsemen rescued their fallen comrade. The next bull that came crashing out was introduced as Randy Newman, though Saltzman thought Tom Russell a more appropriate name. 'By the way,' added the announcer, 'the cowboy trying to stay on him has a brother serving in Eye-raq.' The crowd whooped well enough, but he got no sympathy from old Randy, a monster in size and disposition, who first arched his spine, then unleashed his back legs so forcefully that he practically performed a handstand. The cowboy flew off his back like a stone cast from a catapult, and landed with a thud. One of Randy Newman's greatest hits, you could say. The third bull had obviously gained some understanding of centrifugal force. It just spun around like an old-fashioned 45. Then it stopped dead. But the rider didn't. 'It's a fine line between dirt and glory,' said the announcer. 'In that cowboy's case one more second would have taken him across.' Saltzman was astonished how long eight seconds could seem, and how much drama could be crammed into that brief span.

Dividing the bull riders from the bareback bronco-busters were the Daredevil Darlings, two sisters who were exactly as advertised. When they made their exit (at full gallop) both were standing bolt upright in the stirrups, legs scissored, breasts at attention, and arms aloft holding the Stars and Stripes. The announcer called it the Liberty position. 'As in, "you're all invited to take some",' said Saltzman's neighbour (the one who had been moved to tears by the Dandies). She looked at him. 'You're an Englishman. Am I right?' Saltzman had to admit that she was indeed correct. 'What did you make of the bull riding?' she said. 'Beats cricket,' he said. 'I'm not sure you're right,' she said. 'I am an Anglophile and I follow the sport avidly. With Essex, Middlesex and Sussex it has all the sex a woman on the wrong side of middle age can take. It also has something in common with bull riding. I bet you can't tell me what it is . . .' Saltzman thought for a couple of minutes, then said 'Ball tampering.' 'Explain yourself,' she said. 'Well,' he said, 'in cricket, so it is alleged, bowlers tamper with balls in order to gain an unfair advantage. And in bull riding, so I've read, the animals have their manhood painfully constricted with a too-tight harness, to make them more uppity.' 'You've done your homework,' she said. 'You're a teacher, right?' he said. 'Ex,' she said. 'Me too,' he said. 'My name is Emily Cornstarch,' she said. 'English was my subject. Jailey Tomjack, the prettiest of the Dandies, was my protégée. Oh, she looked so lovely down there I couldn't help but weep. Thanks to me she fell in love with England. Not with its cricket, I admit, but with its writers for sure. Why not? I bet Jane Austen spoke more directly to her than her British counterparts. How many of them are likely to have a gentleman caller turn up at their front door on horseback?' But before it had time to properly blossom, the genteel courtship of Miss Tomjack and her beau was rudely interrupted.

'Born to buck, born to be wild, born to be free – the bronco!' boomed the announcer. And when the first competitor bounced out of the chutes on his spring-heeled steed the announcer couldn't help himself, and actually cried: 'Ride em, cowboy!' Meanwhile, the cowboy was trying desperately to do exactly that. He was leaning back, so that his heels were clamped inches above the horse's shoulders. Like the bull riders he hung on to the rigging with one white-knuckled hand, using the other to keep his equilibrium. And he succeeded. He was still hanging on when the eight-second barrier was broken. Most of the others weren't so skilful or so lucky. A couple even ended up around the horse's neck, at least until the animal lowered its head, when they dropped off like windfalls. 'What's it all about?' said Saltzman. 'What it's about,' said Mrs Cornstarch, 'is men trying to cling on to their youth for dear life.'

Only when he followed her down to where they congregated did he appreciate the acuity of her observation. Most of them were not that young, or if they were they didn't look it. Their bodies were lean, their faces pinched – even gaunt – their clothes stained and scuffed. They stood in groups, hardly speaking. Or sat on benches thinking of falls taken, or of falls yet to come. Some cradled cracked arms set in plaster casts, or wrapped in pristine bandages.

When Saltzman had watched them rattling their skeletons and taking tumbles from his seat in the East Stand (below which he now stood), they had seemed to him as unbreakable as wrestlers. He had completely failed to appreciate the real possibility of damage, and the strain engendered by the anticipation of those eight seconds. Now he could witness it close up in those still awaiting their rides. If the others were taciturn, these were monk-like in their silent contemplation. There could be no doubt that fear was hard at work down here, on the dark side of the chutes. So why did they do it? Saltzman could only guess at the answer: he imagined that fear released its hold as soon as they entered the chutes and mounted their ride (be it bronc or bull). And then, in the clarity of sunlight, every sense was magnified, and time itself expanded until each incredible second stretched an eternity.

'Did you ever see *Junior Bonner*?' said Mrs Cornstarch. 'Several times,' said Saltzman (who regularly screened Sam Peckinpah's movie about rodeo in his course on the director). 'You remember the scene when Junior Bonner's brother, Curly, offers him a job?' she said. 'Word for word,' he said. 'Curly says: "Junior, you're my brother. And I guess I love you. Well, we're family. I don't care what you do. You can sell one lot or one hundred lots. I'm just tryin to keep us together."' Taking Steve McQueen's part, Mrs Cornstarch replied: '"I gotta go down my own road."' Echoing Joe Don Baker, Saltzman delivered the following riposte: '"What road? I'm working on my first million, and you're still working on eight seconds."' 'Of course, every red-blooded male in Cheyenne identifies with Steve McQueen,' said Mrs Cornstarch, 'but somehow they all end up looking like Joe Don Baker.'

Emily Cornstarch had brought Saltzman along so that Jailey Tomjack could meet a real Englishman for the first time. She was probably very disappointed because Saltzman excused himself after only a few minutes, when he caught sight of Mercy Sweetbriar. Some of the indifferent and time-worn cowboys among whom he passed were practising with their lariats in preparation for the steer-roping contest to come. No doubt they would have lassoed Mercy too. Saltzman rather favoured that approach himself but figured that a man in his position required a more subtle manoeuvre, so he decided to draw upon the Virginian's courtship of Molly Wood. The opening round occurred when Wister's hero rode over to her cabin and asked her straight out for a date. 'You can ride my hawss,' he had said. 'He's gentle.' But Molly had rebuffed him, even saying (though not meaning), 'I don't think I like you.' To which the Virginian had replied, 'You're goin to love me before we get through.' And of course the crypto-fascist, sexist pig was right. Okay, Saltzman carried a few disadvantages in the deportment department, but his views on relations – both international and inter-personal – were unimpeachable (in theory if not in practice). Besides, Mercy had (it seemed) fancied Peppercorn, which gave reasonable grounds for hope, since he was far more dashing than his uxorious cousin. Sure enough, her already radiant face shone a little bit brighter when he explained who he

was. Unlike Molly, however, she did not play hard to get, capitulating instantly to the prospect of a gallop with Peppercorn's relative, apparently innocent of the metaphorical weight loaded upon the activity by scores of novels and movies. The only complication was finding an afternoon when Mercy was not burdened by the responsibilities of high office. The CFD ended on Sunday, but her ceremonial duties bled into Monday and Tuesday. However, Wednesday was free. So Wednesday afternoon it was. But where? At the Terry Bison Ranch, of course. Peppercorn, he thought, eat my shorts. Saltzman looked for Emily Cornstarch and Jailey Tomjack to make amends, but neither was in evidence. Nor did the former return to her seat during the steer-roping, or even the chariot and wild horse races.

After dark the cowboys were replaced by country and western singers. Seen from above, the fans in the pits – all male, Saltzman presumed, since they were all sporting white Stetsons – looked to him like bleached-out hasids crowding a wonder rabbi. At first glance the band's lead vocalist lent credence to the comparison, since he was wearing a black hat and a long, black gaberdine. But beneath the hat was a bandanna made from the American flag, and beneath the coat were biceps made for bar-room brawling. 'You know we like to do a little hell-raisin,' he thundered, 'but know this too: we'll never, never, never ever forget the workin man. For all you men out there who work a seventy-hour week c/o the boss – and then like to party hard at the weekend – this song's for you.' One of the guitarists had a T-shirt that read, 'The Dixie Chicks Suck'. The other's displayed the equation: 'MIA = POW'. It turned out that his pappy was a Vietnam vet. As this news was imparted a small, pot-bellied man with long, thinning hair joined the band on stage. 'This man has never got a word of thanks for going over there and doin what his President asked him to,' shouted the singer. 'How's about we show him some appreciation now?' After the roar had subsided the singer said: 'The voice of Cheyenne is the voice of America. Ain't no one gonna invade our town, or our country.' Again the audience whooped in approval. The young man next to Saltzman was an exception. He snorted. 'Cheyenne seems a bit gung-ho,' said Saltzman. 'Yeah,' said the young man, 'it's Dick Cheney territory.' 'Isn't everywhere in the Cowboy State?' said Saltzman. 'Not Laramie,' said the young man, 'some of us think differently there.' He gave Saltzman a dollar to spend should he ever be passing through. Saltzman looked at the note: the bust of George Washington had been replaced by that of George W. Bush. And the country he presided over was now called 'The United States of Aggression'.

While roadies cleared the stage for Willie Nelson, a woman (clearly no gatecrasher) appeared and asked with passion, 'Do you love your country?' She obviously expected a rip-roaring response from an audience of patriots, but received nothing more than a few 'You betchas'. A valuable lesson, thought Saltzman: patriotism and fascism are not synonyms. Moreover, fascists would not have found a place in their hearts for an outlaw like Willie Nelson, who wore a long plait and smoked marijuana. The cheers they denied the unknown rabble-rouser they gave freely to the man who sang, 'Mama don't let your babies grow up to be cowboys / Don't let em pick guitars and drive them old trucks / Make em be doctors and lawyers and such / Mama don't let your babies grow up to be cowboys / They'll never stay home and they're always alone / Even with someone they love . . .'

On Wednesday afternoon Saltzman met Mercy Sweetbriar at the Plains Hotel, and from there he drove her to the
Terry Bison Ranch. For those five or six miles he felt like the
Virginian. But the feeling didn't last. After her initial rebuff
Molly had softened a little – though they never did go riding
on that first day – and offered her hand to her handsome
suitor when they parted. He shook it and exclaimed, 'You're
a gentleman.' 'I've always wanted to be a man,' said she. To
Saltzman's chagrin a similar role reversal occurred when
they entered the stables at the ranch. Although he was on
home territory it was Mercy Sweetbriar who took command.
'I've a fancy for something a little spirited,' she said to Rusty
Nailer, 'but my friend'll be wantin something a bit more
gentle.' 'I'm not afraid of horses,' said Saltzman, 'you
needn't pick out such a docile one.' Throughout his season
as a bus-driver there had been frequent opportunities to
ride, but he had taken none of them. Perhaps because he
was frightened of exposing himself as a greenhorn. He was
sorry now. But how difficult could horse-riding be? Once in
the saddle, all he had to do was stay there. And why should
that be a problem? The creature being prepared for him was
hardly a bronc. He patted its rump tenderly. After all, it was
his Trigger, his Champion, his four-legged friend.

When the horses were ready, Mercy vaulted into the
saddle of hers with a single movement full of grace. How did
she do it? Saltzman had inserted his right foot into the stirrup well enough, but just couldn't raise sufficient leverage
to lift his left foot over the horse's back. By now word had
spread around the stable yard that there was a comedy in
the making, and some of the singing cowboys (employed by

the ranch during the summer) drifted in to enjoy it. In the end Rusty Nailer walked to the other side of the horse, caught Saltzman's left ankle when it briefly showed, and heaved it all the way down the other side. As he attempted to settle, Saltzman heard the chorus of a familiar song: 'Whoopi-ty-aye-oh / Rockin to and fro / Back in the saddle again / Whoopi-ty-aye-yay / I go my way / Back in the saddle again . . .' 'Come on,' cried Mercy Sweetbriar, 'let's feel some wind on our faces.' When Saltzman prodded his horse with his heels it took a few steps. With its first forward movement he understood the meaning of the words, 'rockin to and fro'. He felt himself sliding too much to the right. He attempted to compensate, but did so with excess zeal, and immediately found himself rotating unstoppably in the other direction. As a consequence the ex-scholar fell to earth with a mighty thump (with the exception of his left foot, which remained stuck in the stirrup). Fortunately the horse did not bolt, and Rusty Nailer was on hand to release it. 'Are you okay, Prof?' he said. Having tested his limbs, back, neck and brain for signs of lasting damage, and having found none, Saltzman said that he was. He looked around for his riding companion. But she hadn't registered his fall, and had galloped on, assuming that he was not far behind. 'Tough luck, old chap,' said Rusty Nailer (a touch mockingly), 'but it seems that the sweet bird of youth has flown.'

Saltzman did not attempt to remount. Nor did he even consider waiting for Mercy Sweetbriar's return. No, he fled the scene of his shame, and Cheyenne, just as he had fled Deadwood. He packed his bag, returned his key to his landlady, told her to donate his compact to a charity of her choice, and took whatever it was that All-America Driveaways had to offer. His efficient delivery of Bronco Billy's tomato-red soft-top and the pink Cadillac Eldorado was already the stuff of legend, so much so that the counter clerk felt obliged to apologize for only having a nearly new Chevrolet available, destination Dodge City.

His direction was constant; ever eastward. If he wanted to glimpse the Rockies he had to look in his rear-view mirror. Ahead were only the high plains. So unchanging were they he sometimes had the impression he wasn't moving at all. There were no trees. The only roadside attractions were the signs that changed in nothing but name: Deer Trail, Agate, River Bend, Genoa, Bovina, Arruba, Flagler, Siebert, Stratton, Bethune, Burlington. The last-named claimed ownership of the Kit Carson Carousel. Seeking solace from straight lines, Saltzman elected to give it a whirl.

There were no pedestrians on the sidewalks of Burlington's main drag, nor cars on its tarmac (either in motion or stationary). Nothing stirred in the heat, not even dust. The single movie theatre, the Midway, displayed a poster advertising a film he'd never heard of. Like the rest of the buildings it was locked and deserted. Were the owners merely taking an afternoon siesta, or had they all succumbed to the big sleep? It was impossible to tell. Perhaps Saltzman had stumbled upon the abandoned set of a 1950s sci-fi movie after the town's entire population had been eliminated by aliens or devoured by giant ants (reared on atomic growth hormone). Then he noticed signs of life, or at least a few plastic tables and chairs someone had placed outside a cafe. Sure enough, it was open. True, there weren't any customers, but there was a waitress and (behind her) a cook. Tacked to the porch roof was a sign with the words 'authentic Mexican cuisine' and a caricatured native with sombrero and poncho. Nailed above it was Old Glory. Even Burlington's dumbest bigot could make sense of those signs. Saltzman ordered a couple of tacos, and was given directions to the county fairgrounds, where the carousel was accommodated.

'You might want to join that group of seventh-graders,' said the attendant who took Saltzman's quarter, 'their teacher has just started a little presentation.' The children, a homogeneous bunch of blondies, were standing in front of a twelve-sided structure that housed the baroque merry-go-round. 'The first thing you'll note,' a sun-bonneted young woman was saying, 'is that the carousel has nothing what-soever to do with the famous scout Kit Carson, except for it bein located in Kit Carson County.' Acknowledging the arrival of her mature student the teacher said, 'We have a visitor. Let's make him welcome.' Nodding, Saltzman noted that light threaded its way through the weave of her bonnet and tattooed her cheeks with golden freckles. 'Where you from?' said a little boy. 'Cheyenne, Wyoming,' said Saltzman. 'I've bin to Wyomin,' said a little girl. 'Didn't hear no one speak like that there.' 'Clever girl,' said Saltzman, 'I'm not really from Wyoming. I'm from England.' The children clapped, though Saltzman wasn't sure whether it was to congratulate him for being so far from home, or the girl for unmasking an impostor.

'Okay, children,' continued their teacher, 'the carousel was built about one hundred years ago by the Philadelphia Toboggan Company. Between 1885 and 1930 four thousand such carousels were manufactured in the United States, of which approximately a hundred and fifty survive. In other words, they are as rare as Giant Pandas. And this one here is unique among the survivors in that it still has its original paintwork. What's more, most carousels just had horses, whereas ours has a veritable menagerie – an entire zoo of wild beasts. Just look at them! Have you ever seen such ferocious tigers? And look at the lions, aren't they the roaringest lions you ever saw? And such elegant giraffes! Like the aitches in high society. And camels fit for the prophet! I'm assured that all of the deer are fitted with genuine antlers. And that some of those high-steppin thoroughbreds have real horse-hair tails. How did the animals enter Noah's Ark, children? They went in two by two. In Burlington we were more accommodatin. We let them in three by three. So there'd be plenty for all you young lion-tamers and bronco-busters to ride.' With whoops of joy they mounted up.

The animals were pretty much life-sized, but were made of wood, and would not rise or fall, even when the carousel rotated. Safe in that knowledge Saltzman chose a horse, of course, a haughty grey with a graceful neck, which just happened to be beside the one upon which the teacher sat. 'Veritable menagerie?' he said. 'Children know that proper teachers use long words,' she said, 'and that's what I intend to be.' 'Professor Saltzman,' he said, offering her his hand. His gesture was a little too enthusiastic, and he would certainly have toppled out of the saddle if her clasp had been any less firm. 'Silkie Toper,' she said, 'with one "p", but as in the hat.' Though Saltzman was enchanted, he was beginning to have serious doubts about his ability to retain his balance astride the slippery beast, and considered dismounting voluntarily. But it was already too late.

The fully restored 1912 Wurlitzer Monster Military Band

Organ had begun to bellow its jaunty off-we-go-to-war music, the light bulbs overhead were flashing, and the floor below was beginning to rotate. The faster it spun, the more Saltzman felt like a reluctant member of the Daredevil Darlings, even though he was required to do nothing more daring than sit still. It turned out that he couldn't even do that. The most insignificant of movements unbalanced him, and he began to imagine himself the carousel's first fatality. None other, so far as he could see, partook of his insecurity. All were sitting straight-backed and fearless in the saddle, not least his neighbour. Long before the ride was over, fear quashed pride, and Saltzman found himself hugging his mount's silver mane, as he had seen some of the more inept bronco-busters do back in Cheyenne. In such a way Saltzman managed to survive the 25-cent ride, only to come a cropper when the machinery began to slow. One minute he was upright in Colorado, the next he was in Australia, hanging upside down, with his legs wrapped around the horse's underparts. The child on the giraffe just behind him screamed with delight as his hold slowly failed and he dropped head first to the floor. Unfortunately, the little girl's laughter proved contagious. Finally it overcame even kindly Miss Toper. Saltzman, newly appointed circus clown, took a bow. What else could he do? When Hegel wrote that all great personages are granted two entrances on history's stage, Marx chided him for forgetting to add: the first time as tragedian, the second as farceur. Karl, thought Saltzman, as he dusted his backside for a second time, you were dead right.

Having left one Eden after an ignominious fall, Saltzman bedded down in another would-be paradise called Garden City. The lobby of his motel reminded him of his dentist's waiting room, primarily because both were dominated by an aquarium filled with blue fish. As in Radlett, they darted through the water like turquoise arrowheads, though their journeys were aimless, there being no target at the other end. For Saltzman, it was like looking at his future in a crystal ball. Okay, he was en route to Dodge City, but he had no notion of where he would be going after that. He was from ambitious stock and drift did not come easily to him.

The woman at the reception desk wore a sari, and had an English accent. Saltzman almost told her that he had come for his six-monthly check-up. But he requested a room, and was given the choice of several. He was asked if he had travelled far. Not as far as you, he replied. True, said the woman in the sari. She explained that the interval between her birth in the subcontinent and her acquisition of this fine motel had been spent largely in Northampton. Saltzman congratulated her on taking that final step. To have settled for less would have been immigration lite. You are now an American Indian, he pointed out, and your children will be Native American Indians. You can't get more American than that. If only my ancestors – Ostjuden all – had done me such a favour. Funny you should say that, said the woman in the sari, but some of the Jews who did are buried not ten miles from here. She gave Saltzman directions to the graveyard.

In the morning he followed them. He drove four miles north on US 83, a further four to the west on an unmade road between unbroken walls of ripening corn, and arrived at the junction of Chmelka and Lowe. There it was, a square cut from the infinite cornfield, identified by a standing stone upon which were inscribed the words 'Jewish Cemetery'. Saltzman, not a religious man, nor properly educated in the

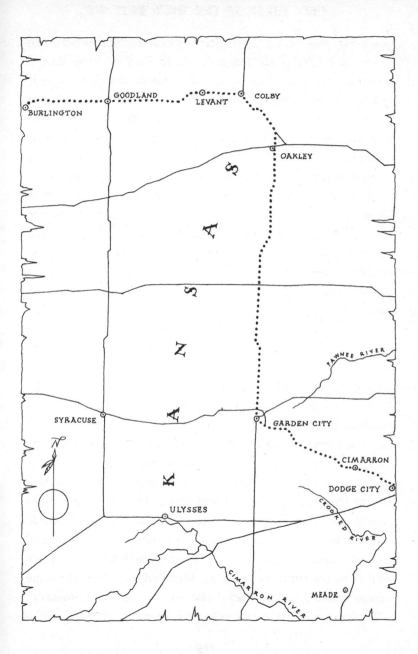

rituals of his people, stepped from the car and immediately felt the need to recite the Kaddish, the prayer for the dead. What a pity he only knew the first line: yisgadol vyiskadash shme raba. The cemetery was established in 1884, and its first resident seemed to have been a woman of thirty-four. Saltzman read the English on her tombstone with ease, and the Hebrew with difficulty, but both amounted to the same thing: Sarah Ochs, wife of S. Teitelbaum, born August 22 1849, died April 12 1884. What was her story? How had she ended up here, in a Kansas cornfield? And so young. Her only identified neighbours were Mr L. Toper (1829–1933) and Mrs L. Toper (1851–1921). How many lives and events had Mr Toper's remarkable span encompassed? His own wife and poor Sarah Ochs for starters. Then the fall of the Alamo, and the martyrdom of Davy Crockett; the acquisition of Texas and California; the Civil War, and the assassination of Lincoln; the winning of the West; Custer's Last Stand; the Massacre at Wounded Knee; the Gunfight at the OK Corral; the careers of Wild Bill Hickok, Calamity Jane, Billy the Kid, and Jesse James; Buffalo Bill's Wild West and Congress of Rough Riders of the World; Hollywood. And then there was the colonization of

Africa; the establishment of Italy and Germany; the First World War; the end of the Austro-Hungarian Empire, ditto the Ottoman; the Russian Revolution. And then, at the death, the election of Adolf Hitler, and the final confirmation of Mr Toper's wisdom in quitting the slaughterhouse. The tombstone was silent on the matter of his descendants. How many children had he had? Grandchildren? Great-grand-children? Was it possible that Silkie Toper of Burlington, Colorado, was a direct descendant? In which case his story certainly had a happy ending.

Twenty-five miles to the east, near the town of Kalvesta, Saltzman came upon an answer to at least some of his questions, in the shape of a marker posted by the Kansas Historical Society and the Kansas Department of Transportation. Headed 'Beersheba', it told the story of the state's first Jewish agricultural colony. Of course, Saltzman knew about the utopian settlements, the kevutzot and the kibbutzim, that had been established in Palestine from the 1890s onwards. But of earlier experiments in Kansas he knew nothing. So he read, and learned. Beersheba was founded in 1882 along the banks of Pawnee Creek (a few versts to the north-east of where Saltzman was standing), by some threescore Jewish immigrants from Russia. Their sponsors were the Hebrew Union Agricultural Society. Later communities included Montifiore, Lasker, Leeser, Touro, Gilead and Hebron. Each family was awarded 160 acres to homestead. Trees were in short supply. They lived in houses built of sod, they worshipped in synagogues built of sod, and their children were educated in schools also built of sod. Cow chips were collected for fuel. Wells were dug (seven, probably, given that Beersheba means 'seven wells'), the prairie ploughed and planted. Saltzman looked around. Every vista was the same: a desert of dry grass. Within the first few months, the marker reported, a wedding took place, a baby was born, and someone died. At the beginning of their first winter the virgin farmers wrote to their benefactors: 'May you ever prosper. All of us have signed our names to this letter. All of the brethren who are at present in the Beer Shebe Colony offer their thanks to you for the kindness and benevolence you have shown to the desperate and miserable fugitives.' But the winter turned out to be harder than expected, and those that followed proved almost too cruel to endure. Things would have been more comfortable, needless to say, had their husbandry proved profitable. But it never did. Then there were the agents, appointed by the sponsors who (perhaps rightly) doubted the settlers' acumen. These agents, according to the colonists, ruled with increasing terror as problems multiplied. If their judgement was challenged, the challenger was expelled without appeal. In order to repay debts some colonists leased part of their land to a cattle syndicate. The agents responded by confiscating the rest of their belongings: tools, machinery, livestock, the lot. One by one the surviving colonists sold or abandoned their homesteads. 'A decade after the colony was established,' concluded the marker, 'none of the colonists remained and the land reverted to prairie.' Not true: Sarah Ochs, for one, went nowhere.

Saltzman thought about the deceased and tried to imagine her as she was in her prime: newly arrived in Kansas, full of conviction, full of hope. Perhaps she had answered the call of a charismatic leader, one whose mesmerizing rhetoric had made nothing seem impossible. Perhaps she had heard him speak in Russia, at the height of the draconian new laws and vicious pogroms that had followed the assassination of Alexander II, and been fired up by his vision of the New Jew in the New World. We have been in Russia for centuries, he had said, yet we are still not considered proper Russians. Nor will we ever be, even if we remain here till the end of recorded time. Why? Because we are divorced from the land. But in America, in the New World, we will at last be able to put down roots. I am not speaking in metaphors, he had said, but telling you the literal truth. In America we Jews can become farmers again, planting and harvesting, as we did in the glory days of our forefathers, in the days of Abraham, Isaac and Jacob. No longer will we be forced to remain as outsiders, parasites, pariahs; on the contrary, we will be producers. And then he had spoken the words that had inspired a generation. In our settlement, he had said, there will be no leaders and no followers, no bosses and no workers. Inscribe these words upon your heart, he instructed his listeners: from everyone according to his ability, and to everyone according to his needs.

At this point Saltzman remembered the carousel, wherein all animals were equal, from the king of the jungle down to the lowly camel, and had all worked in harmony. Had Sarah Ochs and her fellow pioneers also been carved from wood then the experiment at Beersheba would certainly have succeeded, whatever the weather and the condition of the soil. But they were made of flesh and blood, and they were Jews. For every one prepared to obey the sponsor-appointed agents there were two dissenters (who could not even agree among themselves). For every one prepared to be a humanist or a universalist, there were two who preferred to remain as Jews (though what sort of Jew was a matter of dispute). Worst of all, for every Sarah Ochs, there were five or six Teitelbaums (Saltzman hoped that their marriage was the one that, accorded to the marker, signalled the beginning of community life). Many of the eager young men, who gave their all during the day, required something warmer than ideology at night. Adversity demanded unity, and Beersheba (if the ex-professor was right), had none with which to combat it. But failure did not make a joke of Beersheba, not in Saltzman's opinion.

He pictured the decline of Sarah Ochs, the desperate efforts to reverse it, and the despair that overcame all when their best efforts came to nothing. He watched with the community as her coffin was lowered into the Kansas sod, knowing that with it went all their hopes and ideals. Saltzman had long since lost the use of those facial muscles required to cry properly; nevertheless, the involuntary overflow welling from his eyes had the saltiness of genuine tears.

Rousing himself from his melancholy reverie Saltzman drove south to Cimarron. From there it was but twenty-five miles to Dodge City. Many American cities have their heads in the clouds, he thought, but he could see at once that Dodge City was strictly terrestrial. Its tallest buildings were grain silos. Saltzman dropped off the Chevrolet and left his bag behind the counter at the AAD office. According to the monitor outside the Wells Fargo bank it was 14.20 and 109 in the shade. Only madmen were about, but this was Dodge City, Babylon of the Frontier, Buffalo Capital of the World, Queen of the Cowtowns, and Saltzman was still sufficiently in love with his subject to brave sunstroke and seek out what remained of that past, even if what remained had been rounded up and corralled in the Boot Hill Museum.

Saltzman lingered longest before a photograph (taken circa 1960), which depicted a curious meeting: on the left was Ramon House, last marshal of Dodge City, on the right was presidential candidate John F. Kennedy. House was wearing one cowboy hat, and holding another. According to the caption he was offering it to Kennedy on behalf of the 'cowboy capital'. (A fat lot of protection it afforded him when it mattered, thought Saltzman.) After House's retirement, his office was dismantled and reconstructed in the museum. Attached to it were a few words of explanation: 'During his time as marshal, Ramon allowed visitors of Dodge to tour his office, located in the City's Post Office. His office, an air-conditioned replica of *Gunsmoke*'s Matt Dillon's office, housed a roll-top desk, early law books and records . . . House believed his office was "a tribute to the brave men, past and present, who serve as marshal".' Were I still a paid-up po-mo, thought Saltzman, then this would be pay dirt. Here was a real US marshal, who modelled himself upon a fictional TV character, who was himself based upon Wyatt Earp, whose exact role in the history of Dodge City remained uncertain. This was not history, it was a hall of mirrors.

Nonetheless, Earp, rather than equally tough Bat Masterson or Bill Tilghman, had become Dodge City's genius loci. It was Earp who received the glory for taming it in its wildest years (during the late 1870s), when five million longhorns were driven up from Texas by cowboys not attuned to the mores of polite society. Back in 1958, by way of tribute, the city fathers elected to rebrand Chestnut

Street as Wyatt Earp Boulevard, and invited 'television celebrity Hugh O'Brian, star of the sitcom [sic] the *Life and Legend of Wyatt Earp*' to do the honours. He likewise participated in the 'dedication' of the replica of Front Street, the 'first edition' of which was also ready for business. They can dedicate it all they like, thought Saltzman as he peered in its ersatz saloon, but to me Front Street replicated looks about as convincing as a relic of the True Cross. The genius of the Boot Hill Museum was evident in its refusal to acknowledge that there was any significant difference between fiction and history. A fact for its curators was merely something that could be seen; therefore they had no hesitation in billing their facsimile of Front Street as 'Historic old Front Street', when the exhibit was neither historic, nor old, nor even Front Street. It wasn't even certain that the eponymous Boot Hill really was Boot Hill. The museum was noncommittal: 'We like to think bodies are still buried here.'

How Jean Baudrillard would love this place, thought Saltzman. To him it would be proof positive of his contention that Americans offer facts and accept them in equal good faith – even when the facts are what Baudrillard calls 'factitious' (which Saltzman took to be a play on 'fictitious'), as they were in the Front Street charade. To Baudrillard this way of thinking was postmodernism pure and simple – 'nothing deceives, there are no lies, there is only *simulation*'. No, it was more than a way of thinking, it was a religion, the 'religion of the fait accompli'. But what of emotions engendered by the 'play of appearances', by false pretences, by the unquestioning acceptance of simulated facts? Like it or not, they were as powerful as those based upon real tragedy – if such a thing could still be said to exist. It was inevitable that Americans would one day be just as moved by the passing of a fictional president as they had been by the assassination of President Kennedy in Dallas (the city, not the soap opera). In that not-too-distant day death will no longer be death, but being written out of the script.

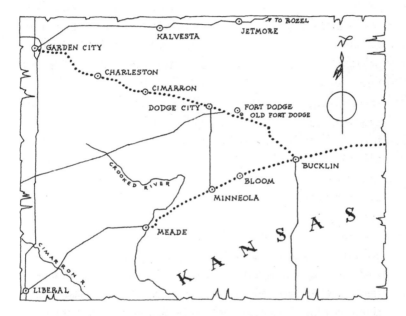

Saltzman had already decided he'd seen enough of Dodge City when he picked up a flyer advertising the Boot Hill Repertory Company in *Gunsmoke: On the Air!*. This is what it said: 'The *Gunsmoke* series, on radio and television, portrayed the wholesome, down-to-earth Matt Dillon as an archetypical man in frontier Dodge City. He enforced the law with a wise mixture of firmness and compassion. Together with Miss Kitty, Doc and Chester, Matt entertained us all and *Gunsmoke* achieved television history as the longest-running series ever. This show is a tribute to that success and those parables that made the *Gunsmoke* series so universally appealing.' Over in that part of the universe called England the show was known as *Gun Law* and broadcast, unusually for a Western, not in the afternoon but at night. Way past young Saltzman's bedtime, in fact. It had taken him many months, if not years, to obtain permission from his parents to watch. These days, however, no one cared – or even knew – what Saltzman was doing. So, having secured a room for the night at the Boot Hill Bed and Breakfast, he gave himself permission to attend the stage version.

GUNSMOKE: On the Air!

The "Gunsmoke" series, on radio and television, portrayed the wholesome, down-to-earth Matt Dillon as an archetypical man in frontier Dodge City. He enforced the law with a wise mixture of firmness and compassion. Together with Miss Kitty, Doc, and Chester, Matt entertained us all and achieve television history as the longest-running series ever. This show is a tribute to that success and those parables that made the "Gunsmoke" series so universally appealing.

FIVE NIGHTS ONLY!
July 26, 27, 28, 29 and 30
Dinner served at 6:30 pm
Tickets $15/Kids under 14 $10/under 6 free

The Boot Hill Repertory Company
at the Homestead Theater
101 E Wyatt Earp Blvd   For reservations call
Dodge City, Kansas 67801   620-225-1001

The price of the ticket included dinner. This meant that the audience members did not sit in rows but at round tables, where they were waited upon by a handsome crew of unemployed actors who were, in fact, only out of work until dessert and coffee was served, whereupon they removed themselves to the stage. The night's performance was prefaced by some remarks from the play's director. He explained how difficult it had been to obtain permission from CBS to reuse the original radio scripts. In the end he had to write to the effect that if he heard no word to the contrary he would assume that it was okay to proceed. Denis Weaver, who had played Chester in the television spin-off, was more

supportive. He had even come to one of the first performances and taken a bow. He was also persuaded to answer
some questions. Of course, everyone wanted to know the
same thing. Why did Chester have a limp? So Weaver had
patiently explained its genesis, which the director repeated.
It seemed that when the pilot show was in pre-production
he was told that his character needed a handicap – any
handicap would do – to ensure that Matt Dillon would never
have a rival for the role of Dodge City's alpha male. The
audience liked being let in on that secret. It could handle a
little alienation. And that's exactly what the play offered.

It began in the office of Harv, a worried man, under
constant pressure to deliver new storylines. While the
scriptwriter was wrestling with the muse, a duo of lovelies
(one of whom had recently been serving Saltzman ice cream)
mooned about the irresistability of yodelling cowboys. Then
the episode proper began. Two brothers were on the point
of fleeing Dodge City with ill-gotten gold, the proceeds of a
fatal robbery, but the younger was reluctant to hit the road
without his girl. Only Mollie didn't have a horse. The older
was not prepared to wait. So the younger decided to steal
her one. Opportunity knocked when the brothers stumbled
upon Matt Dillon and Chester bathing in a stream. Not only
did they steal their horses, but also their boots. Consequently Matt and Chester were forced to tramp bareass and
barefoot across the prairie for one and a half days, until Doc
came to the rescue. Later, in Miss Kitty's saloon, Matt
noticed a young man wearing familiar boots. An arrest was
effected. It turned out the boy was mad because big brother
had run off with the loot, the horses and his best gal. He
offered to lead Matt to their hideout in Texas. Matt accepted

the offer, but as it turned out did not need to lift a finger – the older brother killed the younger, and then was himself gunned down by Mollie.

Both production and the acting were far more sophisticated than Saltzman, in his snobbery, had anticipated. Somehow the director had managed to turn the delivery of a radio script into dynamic theatre. Afterwards Saltzman was able to apologize for his lack of faith. Rather than take a curtain call, Kelly Caroll, Mark Vierthaler, Amy Reinert, Dee Dee Royle, Joe Walker, Kent Ross, Kristina Mortimer and Sarah Simpson lined up to shake the hands of departing spectators. Last in line was the director. The play, he said, was still in an experimental stage. By the time the Boot Hill Repertory Company's ten-million-dollar theatre was complete it should be something really special. So there was life in Dodge City after all, though its climate was Martian: when Saltzman entered the Homestead Theater at 6.00 the temperature had been 106. When he left at 9.00, it had dropped to 99.

Breakfast at the Boot Hill B & B proved to be no less a production. Its Victorian dining room looked like Victoria was still on the throne. Proprietor Julie Thurstin served the pancakes and bacon decked out in a wedding-cake skirt. Her husband Jerry, the cook, was also in costume, notwithstanding the fact that he was a former truck driver (a fact confirmed by a current issue of the Teamsters Union magazine in the downstairs toilet). The man sitting next to Saltzman seemed to be in fancy dress too, unless he always breakfasted in a cowboy outfit. He turned out to be a farmer from nearby Montezuma. Lived in Kansas all his life, save for two years serving Uncle Sam in San Diego. 'Imagine a farm boy who's never seen anything bigger than a thousand-acre lake finding himself on the Pacific,' he said. 'Luckily I was only on a ship for two weeks. I was no sailor. The beaches were not for me. I prefer the wide open spaces and my feet planted on dry land.' He took a gulp of lukewarm coffee. 'Marc S. Ferguson,' he said, extending his hand, 'but you can call me Wyatt, as in Wyatt Earp.' He was, he informed Saltzman, a professional re-enactor, in addition to being a farmer. 'Not only do I step into Wyatt's boots,' he said, 'but I also try to inhabit his mind, to see the world exactly as he saw it.'

After breakfast Saltzman's new friend offered to show him some of Earp's old haunts. How could Saltzman resist patrolling the streets of Dodge City in the company of its most famous lawman? Earp's impersonator conceded that historians had their own ideas about the city's origins – citing the coming of the Atchison, Topeka and Santa Fe railroad, which whisked the Texas beef to the slaughterhouses of Chicago, plus easy crossings of the Arkansas – but in his opinion Dodge City really began when the selling of whiskey was banned at Fort Dodge and two enterprising clerks drove a wagon full of the stuff to a clearing just beyond military jurisdiction, whereupon they loosened its tailgate and opened shop. Marc S. Ferguson pointed to a nearby Dodge dealership, and said the spot they had chosen was under its forecourt. In the 1970s the dealership and its neighbours had banded together to demand the demolition of the real Front Street. Who needed a decaying original when there was a more convenient reproduction on its doorstep? And why did they want Front Street flattened? So as to create a parking lot for their customers. As Saltzman could see, they had had their way. 'You know politics,' said Ferguson. It was politics, he added, that had got Wyatt Earp kicked out of Wichita. In 1876 Wyatt Earp was a policeman there, but had been fired for punching the man standing against his boss in the election for marshal. In Dodge City they weren't so fussy. A month after leaving Wichita, Wyatt Earp was one of its deputy sheriffs. He stayed in the job for a year, then took off with his brother Morgan, only to return in 1878, when he was immediately promoted to deputy marshal.

Ferguson and Saltzman crossed the railroad tracks to the south side of Front Street, where Earp had been busiest. 'This is where the Lady Gay Dance Hall once stood,' said Ferguson. And what was it now? Another Dodge dealership. It was to the Lady Gay that Marshal Ed Masterson (Bat's brother) was summoned on April 9, 1878 to quieten some cowpokes raising Cain. When they saw the marshal they raised their pistols as well as Cain and shot him. Before dying Masterson managed to retort with a fusillade of lead that sent at least one of his murderers straight to hell. 'Being a lawman in Dodge City was not without risk,' said Ferguson, as if he had just recited one of Aesop's fables.

Saltzman suddenly recalled that he had actually seen the ill-starred Ed shot in an old movie called *Gunfight at Dodge City*. And, yes, it had been at the Lady Gay, half-owned (in that version of events) by his more famous brother. As the plot reached its inevitable climax Bat (played by Joel McCrea, in his last film but one) was challenged by the man he thought (wrongly) had bushwacked his brother. His delectable business partner (and future bedmate) had begged him not to accept the challenge, but he insisted he had no choice, and had exited the Lady Gay with these immortal words: 'I don't want to, Lily, but the distance between here and the street is the distance between a man and a rabbit.' This, in turn, reminded Saltzman of the words his wife had uttered when she had slammed the door on their marriage: 'As you've grown older, Saltzman, your mouth has begun to shrink, but your ears seem to be getting bigger by the day.'

'In the same month as Ed Masterson's murder, James "Dog" Kelley was elected mayor,' said Ferguson, as he guided Saltzman to the corner of First and Maple. 'His mistress was a dance-hall singer named Dora Hand. She also caught the eye of a Texas drover named James Kennedy. A real hothead, by all accounts. Anyway, he swore to have her. This vow didn't go down too well with her current beau, who whipped sweat out of the kid over in Hizzoner's saloon. As was the way in those days, young Kennedy swore to kill him. Trouble was, he meant it. He got himself a fast horse. Then he came by stealth to where we are standing, and shot four times into the window of the mayor's house. One of the bullets passed through the mayor's bedroom, through the wall that separated it from a guest bedroom, and into the body of Dora Hand, who (for once) was not sleeping in the mayor's bed. Accused of her murder Kennedy fled, with Bat Masterson and Wyatt Earp hot on his trail. They caught up with him at Meade, where Bat winged him, while Wyatt plugged his horse. Back in Dodge City the fugitive was acquitted for lack of evidence.' Ferguson paused. 'That sorta soured Wyatt,' he concluded. Ferguson pointed out Napa Auto Parts, formerly the swankiest hotel in town. Across the street was Man's Body Shop, where (according to Saltzman's Virgil) they serviced dented automobiles rather than seven-stone weaklings.

Ferguson must have warmed to Saltzman, because he decided to take him over to Fort Dodge to meet his good friend Harley 'Doc' Holladay. They found him waiting outside the Custer House. His face lit up when he saw Ferguson. 'Howdy, Marc,' he said. 'Howdy, Harley,' said Ferguson. He introduced Saltzman. 'I was expectin a party,' said Holladay, 'but it seems that Fort Dodge has been dropped from the itinerary. Seein as I'm all dressed up and rarin to go, why don't I show your Mr Saltzman around instead?' 'Great,' said Saltzman. Holladay sprang up the steps to the porch and unlocked the door of Custer's House. 'Care to guess his age?' said Ferguson. 'Early seventies?' said Saltzman. 'He's eighty-one,' said Ferguson, 'and a multiple gold medallist in the Senior Olympics to boot. What did you get em for, Harley?' 'Long distance,' said his friend. Saltzman believed him. It was easy to picture his lean frame in a loose-fitting singlet and baggy shorts.

'Don't go gettin the idea that just because this house is called Custer's House he ever lived in it,' said Holladay. 'The best guess is that he maybe once had dinner here, during the winter campaign against the Cheyenne that culminated in the Battle of Washita, and created Custer's reputation as an Indian fighter.' After the tour, Holladay took Saltzman over to his house, which he did inhabit, while Ferguson went off to get some colas at the Sutler's Store. 'Sorry I can't invite you in,' he said, 'but Mrs Holladay is not feeling herself today.' He left Saltzman sitting on the porch, and returned holding a large green portfolio. 'Between you and me,' he said, 'I've recently begun a new career as a male model. I haven't had so much fun since I left the army.' He opened his portfolio, which sure enough included photographs of the old devil in the buff. In some he was accompanied by numerous young females, also stark naked. 'I don't show this part to everyone, especially the ladies,' said Holladay. In other photos he was dressed in buckskin, and had long hair. 'That's me in my Buffalo Bill days,' he said. 'I never met him, of course, but I did know the last of the buffalo hunters. I'm also a legitimate buffalo hunter myself, in a manner of speakin, having bagged the only sort of buffalo you're likely to see in these parts nowadays. The first bit of it I noticed was the tip of a horn sticking up in a dry crick. By the time I'd finished I'd dug up an entire skull.' Finally, Holloday turned to a picture of John Wayne (actually a magazine ad for the 'first family-authorized biography'). 'See what he's wearin,' said Holladay. 'Mauve collarless shirt. Leather waistcoat. I sort of modelled my appearance on that look. Though today I missed out the scarf.'

Like his friend Ferguson, Holladay was a Kansas man. After war service he had been invited to stand for sheriff of Dodge City, but he preferred to finish his education at the University of Kansas. Having graduated he had worked for a local brick manufacturer. Several of the modern buildings on the fort were built using its bricks. By coincidence Holladay's great-grandfather Will Hessman (an immigrant from Germany) was one of the labourers who helped construct the fort's older stone cottages. 'You could say that my family's sweat is in Fort Dodge's DNA,' said Holladay. As they walked back towards Ferguson's auto a bird ascended, spitting gold. It looked very like the one Saltzman had surprised at Fort Laramie. 'Does it have a name?' he asked. 'A kingbird,' said Holladay.

'I just love that man,' said Ferguson, as he drove back to Dodge City. 'I think I could too,' said Saltzman. 'You'd be surprised how many don't,' said Ferguson. 'What have they got against him?' asked Saltzman. 'Oh, they think he talks too much,' said Ferguson, 'though I could listen to him all day. They also think he's a bit of a pedant. And maybe he is. But he considers it the first duty of a historian – or anyone interested in history – to get the facts right. That's why he won't have anything to do with the Boot Hill Museum people, nor they with him.'

As they crossed the cracked bed of the Arkansas River, Ferguson said, 'When I was a kid I would never have thought that river would have run dry.' He pulled over on the other side to show Saltzman where the cattle trail once ran. He pointed to a racetrack and a building marked Henton Plumbing Services.

Kansas, when mapped, resembled a chequerboard. Saltzman allowed himself to be moved around it at the whim of All-America Driveaways, but wherever he went – and it was mainly the old cow towns of Dodge, Wichita and Abilene – he kept running into the same old people: General Custer,

Wild Bill Hickok, Wyatt Earp, though not, thank heavens, Calamity Jane. Through these encounters he gradually came to realize how interconnected their lives had been, and how they were all shaped by the booming state of Kansas. It was to Fort Riley, near Kansas City, that Custer had been posted after the Civil War. He considered command of the newly formed 7th Cavalry scant reward for his recent heroics, but decided to make the most of the opportunity anyway. It was an opportunity he severely jeopardized when, after a hard campaign against the Cheyenne, he retired sans orders to Fort Riley, just to spend a night with his beloved Libbie. The romantic gesture earned him a court martial, a guilty verdict and a year's suspension (a plight with which Saltzman could readily identify). Passing the fort late one afternoon, Saltzman decided to visit the scene of this unauthorized tryst but never got to first base. Soldiers guarding its entrance began waving him away as soon as they saw him. Not ready to give up, Saltzman sought another entry and found a gate apparently unmanned. Or that's what he thought, until a bush flagged down his car. 'Can I help you, sir?' The soldier was stern, and not at all friendly. 'I've come to see Custer's House, but can't quite work out where it is,' said Saltzman. 'It doesn't matter where it is, sir,' said the soldier, 'it closed an hour ago, so you won't be seeing it today.' He followed Saltzman's retreat in his Humvee until he was sure that the intruder had quit the post entirely. Only then did Saltzman notice a tank commanding the heights on the opposite side of the freeway. The army was obviously taking no chances.

He had more success gaining access to the real Fort Hays, long since abandoned by the military. It was there, in the late 1860s, that Wild Bill Hickok had been Custer's scout. 'However much Custer fancied him,' Salzman used to tell his students, 'Mrs Custer fancied him more.' Whereupon he would recite a few sentences from her memoir, *Following the Guidon*: 'I do not recall anything finer in the way of physical perfection than Wild Bill when he swung himself lightly from his saddle, and with graceful, swaying step, squarely set shoulders, and well-poised head, approached our tent for orders . . . [H]e looked as if he had descended from a race who valued the body as a choice possession, and therefore gave it every care. He not only looked like a thoroughbred, but like a racer, for he seemed even in repose to give evidence of great capabilities of endurance – of fine "staying powers" in his own vernacular. The days of the Greeks are slowly returning to us when the human form will be so cared for that no development it is capable of will be neglected . . .'

In 1869 this paradigm of masculinity had been elected sheriff of nearby Hays City, but within the year he was unelected by a vote of 114 to 89. One of the reasons for his unpopularity was his ongoing campaign to improve the manners of the free-spending 7th Cavalry. Custer's younger brother, Tom, took especial exception. One night he rode into Hays City followed by three enlisted men, all intent upon giving Hickok a taste of his own medicine. By the end of it Tom Custer's enforcers were all dead. And Hickok, soon to be an ex-sheriff anyway, was advised to quit town toot sweet, unless he wanted to face the army's retribution. Tom's big brother was more forgiving, however, maintaining (in his memoirs) that Hickok was guilty of nothing worse than justifiable homicide.

Meanwhile, over in Abilene the locals were getting

twitchy. They liked the wealth associated with being the railhead of the Chisholm Trail, but not the anarchy. And anarchy was on the cards ever since the man they had relied upon to preserve order, the unflappable Tom Smith, had been unexpectedly butchered with an axe. Who could replace their assassinated peacekeeper? The answer came when Abilene's mayor offered Hickok the marshal's star, and he (on the rebound from Hays City) accepted it. Saltzman, searching the modern city for evidence of that old employ, entered a coffee shop on Third seeking guidance and renewed energy. Its proprietess introduced herself as Jan. Before she opened the cafe she had taught art. The flamboyant flower paintings on its walls were her work. She wore a cross, and confided in Saltzman that she had a bad heart. But she served good coffee.

She explained to Saltzman how Hickok had ended up persona non grata in Abilene as well as Hays. 'I know what I'm tellin you's the truth,' she said, 'because I heard it from an old-timer whose father had heard it from his. Well, they hired Wild Bill Hickok because they wanted someone mean enough to keep the Texas longhorns (hundreds of thousands of them), plus their two thousand Texican minders, around the train depot where they belonged. And Hickok did what they wanted right enough. But one night a bloody-minded cowboy got bored with the whores and the card sharps, the pickpockets and the gunslingers who infested the south side of the railroad, and crossed over into the respectable part of town, ending up somewhere round here, where he created a major ruckus. Wild Bill Hickok was called and there was a fight, which cost the foolhardy cowboy his life. That was no problem. But then Wild Bill's deputy came running up behind him, and Wild Bill, thinkin it was a friend of the deceased, spun around and shot him too. After that he was thrown out of Abilene. And he's yet to be welcomed back with any real enthusiasm. The best we can muster is a rodeo named in his honour, which features a Wild Bill lookalike contest, and was graced last summer by the two times Wild Bill lookalike world champion.'

In Wichita weeks later Saltzman recollected that Wyatt Earp, like Hickok, had been shown the door by citizens concerned by his overzealous behaviour. It was a pattern he would have thought worth exploring, were he still an academic. Instead, here he was at the wheel of a feisty 1969 Ford Mustang – not his, of course – approaching a Scottish castle (erected by an American Campbell in 1888) turned guest house, at which the auto's new owner was staying. He had long since come to accept that his clients never engaged him in conversation. They always asked the same question: 'How did she drive?' To which he had learned to reply, 'Like a dream.' And that was that. What to do next? Although he had come to resemble a hippie who hadn't shaved or cut his hair since the Rolling Stones played Altamont, Saltzman still enjoyed his creature comforts, and he still had credit on his Amex card. So he presented himself – and it – to the proprietor of the Castle Inn. The proprietor, whose name was Terry Lowry, didn't really resemble William H. Macy, but if you were looking for an actor to play him in a movie it would undoubtedly be William H. Macy you'd choose. When asked if there was a room available he laughed, the sort of resigned, self-deprecating laugh that was William H. Macy's trademark.

'All bar one,' he said. 'That leaves you the Royal Court done up in a Greco-Roman style, complete with pillars and

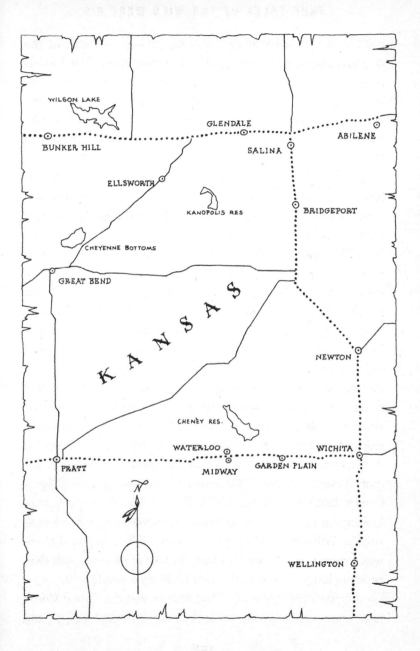

pediment over the marbleized jacuzzi area. It sits at the top of the turret, and offers spectacular views of the Little Arkansas River, and the city's skyline. To be candid, it's really for couples, but if you ever wondered what it felt like to be the Emperor Nero, now's your chance. No? Then perhaps, considering your nationality, you might prefer a cosy room whose stately-home atmosphere is complemented by images of fox hunting. Or, if your fancy's for something completely different, you might be tempted by the Native American room, in which a fourteen-foot-tall tepee bedchamber accents the tribal motif.'

'That sounds perfect,' said Saltzman. 'Good choice, Professor Saltzman,' said Lowry, as he examined the Amex card, 'you've lighted on one of my favourites.' Assuming he was addressing a gay interior designer, Saltzman asked, 'Is this all your own work?' 'I can only claim half the credit,' replied Lowry, 'the other half belongs to my wife. We both grew up in Wichita, and knew the Castle only as a majestic wreck. But something about it caught my imagination early, and even then I dreamed of one day owning and restoring it. The dream stayed with me all through my studies, and my twenty-year exile in California, where I practised as an orthodontist.' Okay, thought Saltzman, who didn't like admitting his errors, what is an orthodontist but an interior designer of the mouth?

'In 1994,' Lowry continued, 'we decided it was time to turn my dream – by then our dream – into reality. We sold our home in California, returned to Wichita, and somehow raised the two and a half million dollars required to rescue the Castle from total ruin. My wife supervised the restoration. No expense was spared. For example, that staircase in the Grand Foyer was shipped from London and is over two hundred and fifty years old, while the Grecian-style fireplace is even older, weighing in at six hundred and fifty years. What you are looking at is a dream come true.' Oh no, it isn't, thought Saltzman, you don't remind me of William H. Macy for nothing.

'Or it would be,' said Lowry, 'if it weren't for the ever-present possibility of it becoming a nightmare. Already the strain has turned my hair prematurely grey. You see, Professor Saltzman, for all our efforts, it's just not working. The Kansas mentality is simply too narrow to accept something so different. It turns out that, given the choice, people would prefer to go to a hotel chain than risk novelty. And even if we wanted to sell up we couldn't, because the Castle is a white elephant. Not that we intend to abandon it, but a white elephant is a very demanding creature. And this one is costing us a small fortune every month to maintain. Since we do not possess a fortune, large or small, in two weeks' time I shall be returning to my old profession. Not in Wichita, nor even in California, but in Holland. I only hope our marriage will survive all this.'

As if on cue Lowry's wife suddenly appeared. 'For goodness' sake, Terry,' she said, 'stop talkin, and let the man go wash up.' 'It's okay, ma'am,' said Saltzman, 'I'm pretty much washed up already.' 'Do you know who you remind me of?' said Lowry. Saltzman hadn't a clue. So Lowry told him: 'Krusty the Clown.'

Sitting on the bear-skin rug within his tepee, Saltzman wondered whether he ought to have Terry look at his teeth. He was pretty certain that a reminder from Mr Wolffe would be among the many letters that had been accumulating behind his front door, unopened these many months. It was one thing to let hair and whiskers grow unchecked, but another to let plaque spread like coral. That was a sure sign that all hope had been abandoned. And Saltzman was not quite ready to do that. Not in the presence of a man fighting tooth and nail to save his dream. It suddenly occurred to Saltzman that Terry Lowry was the Jay Gatsby of Wichita. And with that, Saltzman's respect for him grew. Poor Gatsby had seen his dream slip from his grasp. But Terry Lowry was determined to hold on to his, even if it meant filling Dutch cavities. That night Saltzman brushed and flossed his teeth with renewed vigour.

Although Saltzman had spent most of his time in Kansas hanging out with the lawmen, his true blood brothers remained the outlaws. Did they not want the same thing as he: to vanish – if not from the eyes of God, then at least from those of man? As a consequence they did not dwell in houses, like law-abiding folk, but in hideouts. And according to the sign Saltzman had just passed, there was a not-to-be-missed example in Meade, much used by the notorious Dalton Gang. Saltzman was on the road from Wichita to Dodge City (not the 50, but the 54, slower but supposedly more scenic) when he noticed the sign. Checking the map he worked out that a visit would add fifty-five miles to his journey. But he was in no hurry, and he was not alone in that. It was a Sunday morning in late September, and the whole world seemed to be turning at a slower pace. Lines of combines were moving across the ripe fields like grazing dinosaurs. The air sparkled with golden dust. At Mullinville, Saltzman ignored the exit for Dodge City. The only cars he saw thereafter, as he passed through the townships of Bucklin, Bloom,

Minneola and Fowler, were clutched around wooden churches, the doors of which remained open, so that he could sometimes hear the raised voices of those who thought God still gave a damn.

Arriving in Meade, Saltzman discovered that the Dalton House Hideout, poised on the corner of Pearlette and Green, was closed until after lunch, to avoid competing with the Lord for business. So he took himself off to the Chuck Wagon Restaurant on West Carthage, arriving just after the hungry churchgoers. Their automobiles – which filled its forecourt – all displayed the same sticker on the rear fender: 'Remember Korea'. Looking around the restaurant's interior Saltzman began to suspect that its entrance was no entrance, but a time portal to the lost world of the 1950s, where Rock Hudson was a heterosexual, Peggy Sue a virgin, the Sioux and the Apache, the Kiowa and the Comanche injuns, and the blacks invisible. In Wyoming all the men wore Stetsons, but in the Covered Wagon the headgear of choice was the baseball cap – though more often than not the caps bore the name of a battleship rather than a favourite team. Saltzman could not be certain, but was pretty sure that most of them were sporting 'I like Ike' pins in their lapels. Their wives, without exception, had lilac perms, as if a single brand of hair dye held a monopoly in south-west Kansas. The men's skin was pulled tight over their cheekbones and shone red in the neon light. The women's faces were matt, having been dusted with rouge. All the couples appeared childless, though some shared tables. Saltzman, however, preferred to sit alone. 'Whatcha havin, honey?' said the waitress. Had such honest folk (or their ancestors) really once turned a blind eye to the presence of the godless Dalton brothers: Emmett, Grattan and Bob?

The answer, as it turned out, was probably, 'No.' The hideout was a small white house with a single gable, raised upon a hillock and backed by a wooded creek. It was built in 1887 by John Whipple, a merchant, for his new bride Eva Dalton, a milliner and sister of Emmett et al. No evidence exists to show that Whipple's new in-laws ever so much as paid a courtesy call. Nevertheless, when a deep drainage ditch was found connecting the house to a barn (some thirty yards distant), imaginative locals immediately pronounced it a tunnel. The only people who would need to commute secretly between the two buildings were Eva's nefarious siblings. Therefore her house must have been as much hideout as home. So much for wishful thinking. Analytical thought, as practised by ex-Professor Saltzman, quickly demon-

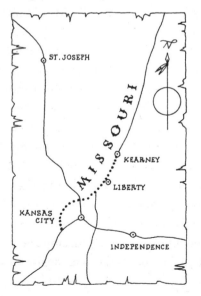

strated its fragility if not its falsity. Horses did not arrive invisibly, and surely any posse worth its salt would ensure both house and stable were watched to prevent a getaway. But why spoil a good story?

During the New Deal the barn was demolished, replaced by a more imposing structure, and called a museum; at the same time the tunnel was enlarged by ex-farmers engaged by the

Work Projects Administration, so that visitors to Meade's only attraction could pass through it more easily than their desperate predecessors. The museum had two levels: shop on the ground, artefacts in the loft. Climbing the stairs Saltzman found an illustrated history of the Daltons awaiting him. The exhibit relied upon facsimiles of old newspapers, and concluded with a reproduc-

tion of the famous photograph of Bob and Grattan handcuffed and upright on a board after the failed raid at Coffeyville, over in south-east Kansas, where they had designs to be the first gang to rob two banks simultaneously. Emmett alone survived the massacre, and kept alive the Dalton name in more ways than one. Having served his time in the state pen, he went on to write two books about his lawless brethren and lived long enough to see Hollywood make a movie of the second, with Brian Donlevy playing his part. In fact, he died in Hollywood a wealthy man, so you could say that he didn't do so badly out of bank robbing after all. Better yet, he had been reincarnated and given literary immortality as the narrator of Ron Hansen's *Desperadoes*, a novel Saltzman had placed high on the Contemporary Western Fiction reading list – the course he was destined never to teach.

Emmett Dalton's own efforts had no such claim upon literary greatness, as their author was the first to acknowledge, but he was equally insistent that they possessed another quality, one which he rated even more highly, claiming that 'every statement herein contained, regarding myself and brothers, is absolutely true in every detail and is the first true and only authentic history ever written about us'. It always seemed odd to Saltzman that such cod-legalese phrasing should preface a book called *Beyond the Law*. Instead of refuting Emmett Dalton's claim to papal infallibility with his postmodern sensibility and sharp tongue, Saltzman simply pointed to the museum's biggest draw, its Rosetta Stone as it were, and said softly, 'Behold truth, in all its majesty.' Truth was a two-headed calf. It stood looking both ways out of its glass case, which had been placed plumb in the middle of the museum. Here was truth, Wild West style: for every story, a counter story; for every tall tale, a taller tale. 'Do you remember the calf that was born over at ol Doniphan's place with five heads?' said an entranced visitor to her husband. Even better, thought Saltzman.

Not long afterwards he took the opportunity afforded by a Kansas City run to cross the wide Missouri, and amble north through fertile and rolling land, still punctuated here and there by ancient woodland. The glory of trees is something easily forgotten, thought Saltzman, in the wheaten desert that is Kansas. After twenty miles or so he came to Kearney, and just beyond that to the farm that nurtured the nefarious brothers Frank and Jesse James, role models and Irish cousins to Emmett, Bob and Grattan. Before being allowed entry to the farmhouse itself Saltzman was required to view a short docudrama in the museum's small movie theatre. The James boys, it seemed, were victims of neither nurture nor nature, but circumstance. Nurture was provided by a stiff-necked mother, and, for their first years at least, by a father who interpreted God's ways

JESSE JAMES FARM & MUSEUM

21216 Jesse James Farm Road
Kearney, Mo. 64060
(816) 628-6065

from the pulpit of the New Hope Baptist church. In 1850, however (when Frank was seven and Jesse but three), the Lord ordered him to minister to the Forty-niners, so he set off for California, where he immediately died, and was buried with his good intentions in Placerville. Zerelda's second husband, older and richer than her, expired within months. It was her third, a country doctor, who was the true father to the boys. Nothing much wrong in the nurturing the boys received, then; strict, but always fair. Their natures, claimed the film, were honest and open. Nor was poverty an issue. The farm was nearly three hundred acres, and the family was sufficiently well off to own several slaves. No, it was circumstance that turned them bad, if bad they really were. Antebellum Missouri, according to the film, was a prelapsarian paradise. The Civil War was the Fall. Afterwards was paradise lost. Whatever they did during those chaotic years, the film could not find it in its heart to condemn them. Indeed, the iconography of Jesse's death – nay, martyrdom – suggested that it would have been much more comfortable hymning his praises. Standing on a chair, arms outstretched, in order to dust (or hang) a framed sampler, he was shot in the back by a member of his own gang, for the equivalent of thirty pieces of silver. The film never actually said it, but obviously wanted to: 'Jesse died for our sins.' What it did say, at the end, was this: 'For reasons best left unexplored Jesse still lives.'

He certainly did in the rebel heart of the prim devotee who led Saltzman down into the hollow where stood what was, in effect, the First Church of Jesse James, a long farmhouse lacking only a steeple. It became a place of pilgrimage very soon after his death, when Zerelda opened it as a roadside attraction. She told visitors stories of her more sinned against than sinning sons, and sold stones from Jesse's grave (replacing them with pebbles from the river bank whenever the supply ran dry). She wept openly, and visited imprecations upon the heads of the Pinkerton detectives who, so she claimed, had maimed her arm in a bungled attack on the farm and hunted her courageous son to his doom. The grave site looked much as it did then, though Jesse's body was no longer in it, having been removed to the Mount Olivet cemetery in Kearney proper. Near it, in untrodden grass, Saltzman noticed a shucked snakeskin. A red-tailed hawk circled over woods (having recently acquired a copy of Roger Tory Peterson's *Field Guide to Western Birds* Saltzman could now do his own identifying).

The woman unlocked the farmhouse. Its interior was chill from the air conditioning, and smelt of mothballs, which were scattered throughout the attic to prevent infestations. It was within these walls, from which the paper was peeling, that Frank and Jesse were born. And it was here in 1915 that Frank died peacefully in his own bed, having led a blameless life since his brother's apotheosis. A framed photograph taken in those last years showed him tall, top-hatted and old, waiting beside the gate for visitors, or maybe death. A few signs, easily legible, had been nailed to it: 'Home of the James. Jesse and Frank James. Admission 50c. each,' and 'Kodaks bared.' Frank apparently liked to read Shakespeare, but he obviously couldn't spell. Neither could he act. He started a Wild West show with his cousin Cole Younger, another notorious survivor, but it flopped. No doubt it peddled the Authorized Version, which presented the Confederate outlaws as White Indians: equal victims of Northern expansion, and of land grabs by the robber barons who ran the railroads.

This image had been developed even while the gang was still in business, credit for which properly belonged to Jesse's own Ned Buntline, a journalist named John Newman Edwards. In an editorial headed 'The Chivalry of Crime' he lauded the exploits of Jesse and Frank, compared them to King Arthur's Knights of the Round Table, and called their latest robbery 'poetic; superb'. No slouch at self-promotion himself, Jesse followed that with a letter to the *Kansas City Times*. 'Some editors call us thieves,' he wrote. 'We are not thieves – we are bold robbers. I am proud of the name, for Alexander the Great was a bold robber, and Julius Caesar, and Napoleon Bonaparte.' The bold robber then boldly claimed that he only robbed the rich and gave to the poor, that he was (in other words) Robin Hood reincarnate. Many on the left took this self-assessment at face value. Even the great Eric Hobsbawm was ready to place Jesse James among the peasant outlaws, saw him as one of those 'who remain within peasant society, and are considered by their people as heroes, as champions, avengers, fighters for justice'. But history, being a two-headed calf, had an alternative view to offer. This other Jesse James was a racist, who took in hatred of equality with his mother's milk, and a psychopath who learned his craft from guerrilla leaders whose pièce de résistance was the massacre of unarmed civilians. Moreover, the peasants who supposedly worshipped him as a righter of wrongs were anything but; were, in fact, what passed for gentry in Missouri's Little Dixie. And what John Newman Edwards saw in Jesse James was not an unrequited lover of humanity but an unreconstructed champion of the defeated Confederacy. But maybe he was wrong.

Either way, the criminal career of Frank and Jesse got under way on 13 February 1866 when they robbed the Clay County Savings Association over in Liberty of $70,000 in cash, though even that basic fact was disputed, since there were those who said Jesse was sick in bed on that day and Frank was in Kentucky. No he wasn't, insisted Kissee Mills, who was looking after the former bank turned museum, he was right here with a neckerchief wrapped around his face and a six-shooter in either hand. Jesse had spent several days planning the raid, and now it was in full swing. Ten men at least were involved, all dressed in Union overcoats (it was 2.00 p.m. on a winter's afternoon and they needed them for warmth as well as disguise). Greenup Bird, the cashier, was forced to fill a large wheat sack with the contents of the vault. Then he was locked in it. So far, so good; no casualties, no shots fired. But as the robbers were making their escape they shot at two passersby, who just happened to be strolling across Liberty's main square at the wrong time. One of the pedestrians was untouched, the other took a bullet in the heart and died instantly. The unfortunate youth turned out to be a student at a seminary founded by the Revd Robert James, co-founder of the James Gang too, in a manner of speaking. Kissee scoffed at the idea of extenuating circumstances and at the idea that Jesse sent a letter of apology to the dead student's family.

'My aim is to tell the truth,' she said. 'And the truth is that Jesse and Frank were common criminals. They did not rob the rich to assist the poor. Or if they did they were worse than useless, because the bank and all its investors were ruined by their act. But do people listen to me? Of course they don't. They come here with this romantic notion of Jesse James – the compassionate bandit who gave an old lady the money to pay off her mortgage, and then ambushed the banker in order to steal it back again – and they fully intend to leave with it intact. In the same way they have a pretty fixed idea of how the inside of an old bank should look. When we first opened there were no bars above the teller's desk, which led to a lot of complaints from our visitors. The problem was that in all the Westerns they had seen there were bars, and that's what they came expecting to see. In the end my boss got so fed up with explaining that

Hollywood had got it wrong that he went and had bars fitted after all. Since when there have been no complaints. It just goes to show . . . Hollywood turns your brains to mush.'

But if it weren't for Hollywood would Jesse James still be the Coca-Cola of outlaws? According to Kissee he'd had more films made about him than any other character in American history, excepting Billy the Kid. So far the score is 47 to 48 in Billy's favour, though Kissee had heard rumours that Brad Pitt would be starring in a version of Ron Hansen's *The Assassination of Jesse James by the Coward Robert Ford* (another title on Saltzman's ghost reading list). She also threw in these other facts. One of the first people to play Jesse James in a movie was Jesse James Jr. The one Jesse James movie to avoid at all costs is *Jesse James Meets Frankenstein's Daughter*. Before he reached the age of eleven Robert James (son of Frank) met about a dozen men claiming to be his Uncle Jesse. Notwithstanding a report in *Scientific Sleuthing Review* (dated February 23, 1996) by James E. Starrs (Professor of Law and Forensic Science at George Washington University), proving by use of DNA samples that the corpse buried in the grave marked Jesse James really was Jesse James, several families and autodidacts had claimed that the real Jesse James faked his own death and went on to enjoy a ripe old age. In Granbury, Texas, Jesse Frank Dalton, who lived to be 104, was exhumed on the strength of an alleged deathbed confession. And again in Neodesha, Kansas, the eternal rest of one Jeremiah James was disturbed before an audience of family members and cowboy re-enactors (who said they had come to honour the outlaw's legacy). 'So,' asked the man filming the event for the History Channel, 'was Jesse James shot in the back of the head by the cowardly Bob Ford, as conventional wisdom has led us to believe? The truth is, we still don't know for sure. Which leads us to explore other theories as they emerge.' The man's a po-mo and doesn't know it, thought Saltzman, he should apply for my old job. Kissee Mills just laughed. Saltzman feared for her safety. If Jesse James were ever to become a demigod his acolytes would certainly call her a heretic and burn her at the stake.

The man who ran the AAD office in Kansas City wondered if Saltzman would be interested in driving a 1990 VW Beetle all the way to Lawton, Oklahoma. Why not? The last time he had been in Oklahoma he had still to marry his ex-wife, though they were travelling together by then. One Saturday night they had ended up in Tahlequah, capital of the Cherokee nation, and with little else to do had booked to see a play that ran all summer in a huge open-air amphitheatre called Tsa-La-Gi. The play told the story of the Cherokee, or at least one version of it. At its core was deracination. In 1838 the tribe had been driven from its homeland in the Allegheny Mountains, forcibly marched across half a continent and the remnant dumped in what would become Oklahoma. It wasn't called *The Trail of Tears* for nothing. Though, America being America, the play's conclusion was anything but lachrymose, being a rousing celebration of Oklahoma's statehood.

Nearly thirty years later Saltzman remembered few details of the play, though one scene remained vivid. Corrupt Indian Agents (knowing they had Washington in their pockets) were shown traducing and cheating the Cherokee with impunity. Observing them at work an honest colleague couldn't help but exclaim, 'The United States as usual is backing the wrong side.' The spontaneous applause that followed the remark revealed just how unpopular the Vietnam War had become, yea even in Oklahoma. At breakfast next morning, he and his future ex-wife had sat at a table for two. Nearby was a quartet of elderly spinsters, who were soon approached by an old gentleman. 'How come you four pretty girls are all sitting at the same table?' he asked. They all twittered. 'Oh, we all hurried back from church,' replied one, 'didn't even have time to shake hands with the preacher.' 'Well, I'm getting together a picnic for our Vietnamese orphans,' he said. 'Had em round last week for hamburgers and hot dogs. That's what they like. I'm gonna supply the food, and Mrs Morell's gonna supply the place.'

History would soon be repeating itself, thought Saltzman, except that this time the cook-outs would be for Iraqi orphans. As yet he had not detected any great anti-war sentiment in the West, but it would come, of that he was sure. Unlike his po-mo and po-co colleagues at the University of St Albans, Saltzman had not been an a priori opponent of the invasion of Iraq.

American interventionism was not, to his mind, necessarily a bad thing, especially if it brought down a regime of exceptional barbarity. For that reason he had declined to join any of the anti-war marches. Besides, he was choosy about the company he kept. However, he could no longer deny that America's initiative had actually made things much worse, even if on this occasion (or so it seemed to Saltzman) the country's mistake had not been in backing the wrong side but in electing the wrong leader. Saltzman sometimes suspected that President Bush had based his entire war strategy on sentiments seen on the Official State

Highway Map of Wyoming: '. . . [A]lthough they are typically individualists, cowboys most often are willing to "circle up the wagons", to join together in a just cause . . . It is in the spirit of this rangerider that we . . . urge all freedom-loving people to "Cowboy Up" with us and with America, in this time of national and, indeed, worldwide need – until what needs doin is done.' Could it be that Bush really was persuaded that all his army had to do was run the bad guys out of Baghdad?

The first thing Saltzman saw as he entered the National Cowboy and Western Heritage Museum in Oklahoma City was the sculpture loathed more than any other by the curators of *The American West* show at Compton Verney (which he had visited in a previous life). Near twenty feet high, and made of gleaming white plaster, it presented a dispossessed and defeated Indian slumping over his horse's neck, which seemed to be folding under the burden. The pair could obviously go no further, hence its title, *The End of the Trail*. Yet despite all the likelihood of falling, the horse remained standing. Perhaps there was some hope to be found in that. Though, to be honest, its rider didn't look like he'd be picking up a guitar and singing Gene Autry's 'Back in the Saddle Again' any day soon.

If you wanted to see that, you had to take yourself to a small screening room where a short documentary called *Silver Screen Cowboys* was playing. Buffalo Bill was the hero of more than seventeen hundred dime novels, said its narrator. His near namesake, Broncho Billy Anderson, created the cowboy's screen image. Gary Cooper appeared, misquoting Owen Wister: 'If you want to call me that, smile.' By 1932 Hollywood was making over a hundred Westerns a

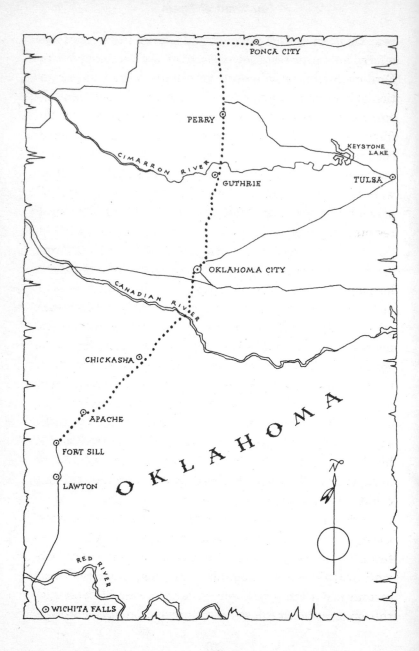

year. Gene Autry, Roy Rogers and the other singing cowboys offered an escape from the miseries of the Depression. John Ford made films with a deep sensitivity to the transformation of history into myth. *The Searchers* was a psychological epic set against a mythical landscape. As long as there are films there will always be Westerns, the narrator concluded, celebrating the truth and revealing the myth, though (in a postscript) he did express doubts about the direction some were taking. The demise of cowboy heroes, and the cynical presentation of the heritage of the West, he said, frequently resulted in shorter lines at the box office.

As he passed through its various displays Saltzman sensed that the museum's curators were having a hard time keeping the two-headed calf on the straight and narrow: one head wore a mortar board and wanted to go to school, the other wore a Stetson and just wanted to have fun. They did not shy away from phrases such as 'inventing the American West', but nor could they resist exhibiting John Wayne's movie costumes as if they were historical artefacts. Spread out in a glass case was the uniform he sported in *She Wore a Yellow Ribbon*: jacket, shirt, trousers, belts, kepi, boots, spurs. Alongside it was the special Bowie knife presented to him by Gucci after the release of *The Alamo* in 1960. Wayne liked it so much he kept it in his desk drawer, where the only combat it saw was opening fan letters.

And (God help him) young Saltzman had written one of them, though John Wayne was never more than his second-favourite cowboy: he'd always found it easier to identify with Gary Cooper's vulnerability than the Duke's cast-iron certainty. But there was another, more personal, reason for this preference. One of the few things that had made growing up in Luton half bearable (this was before Saltzman's father made a lot of money and moved the family to Hendon) was the astonishing discovery that Gary Cooper – son of an English mother – had been removed from his native Montana and sent to Ashton Grammar School in nearby Dunstable. Thereafter, Saltzman regarded the gloomy, neo-Gothic pile with its nightmarish spires as a place of pilgrimage just a short bus-ride away. Had I but been born forty-seven years earlier, he had thought while standing on the other side of the A5, we could have been playmates. So what choice did the grown-up Saltzman have when he heard that Virginia Campbell would be introducing a gala screening of Cecil B. DeMille's *Unconquered* (in which she co-starred with Gary Cooper) that very afternoon? At 3.00 p.m. prompt, Saltzman took his seat in the Sam Noble Special Events Center.

Virginia Campbell was just about the best advertisement for longevity Saltzman had ever seen. She must have been in her nineties, but was as kittenish as a schoolgirl. She wore a turquoise cap and a black dress. When she smiled she looked like happiness personified.

'Jessica Tandy was a very good friend of mine,' she said, 'and Jessie was offered this part in *Unconquered*, but she was going for something else, so she said, "Ginny, why don't you go for it?" And I said, "Why not?" So she arranged with her agent to send me in her place, and I went for the interview.' She paused. 'I had thought that Cecil B. DeMille had been dead for some time,' she said, 'but obviously I was wrong.' The audience hooted. Virginia Campbell smiled sweetly, then continued. 'So I went for the interview. And he said, "Well, yes, Miss Campbell, how do you intend to play this part?" And I said, "Mr DeMille, I've never done film. Don't you have things called screen tests?" And he said, "Yes." And I said, "Shouldn't I do one?" And he said, "Miss Campbell, I'm offering you the part." And I said, "Mr DeMille, I want you to be really sure, so shouldn't we do this?" And he said, "All right, let's arrange for Miss Campbell to have a screen test." So I had a screen test, and then there was another interview. And he said, "Well, Miss Campbell. are you happy with that?" And I said, "It's *you* who has to be happy. I don't know anything about filming." So he said, "Miss Campbell, Yes or No?" And I said, "Yes, Mr DeMille." And that's how it began.

'The first scene in which I participated was on a huge new set. Louella Parsons was there – Cecil B. DeMille always had other people watching. As I recall, Gary Cooper comes to the house of his best friends, who are me and Ward Bond, play-

ing husband and wife. And then he picks me up, and puts me on his knee, and we have a lovely hug, and I say, "Why are you here?" And he says, "I've come to trap a skunk." The skunk being the villain who's selling arms or whiskey to the Indians. It's at this point we see his new acquisition, Paulette Goddard, who's looking quite raggedy and everything. In an earlier scene Gary Cooper had bought her somewhere in England, where she was being auctioned as an indentured slave, and brought her back to America, because he felt sorry for her. Well, we did the beginning of the scene all right, and Mr DeMille called, "Cut!" After that he planned to do a close-up of me during which I deliver my reply to Gary Cooper, which is: "It appears to me you've already trapped a chipmunk." Meaning Paulette Goddard, of course. In close-ups you're on your own, the director doesn't give you the cue, so I was especially careful when they took the scene, and felt pleased with myself when it was done, because I assumed I'd said my line perfectly. But there was a terrible silence and people went different colours, and Gary Cooper (who was a darling) didn't put me down – remember I was still sitting on his knee – he just picked me up and took me through the set out onto the alley. He stood with one leg raised and resting on a bench, took out a packet of cigarettes, gave me one. And I said, "Why are we doing this?" And he said, "Well, you don't know what you said?" And I said, "I said my line." And he said, "You may think you did. But unfortunately what you said as you gazed at Paulette Goddard was, 'It appears to me you've trapped a skunk.' And given what everybody's feeling about her at the moment, it was the wrong thing to say." Because apparently she had done – I don't know what, something terrible. So that was my first thing.

'And then I went and did something else that rather shocked people – I spoke to Mr DeMille directly. Apparently it was the custom that if you wanted to speak to Mr DeMille you spoke to an assistant, who spoke to another assistant, who spoke to another assistant, and then – if you were lucky – you got to speak to him. But I didn't know that, and I said straight out, "Mr DeMille!" And he came over. It was a shock. I don't think anyone had seen him behave like a human being in years, and I think he rather liked it. Otherwise he would have ignored me, because he could be awfully cruel. So you could see why anyone who was a friend would think, "Oh God, Ginny's going to end up in his bad books." And that was not a good place to be. But he apparently understood that I was just being very earnest, and sincere, and trying to do a good job. And I said, "Come over," and he came over. And I said, "Don't leave my side, I'm very nervous." And he was very, very sweet.

'The last big scene was the ballroom. And again I said, "Mr De Mille, could I speak to you?" But this time he said, "Miss Campbell, just do it!" He'd had enough. And I said, "Yes, Mr DeMille." And I do it. I go over to Gary Cooper to talk about something, and then the villain barges in. I think there's a challenge with guns or something and Gary Cooper pushes me gently out of range of the guns. And that was the last scene we had together.'

During the post-screening reception, at which Miss Campbell was the guest of honour, Saltzman asked her if there had been much camaraderie on the set. 'There was in my dressing room,' she said. 'We used to have meetings there, the way you do between scenes. Everyone was welcome, there was no – what do you call it? – hierarchy as there tended to be elsewhere.' 'Did Gary Cooper come?' he asked. 'Of course,' she replied, 'he was a very nice man. Once, on location, he even let me have his dressing room. Though, I am sorry to say, he was not in it at the time.' 'Did you work with him again?' asked Saltzman. 'I never saw any of the cast again,' she said, 'except for Boris Karloff, who played Guyasuta, Chief of the Senecas, though we never actually met on set. It was much later that we became good friends. When we all lived in Rome. He was such a cultured man. And he loved reading bedtime stories to my daughter. Do you have any children, Professor Saltzman?' 'No,' he said. 'A wife?' she said. 'Not since the divorce,' he said. 'Your accent tells me that you are English,' she said. 'Do you live there?' 'I have a house in St Albans,' he said. 'Well, I have a flat in Chelsea,' she said. 'So next time you are in residence you must call me, and I'll take you to meet my daughter, who is very talented, very beautiful, and a divorcee. Do you promise you will?' Saltzman promised he would. She wrote her telephone number on his ticket stub: 0207 352 XXXX. Peppercorn's family, he recalled, had once lived at 352 Watford Way. It occurred to Saltzman that he hadn't spoken to his cousin in many weeks. He called him before he left the museum. Peppercorn had no news, except that Mrs Peppercorn was unwell.

Back in the days before his life became a series of unconnected journeys on the freeways and interstates of the American West, Saltzman had had occasion to deliver a lecture on Geronimo, last of the free Apaches, who would certainly have envied such a lifestyle. Being more of a cultural historian than a proper historian, he did not delve into the causes of Geronimo's rebellion or offer a detailed biography of the man. Instead, he chose to concentrate his attention (and that of his audience) on two photographs, which told the same story in sign language. The first was the work of Camillus S. Fly of Tombstone. It was taken in 1886 at Geronimo's special request, and showed five Apaches in a line. Left to right they were Perico, a warrior (who was holding a child); beside him, mounted, was Geronimo himself; next, also mounted, was Naiche, son of Cochise and hereditary chief of the Chiricahua Apaches; leading his horse was Geronimo's son, Tsisnah.

'Take a good look, ladies and gentlemen,' said Saltzman, 'you will not see their like again. Geronimo appears exhausted, but by no means broken; his eyes are fierce, and his jaw determined. And he is dressed to kill, meaning (on this occasion) to impress. His jacket is tailored, as if for the hangers of Abercrombie & Fitch, his calico shirt is new. Naiche, for his part, is wearing a fancy hat. Perico and Tsisnah are decorated with face paint. Geronimo's saddle and tackle are American, as are his guns. But his spirit is unpasteurized Apache. For nearly a year, as Naiche's Minister of War, he has been humiliating both the American and Mexican armies, but he is leading a hundred and ten against thousands, and he knows that he cannot run forever, not with women and children in tow. So it is time to sue for peace (though the Americans prefer the sound of "surrender"). They are heading for a rendezvous of Geronimo's choosing, the Cañon de los Embudos, a beautiful spot, with clear running water shaded by sycamores, ash, cottonwoods, willows and blackthorn, a strand of which, you'll note, spreads before Geronimo's horse like a line of barbed wire. In his heart Geronimo must know that when he crosses that line he will be leaving the old ways behind forever, that the Cañon de los Embudos is the end of the trail. Even so, when Fly had taken the picture, he crossed it.'

General Crook was impressed by what he saw approaching him. The hostiles were, he wrote, 'in superb physical condition, armed to the teeth', and as 'fierce as so many tigers'. One of his aides, Captain John G. Bourke, was even more taken with their physiques, noting that 'every muscle was perfect in development and hard as adamant, and one of the young men . . . was as finely muscled as a Greek statue'. (Or even Wild Bill Hickok.) Another thought that if only the American army could boast twenty-five thousand such recruits it would whip the best Europe had to offer. Fly went about his business of photographing the negotiations with such bravado, coolly asking Geronimo to turn his head a little so as to improve the composition, that Bourke thought him suicidal. Despite the understandable tensions a deal was negotiated that, after a symbolic period of imprisonment, would allow the Apaches to return to their native Arizona. It lasted no longer than the time it took President Cleveland to read its terms. He ordered Crook to tear it up and insist upon nothing less than unconditional surrender. 'I want no more of this,' said Geronimo, and left with Naiche and thirty-two others. But it was an encore, nothing more. Five months later Geronimo surrendered for good, at Skeleton Canyon, on the American side of the border, from where he was sent to a prison in Florida.

The second photograph was taken in 1905 at Ranch 101, situated about a hundred miles north-east of Oklahoma City. 'At first glance it appears that Geronimo has become more than assimilated in the intervening years,' said Saltzman. 'He's done up like a prosperous Yankee businessman, with a black waistcoat, a white shirt and a black top hat. What's more, he's at the wheel of a brand-new Locomobile Model C. Perhaps he has only just taken delivery, and is showing it off to his chums. Beside him sits Edward Le Clair Sr., a Ponca notable, in full headdress, beaded waistcoat and related finery. In the back sit an unknown pair. One is wearing the single-feather signifier, while the other sports a cap made of horsehide tanned soft, with peaks on either side like erect ear muffs. But look more closely and you'll see that the car isn't even on the road, let alone in motion. It is stationary in long grass. Geronimo's prosperity is a bubble, and his freedom an illusion.'

Ranch 101 was a working ranch – (Tom Mix was its foreman), but it also mounted Wild West extravaganzas – which were Tom Mix's springboard to Hollywood and universal stardom. On 11 June 1905 the notorious Apache warlord was the main attraction. Thousands turned up to witness what was billed as Geronimo's Last Buffalo Hunt, an atrophied skill, old Geronimo had not hunted buffalo since his earliest youth. But that was of no consequence. While someone else drove the Locomobile, Geronimo directed three arrows into the flank of the sacrificial offering. But, as in John Ford's *The Man Who Shot Liberty Valance*, it was an unseen marksman who fired the fatal bullet. After that Geronimo had to pretend to skin the unfortunate creature. And when the day was done, armed guards returned their prisoner to Fort Sill, where he had been confined since 1894, and where he died in 1909.

Having left for Lawton at 5.00 p.m. Saltzman passed Fort Sill at 7.00. Although it was surely after closing time there was a line of cars waiting to gain entry. Deciding to try his luck Saltzman joined it. The military policeman at the gate did not turn him away, but forwarded him to a checkpoint manned by soldiers, one of whom demanded a picture ID. That being in order Saltzman felt emboldened to request directions to Geronimo's grave. 'They're yours,' said the soldier, 'so long as you can show me a valid Department of Defense sticker.' Saltzman couldn't, and was dispatched to a second checkpoint, where he was greeted by a bull-necked sergeant with a shorn head and beads of sweat on his tan skin (as late as it was, the temperature was still close to body heat). 'I assume you are here for the graduation,' said the sergeant. 'No,' said Saltzman. 'Fancy,' said the sergeant, 'you're the first one tonight who isn't. So just why have you come to Fort Sill?' 'I'm hoping to visit Geronimo's grave,' said Saltzman. The sergeant asked if Saltzman wouldn't mind opening the glove compartment. Saltzman had no objections. 'How about the console?' said the sergeant. 'What's a console?' asked Saltzman. 'Don't worry,' said the sergeant, 'you probably don't have one.' He instructed Saltzman to pop the trunk and hood, then ordered him out of the vehicle. An officer approached and took his passport and driving licence, which were both subjected to careful scrutiny. Meanwhile, a grunt examined under the car with a mirror that looked like one of Mr Wolffe's instruments manufactured on a Brobdingnagian scale. That done, the boy checked the engine and Saltzman's single bag, and finally issued a clean bill of health.

Having been admitted, Saltzman tried to remember the directions grudgingly given him by the sergeant, but discovered himself bewildered in the back country, and not helped by signs such as: Howitzer range; Bivouac site and Model village. An armadillo rattled its articulated plates along the dusty gutter, and scurried into the woods. Lucky creature, thought Saltz-man, you get to retain your armour at all times, whereas I have to shed mine every time I get out of the car. Lost, he flagged down a breathless jogger, who politely directed him across a single-track bridge before staggering off into the uninhabited wilderness.

Saltzman knew he had arrived because he could see a marker headed 'Apache Prisoner-of-War Cemeteries'. Below it, cast in bronze, were the following observations: 'Under Oklahoma skies far from their native haunts in Arizona, New Mexico and northern Mexico is the resting place for more than three hundred Apaches of the Chiricahua, Warm Springs, and Nedni tribes. During and after the Geronimo campaign of 1886 these people – hostiles, friendlies, and scouts alike – were sent as prisoners-of-war to Florida, then to Alabama. In 1894 they were brought to Fort Sill where they remained for the next nineteen years. Living in twelve villages, with many of their leading men serving as soldiers and US scouts, they built their own houses, fenced the entire military reserve, dug water tanks that still dot the landscape, raised ten thousand cattle, and grew bountiful crops. Granted freedom by Act of Congress in 1913, a hundred and eighty-three returned to New Mexico while eighty-two settled on farms near here. This burial ground is a memorial both to their historic past and to their industry and perseverance on their long road to a new way of life.' So that was how you measured progress, thought Saltzman, the time it takes to travel from 'native haunts' to a 'new way of life'. Who knew? Perhaps he had been wrong in his lecture, perhaps the Cañon de los Embudos had not been the end of the trail for all the Apaches, though he was certain he wasn't wrong about Geronimo.

The obstinate warrior's tomb was a miniature pyramid made of rocks and topped off with a metal eagle. It was shaded by a cypress, to which neckerchiefs and multi-coloured bandannas had been knotted. As the wind blew they fanned the stones. On the steps of the pyramid visitors had left offerings of cigarettes, cigarette holders and pouches of tobacco. Someone had left a white plastic horse. It was peaceful in that place, but not quiet. Crickets sang their song of the body electric. A large hornet, the size of a humming bird, collected nectar. Its wings made a purring sound, like a perfectly tuned motor. Large red ants had carved a path through the dry grass. A raiding party was transporting a captured wasp, as if bringing their own tribute to the fallen hero. Mosquitoes buzzed Saltzman continually, like a swarm of phantom arrows. The graves of Geronimo's wives and children were small and white. They stood before his, like pawns before a king. As did Saltzman.

When he went to collect his pay cheque at the AAD office in Lawton, the counter clerk said, 'We've got the big one if you want it. A 1970 Dodge Challenger to be delivered to Los Angeles in forty-eight hours. Think you can hack it?' 'How many miles would that be?' asked Saltzman. 'About thirteen hundred,' replied the clerk. 'No time for sightseeing, then,' said Saltzman. 'Unlikely,' said the clerk. In the days when 'hip' was still acceptable currency – in other words, when he had made the same trip with the future Mrs Saltzman – he had taken Route 66, and saw Amarillo, Gallup, New Mexico, Flagstaff, Arizona, Winona, Kingman, Barstow, San Bernardino. But now Route 66 was closed – like the Frontier – and a new interstate bypassed the towns and cut out the romance.

And so, after months on the road, Saltzman found himself almost back where he started: not at Gene Autry's Melody Ranch, to be sure, but at the Autry Museum of Western Heritage, some twenty miles distant. In the plaza around which the museum was designed, he saw another statue of a man and his horse. But this man was cast in bronze, not plaster, and was looking towards the heavens, not the grave. He was sitting on a rock, strumming his old guitar, while his horse turned its head the better to hear (if it is proper to call Champion an 'it'). The statue was called *Back in the Saddle Again*. That'll be the day, thought Saltz-

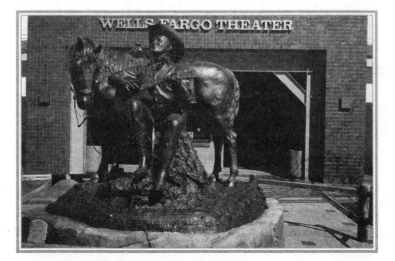

man. He found his way to the 1950s boy's bedroom that had seduced even Richard William Hill, Cree co-curator of the anti-Wild West show at Compton Verney. Its manifold images of cowboy heroes had an even more dramatic effect upon Saltzman, who felt his facial muscles pull in such unfamiliar and forceful ways that he feared he might be having a stroke. Try as he might there was nothing he could do to keep them under control, and he began to bawl like a baby, with no mother or father to comfort him.

True Tales of the
WILD WEST Nº4

Tombstone's
Femme Fatale

After the death of his wife Peppercorn received numerous letters of condolence, but none could tell him how to raise the dead. One (postmark illegible) came from Saltzman. His cousin's expressions of grief sounded genuine, but he said nothing about returning to St Albans. Peppercorn's guardian angel at *Terra Incognita* proposed several assign-ments, but Peppercorn declined them all, preferring to re-establish himself upon terra firma. His GP, a divorcee, began to look in upon him from time to time. Before long it became their habit to dine together on Friday nights. Since Peppercorn was the better cook he took on that role, while Dr Helman played the sommelier. He would telephone on the Thursday to enquire whether they were having meat or fish, and show up on the morrow with the appropriate colour. For example, when salmon was named as the plat du jour he purchased a bottle of Bonny Doon's well-regarded Clos de Reynard.

'And what is your adventurous son up to this week?' he said, as he filled two glasses with the honey-hued wine. 'Still working as a bellhop at that hotel in Desert Hot Springs, and loving every minute,' said Peppercorn. 'I know it wasn't easy,' said Dr Helman, 'but you were quite right to insist that he stuck to his gap-year plans.' 'We speak every day,' said Peppercorn. 'He likes to reassure himself that I've made it through another night, and I'm just glad to hear his voice. I can't help worrying, him being so far from home for the first time.' 'Maybe he's safer in California,' said Dr Helman, whose daughter lived with her mother in Finchley but attended school in the City. 'It's now routine for me to interrupt my surgery at 9.00 a.m. to listen to the news, in case some meshuggener has blown himself up on Zoe's train.' As far as Dr Helman could tell, the world's store of madmen was increasing by the minute. His diagnosis of what ailed the planet allowed for no second opinion. 'I blame your cousin Saltzman and his ilk,' he said. 'For years they've been going around maintaining that everything is relative, and that truth is a fairy story. Equally outmoded is any distinction between right and wrong. Morality, we are assured, is merely the lapdog of the powerful. And shame is so last century.' 'Not for Saltzman,' said Peppercorn, 'not since Deadwood.' 'Good,' said Dr Helman. 'He learned his lesson. But his legacy remains: an unhinged world, swinging aimlessly while dogmatists slowly turn the screw.' 'Sometimes,' said the widower to the divorcee, 'I feel that we are like characters in a Chekhov play. Talking and talking, while the house in which we sit is collapsing around our ears.'

And so the weeks passed, and the months, until it was time to light the candle for Mrs Peppercorn's yahrzeit (which happened to fall on a Friday). 'I wish you long life,' said Dr Helman when he saw the flame flickering in the glass. Over dinner they also proposed a toast to the memory of Theo van Gogh, lately murdered by a jihadist in Amsterdam. Peppercorn saw the crime as inexcusable butchery, and was astounded by the equivocal response of others, the worst offender, in his opinion, being Rohan Jayasekera. 'He's an associate editor of *Index on Censorship*, for God's sake,' Peppercorn said to Dr Helman, 'a magazine dedicated to the defence of free speech. But instead of defending van Gogh, he rounds on him, calls him a "free speech fundamentalist on a martyrdom mission", and finally applauds his cruel end as a "marvellous piece of theatre". It's a disgrace.' Dr Helman had to concur. 'There can only be one explanation for this monumental perversity,' concluded Peppercorn. 'In Jayasekera's eyes, Theo van Gogh was not Theo van Gogh but Uncle Sam. To the Jayasekeras of this world, America is exactly what Ayatollah Khomeini said it was – the Great Satan.' 'And not only to the Jayasekeras,' said Dr Helman, 'but also to otherwise decent people. Only the other day I heard one of the grandes dames of Eng Lit publicly declare her loathing for all things American. It seems that anti-Americanism is the one hatred left that dares to speak its name.'

'I'm surprised about her,' said Peppercorn, who had photographed the writer on several occasions, and well remembered the last time they had met. On the morning of 11 September 2001 he had taken the train from St Albans to King's Cross, accompanied by his son, who happened to have the day off school. They had walked from the station to the British Library, where they saw an exhibition called (cunningly and punningly), 'The Lie of the Land'. Its subject was the secret life of maps. Among those on display was one of Paradise (circa 1685), which confidently situated the Garden of Eden, the Tower of Babel and Nineve ('where Jonas preacht') in the region of the Euphrates. Also on display was a chart labelled as an Ethnic Map of Slovakia (drawn by German civil servants in 1941). From a distance it looked rather attractive, being dotted with coloured circles in the manner of a Kandinsky, but closer inspection quickly revealed that these discs represented high concentrations of Jews and gypsies. 'It was probably a map like this, for the neighbouring province of Moravia,' noted one of the curators in the catalogue, 'that in 1941 and 1942 assisted the Nazi authorities in planning the deportations and the eventual deaths in concentration camps of most of my mother's family.' Near this was a map that could have passed for a Mondrian, but was actually a Zone Map of Dresden (circa 1944), created for the benefit of the Royal Air Force. The catalogue contrasted the precision of the map with the chaos it engendered.

As Peppercorn and son quit the exhibition the latter received a call on his mobile phone. A friend was watching CNN and needed to share the horror. The story he had to tell sounded incredible: that two hijacked jets had flown into the Twin Towers, causing at least one of them to fall. And there were rumours of even worse in the offing. Much shaken, father and son turned left on to the Euston Road and walked towards King's Cross, where the offices of *Terra Incognita* were located. Peppercorn had a 3.00 p.m. appointment to discuss future projects, including the possibility of photographing Governor Bill Janklow's Buffalo Roundup (one of the more insignificant side effects of the attack upon New York City had been the postponement of that project until the following year). Waiting to cross Pancras Road he had found himself standing beside the celebrated scribe. 'Have you heard the news?' he asked. 'I had an inkling that something untoward had occurred when I left the Library,' she said, 'but I didn't exactly know what.' Peppercorn, of course, did. 'From now on I'll always remember you as the man who told me about the destruction visited upon New York,' she said, 'while we waited for the lights to change outside King's Cross station.' She seemed pretty upset to me back then, thought Peppercorn, so what had changed? As if he didn't know! 'President Bush prattles on about an Intelligent Designer,' he said to Dr Helman, 'but what kind of Intelligent Designer would have placed him at the head of the forces of light, when darkness was a real threat?' 'A malign one?' said Dr Helman.

A few minutes later full-bladdered Dr Helman went to the bathroom, and returned looking more satisfied than his achievement merited. 'I see you have a new woman in your life,' he said.

'You noticed the photograph?' said Peppercorn. 'I could hardly miss it,' said Dr Helman. 'You don't see breasts like that every day. Even in my profession.' 'That was part of her appeal, certainly,' said Peppercorn. 'But I also saw a touch of Thanatos in the black veil that draped them so transparently.' 'Where did you find her?' said Dr Helman. 'I bought her last Tuesday for £16 at the weekly auction in Sandridge Village Hall,' said Peppercorn. 'Did you know who you were bidding for?' said Dr Helman. 'Hadn't a clue,' said Peppercorn. 'I fancied she was a daring Viennese beauty who shocked her strait-laced parents by posing for Klimt in the nude.'

'Not a bad guess,' said Dr Helman. 'Her parents were not Austrian, but German. German Jews, to be precise. However, she was born neither in Berlin nor Vienna, but in New York. Just a few months before Klimt, as a matter of fact.' 'Are you going to tell me her name?' said Peppercorn. 'Josephine Marcus Earp,' said Dr Helman. 'As in Wyatt Earp?' said Peppercorn. 'As in Wyatt Earp,' said Dr Helman. 'She was his wife for fifty years.' At that the photograph changed character. No longer was it simply a photograph. It had gained a personality, become a portrait. Ever the sceptic, however, Peppercorn demanded evidence to back up the doctor's astounding pronouncement.

'Since when were you such an expert on the subject?' he said. 'Since 1986, actually,' said Dr Helman, 'when I received an invitation from my friend Leslie Brody to attend the first night of her play about Josephine. *Quiet, Wyatt!* was performed at the Weyerhaeuser Auditorium in St Paul, and again in San Francisco. Unfortunately, I could get to neither production, but I still have posters from both. There's no doubt that the young woman featured on them is the young woman in your bathroom.' 'Do you know anything else about her?' asked Peppercorn. 'Not really,' said Dr Helman. 'Only that she was raised in San Francisco, and that she met Wyatt Earp in Tombstone.' 'So she was there when he took part in the Gunfight at the OK Corral?' said Peppercorn. 'Some say she was its cause,' said Dr Helman. 'They call her Tombstone's Helen of Troy.' 'Looking at her portrait I can believe that,' said Peppercorn. 'But there is one thing that puzzles me: if it's of who you say it is, how come the mount has the name Kaloma embossed upon it? And why is it dated 1914? By when Josephine must have been well into her fifties.' 'Don't ask me,' said Dr Helman. 'If you want to know the answers, you'll have to find out for yourself. In fact, my prescription for you, old friend, is cherchez la femme.'

'Always good advice,' said Peppercorn, 'but I might just cherchez l'homme first.' Josephine's husband, in the shape of Hugh O'Brian, had been one of the four just men of Peppercorn's childhood, along with his late father, King Arthur and Robin Hood. So great was his enthusiasm for the TV series based upon Wyatt Earp's life that, when its star came to London as the leading act in a Western variety show, his parents obligingly booked front-row seats. One of his greatest joys, on hearing the news, was that Saltzman's hadn't. Decades later he rather wished he had seen it too, because all Peppercorn could recall of the event was the enchantment of the Dominion Theatre on Tottenham Court Road, and the grand entrance of Hugh O'Brian on a golden horse. But of what happened thereafter Peppercorn had no memory at all.

Filling those gaps would make the subsequent search for Josephine more personal, part of the campaign to recapture the pleasures lost with his childhood. Peppercorn began at Hugh O'Brian's official website, scrolling through the section called 'memorabilia', until he found a souvenir programme circa 1957, which seemed about right. He ordered a copy. It arrived autographed by Hugh O'Brian himself, but contained no useful information. So Peppercorn sent a further email to Mr O'Brian (via his webserver), posing specific questions, though not expecting answers. To his surprise he received a response from Dolores Drumbeater, Mr O'Brian's PA, who reported that her employer would be passing through London in the near future and would be happy to answer Mr Peppercorn's questions face to face, 'if things work out advantageously'. By return, Peppercorn offered to make sure they did, and was asked by Ms Drumbeater to secure a double room in a budget hotel near Mayfair or Piccadilly. He made a reservation at the Regent Palace, from the last days of December through to the first few of January.

Peppercorn waited until after Christmas, then emailed Dolores Drumbeater. Among other things he wished her a Happy New Year. How could he have known that her fiancé of fifteen summers had died in his sleep, right after their Christmas vacation? The suddenness of his passing had, she wrote, left her devastated and emotionally depleted. Peppercorn felt obliged to respond as openly as he could to this personal revelation. 'It would be foolish and arrogant to claim that I know how you feel – most of the time I don't even know how I feel,' he wrote. 'But I do know what it's like to lose a partner, my wife having died about eighteen months ago.' Dolores thanked Peppercorn for his caring thoughts and expressed sorrow for his loss. She wondered, given his own experience, if he had any advice that would enable her to carry on. Peppercorn the counsellor? How Mrs Peppercorn would have laughed. But he had to say something. He advised Dolores to retain the form of her life, in the hope that some content would return. She thanked him, but his words hadn't helped. If anything, the days had become rougher. She no longer knew where to turn. Peppercorn urged her to trust her feelings. 'Don't let anyone – or any book – tell you how you should be feeling,' he continued. 'Hit any person (gently, of course) who utters the dread word "closure". Better to live with the dead (not exclusively, of course) than shut the door in their faces (they've always got their foot in it anyway).' Dolores thanked Peppercorn for his support from the bottom of her heart. She begged him to stay in touch, adding that his friendship brought comfort to a 'lost soul'. This was what Peppercorn loved about Americans: their openness. Within minutes of meeting, complete strangers revealed their innermost beings to one another, and declared eternal fealty, even though their paths were unlikely ever to cross again.

Peppercorn did not recognize Hugh O'Brian when he first saw him in the lobby of the Regent Palace. This was probably because he was expecting an aged version of the Hollywood dandy he remembered, but what he got instead was a rather shabby golfer, dressed in a thin windcheater, shapeless pants and worn sneakers. What's more, he was wheeling a small bag, out of which an umbrella with a duck-head handle protruded. A shiny patch on the bag read 'US Marines'. They found two seats in the coffee shop, but conversation was difficult on account of O'Brian being deaf in his right ear (thanks to all the gunshot to which he was exposed during his working life, he said). Could this really be the man who had looked so untouchable on the stage of the Dominion? Would he be able to answer Peppercorn's questions about that night? Would he even be able to hear them?

'Am I right in thinking that you made your entrance on a horse?' Peppercorn said emphatically. 'Absolutely,' said O'Brian. 'That horse was our big gimmick. It stood on its hind legs, and performed all manner of other tricks.' 'And it was a palomino?' said Peppercorn. 'It was a palomino,' said O'Brian. 'You have a good memory, my friend.' 'That may be,' said Peppercorn, 'but try as I might I cannot remember what else happened.' 'I'm not one hundred per cent certain myself,' said O'Brian. 'It was a variety show, and there was certainly a shoot-out, and a square dance. Altogether, including the interval, it lasted close to two hours.' After the show Peppercorn had returned to the suburbs, of that he was certain. O'Brian, meanwhile, had been whisked away by the daughter of the American ambassador, who had married into the aristocracy (the Queen's equerry, or some such). Arriving at her country seat, he was led by a liveried lackey into the dining room, where every guest had at least one butler in attendance. His presence was announced, but ignored. Everyone was much more interested in the ongoing food fight. Eventually the ice was broken, not by a kind word, but by a bread roll hitting O'Brian on the forehead. You can push an American only so far. O'Brian shrugged, and lobbed a roll in the direction of his assailant. The crossfire had escalated until it made the battle of Bunker Hill look like a tea party.

Peppercorn asked how O'Brian had landed the role of Wyatt Earp in the first place. 'Money,' said O'Brian. 'I came at the right price.' But that was only half the answer. 'I think it was also because Stuart N. Lake, who knew Wyatt Earp, wrote the first and only authorized biography of him, and was retained by ABC as a guarantor of authenticity, wanted me for the part. Lake wanted me because we had both been marines. He had lost a leg in the First World War, and I had been, at seventeen, the youngest drill instructor in its history. He liked the way I carried myself. A marine is trained to strike suddenly and unexpectedly. Like a snake. And that's how I played Wyatt. Like a coiled spring. Always easy and casual, right up to the point of action. Then, boom! Lawbreakers on the show soon learned to wear three shirts or coats, because they knew I'd rip the fucking top one right off them.'

It was while he was still a marine that O'Brian had first encountered John Wayne. Every Friday night, by way of entertainment, there'd be a boxing match at boot camp. Each platoon consisted of thirty men. So thirty pieces of paper would be dropped in a hat, only one of which had the word 'boxer' written upon it. The Friday came when O'Brian drew it. His opponent from a rival platoon was a giant. 'The biggest guy I've ever seen,' said O'Brian. 'A huge Afro-American. Over six feet six tall, and weighing well in excess of two hundred pounds. Turned out that he'd been the tackle on a Texas football team. Me? I'm a hundred and fifty-five pounds soaking wet, and as skinny as a rake. But the rule was, you had to box, whatever the size of your opponent. Because when you're fighting for real, you don't get to choose an enemy of a similar build.

'Just as we're about to climb into the ring, the announcer says: "We've got someone special to referee for us tonight. He was shooting a movie in the vicinity, and agreed to help us out, because he loves the marines." So John Wayne steps into the ring ahead of us, takes one look at me, takes another look at the man mountain waiting for me, and shakes his head. "Take your pick," he says, "you can fight by the Queensberry Rules, or by my rules." "Your rules," we say, as if we had a choice. As I slip through the ropes I swear John Wayne gives me a wink. He hits the gong, and that's it for the next twelve minutes. Had we elected to fight by the Queensberry Rules, there would have been a two-minute break between each of the three rounds. Wayne must have figured that the only chance I'd have would be to outrun the son of a bitch, and wear him down. And that's what happened. He chased me around the ring for eleven minutes, trying to knock me into kingdom come. But by the twelfth he was winded, and I took my opportunity well. That must have been in about '43.

'Twelve years later Rhonda Fleming, who played Burt Lancaster's love interest in *Gunfight at the OK Corral*, asks me to accompany her to a black-tie dinner in the Beverly Hills Hotel. When we arrive we're led past table after table – because Rhonda is a big star – until we're right at the front. At John Wayne's table, in fact. John Wayne gives her a big hug. To me he says, "Hey, you're doing a great Wyatt Earp."' So saying, O'Brian punched Peppercorn on the shoulder, as if he were John Wayne and Peppercorn Hugh O'Brian. 'Between courses Rhonda Fleming decides it's time to powder her nose,' he continued, 'and as often happens all the other women at the table simultaneously feel the same need. "I'm not giving you any shit," repeats John Wayne, "you're doing a great Wyatt Earp."' Once again O'Brian thumped Peppercorn's shoulder. '"Thank you, Mr Wayne," I say. "No more Mr Wayne," he says. "Call me Duke." "Okay, Mr Duke," I say. "Do you remember the time you refereed a boxing match between two marines?" "How could I forget?" he says. "It's not every day you get to see a skinny little shit beat the crap out of a fucking eight-foot gorilla. Though, as I recall, he had a little assistance from me and my rules. Why do you ask? Were you there?" "Well, Mr Duke," I reply, "I was that skinny little shit." "You don't say!" cries John Wayne.' At which point Peppercorn took a third blow on the right arm. 'Then Wayne stands up,' continued O'Brien, 'puts one foot on a chair, in a typical pose, and yells, "Listen up, everybody. Wyatt Earp wasn't a marshal. He was a marine!"

'When Duke came to make his last film, *The Shootist*, I volunteered to be a part of it, like most of the cast. He was already stricken with cancer, and he played a gunman dying of the same disease. Not wanting to waste away in bed, Wayne's character engineered a gunfight during which he intended to be killed. I took part in the final shoot-out, and got plugged right between the eyes. Duke was supposed to shoot another of his opponents in the back. But after it was filmed Duke decided that he didn't like the idea. "I've made over two hundred films, without ever shooting anyone in the back. I don't intend to start now." So the scene was redone. That was the Duke.'

In a like manner, Stuart N. Lake was paid by ABC to certify that neither Wyatt Earp nor any of his cohorts acted out of character on its show. 'We always tried to base our dramatis personae on real people,' said O'Brian, 'and Stuart did his best to make sure we didn't put unauthentic words in their mouths. Ned Buntline appeared in a few episodes. Actually, Wyatt eventually ran him out of town, but not before he'd presented Wyatt with a unique order from Colt, the Buntline Special. I doubt whether Wyatt ever fired it. We used it in the show as a gimmick, for long shots in place of a rifle, or for whacking miscreants over the head. As far as I know Wyatt only killed but two men, and one of those had murdered his brother. Nevertheless, he was generally considered to have the quickest draw in the West.

'Determined to become his equal I began to practise in front of a mirror, but never got far, because the holster kept falling apart. I asked the producers for a stronger one, a request they rejected when they discovered that it would cost fifty bucks. So I bought it with my own money. Then it was back to the mirror for a hundred hours or more of hard graft, until I was so proficient that I could be filmed pulling my own gun without any trick editing. It was a small detail, but in my opinion added greatly to the show's appeal. My agent agreed, and figured I should be getting some more money, but the producers weren't very sympathetic to the idea. So I found out from the props man where the studio hired their guns, and how much they were being charged. Then I went to the producers and told them that I knew a place where they could get them cheaper. This idea they liked. They wanted to know the name of the company. I said it was called the National Gun Association, a name I made up on the spot. Once they swallowed the bait I went to my bank, withdrew my savings, and invested in a boxful of guns, which I proceeded to hire out to the studio. That augmented my salary nicely.'

The spirit of Wyatt Earp re-entered O'Brian as he relished the memory of that victory. Firmness replaced slackness in the slant of his jaw. Peppercorn stared as

a child would, quite transfixed by the sudden rejuvenation.
Steely eyes aglitter, O'Brian stared right back. 'By the
look of you,' he said, 'I'd guess you grew up watching
Westerns on TV.' 'It was a golden age, an age of heroes,' said
Peppercorn. 'There was Wyatt Earp, of course, and
Matt Dillon; Hawkeye, Kit Carson and Davy Crockett; the
Lone Ranger, the Range Rider and the Cisco Kid; the
Cartwrights; Rowdy Yates; Roy Rogers, Gene Autry and
Hopalong Cassidy; Seth Adams; Cheyenne Brody and
Bronco Lane; Paladin and Maverick.' All these and more
were Peppercorn's birthright. 'Do you know why there
are so few of em on TV these days?' O'Brian asked. Pepper-
corn considered various political and financial causes, but
ended up just shaking his head. 'Because there are only so
many ways you can crash a horse,' said O'Brian tri-
umphantly.

'The funny thing is that I can't remember seeing
you actually ride one,' said Peppercorn, 'except for that
time on stage, of course.' 'That's because in "adult" Westerns like *The Life and Legend of Wyatt Earp*, a horse was
just a horse,' said O'Brian. 'Mine wasn't anything special.
It didn't have a name like Champion or Trigger or Silver,
it didn't get sung to, and it didn't get kissed.' Women got
much the same treatment in the show, noted Peppercorn,
not least Josephine, whose existence it declined to acknowledge. Yet O'Brian seemed to know all about her. According
to him, she first showed up in Tombstone en route to San
Francisco, having just graduated from Stevenson College
in Missouri. 'I don't know what a Stevenson graduation
gown was like,' said Peppercorn, 'but you should see the
one she wore in Tombstone.' He described its revealing

quality, and explained that a photograph of her modelling it now hung in his bathroom. 'I'd heard that she was a looker,' said O'Brian, rising from his seat, 'and rumours that she'd posed for some risqué shots.' He began to walk away, then turned. 'Don't leave,' he said, 'I've got something for you upstairs.' Peppercorn waited with nothing but the duck-headed umbrella for company, until its owner returned from his room holding aloft a publicity photograph from his glory days as a lawman extraordinaire. In it he was wear-ing his signature black hat, a fancy waistcoat, a tin star, and resting a Winchester rampant on his hip. It was inscribed to Peppercorn with the words, 'You are a "Top Gun" and can ride shotgun anytime.' 'Be sure to hang it alongside Josephine,' said O'Brian, 'with apologies from me for the years of neglect.'

And so it came to pass that Josephine Marcus Earp became the centre of attention. As Peppercorn saw it, he had two entwined tasks: to find out all he could about her, and to establish the authenticity of her portrait. He contacted Leslie Brody – playwright, autobiographer, unrepentant sixties rebel, erstwhile editor of *Boxcar Bertha*, longtime friend of Dr Helman – on the campus in southern California where she taught creative writing. Seeking its location on a map, he realized it was within fifty miles of where his son was waiting tables, and felt the first stirrings of inner locomotion. She mailed him a typescript of her play.

Quiet, Wyatt! contained no reference to Stevenson College, Missouri. Its version of Josephine's higher education was altogether less conventional – in fact, it verged on the scandalous. Aged eighteen she had run away from her bourgeois Jewish home in San Francisco to join Pauline

Markham's portable production of *HMS Pinafore*. The company had taken ship to Santa Barbara, then travelled overland to Tombstone. Crossing the blood-red deserts of Arizona the company's stagecoach was threatened by Apaches. Her saviour was a dashing ladies' man named Johnny Behan, Deputy Sheriff of Yavapai County. Such was his way with words that he

charmed the pants right off her. Ignoring the advice of her parents she set up home with the bold Irishman, only to discover that her parents were right – Behan's blarney was not available on an exclusive basis. As he was cast adrift, another handsome lawman was permitted to dock. Was the transference of sexual favours from Johnny Behan to Wyatt Earp the spark that set Tombstone ablaze? Leslie Brody liked to think so. In any event she considered her play to be pretty close to the truth, since it was based upon Josephine's own memoirs, *I Married Wyatt Earp*. She had, she wrote, spent an entertaining afternoon in Bisbee, Arizona, with the man who had edited them.

Peppercorn ordered his own copy. The first thing he noticed when it arrived was that his photograph of Wyatt's bride – albeit with the peignoir rendered opaque for modesty's sake – was on its cover. It reappeared as the frontispiece, where it was captioned, 'Josephine Sarah Marcus Earp, c. 1880'. Its provenance was not supplied. Nor did its subject make any reference to the photograph's creation or later existence in the text. But everything else Peppercorn read confirmed Leslie Brody's characterization, most especially when Josephine pointed the finger of blame at the men who had led her astray, whose Bohemian rhapsodies had danced her to a diaphanous chemise rather than a wedding gown. 'My upbringing was all directed toward taking my place some day as a proper matron in a middle-class setting,' Josephine wrote. 'I probably would have fulfilled this destiny if it hadn't been for Gilbert and Sullivan.'

Peppercorn understood why the widow of a famous lawman, when composing her memoirs, would want to erase nude photo sessions from the record. But there were other, more curious, omissions. For example, Josephine offered a vivid description of the stage fright she had experienced when performing in *HMS Pinafore* for the first time, but neglected to add what role she had been assigned by Miss Markham. In an Epilogue, the book's editor explained that Josephine had not composed her memoirs in any coherent manner, nor did they exist in a single manuscript. His task had been to bring order to a mishmash of manuscripts, to give shape and breathe life into a heterogeneous body of words. Nor was that the only requirement. He had to ensure that the voice remained consistent throughout.

However, this approach left its practitioner vulnerable to criticism. Researching further, Peppercorn discovered there were those who maintained that the editor of *I Married Wyatt Earp* was more author than editor. Some even accused him of being a fraudster, of making the whole thing up. Glenn G. Boyer, the accused, did not deny that he had, when required, put words into Josephine's mouth, but insisted they were always in character. He called his genre 'creative nonfiction'. Peppercorn liked the sound of that. If the truth were told he had used a similar method when writing his commentary on the Buffalo Roundup for *Terra Incognita*. But Boyer's fiercest critics would have none of it; what he called 'creative nonfiction', they called 'lies'. Boyer was not shy in defending himself. The weapons may have been words, but in every other respect the enmity between Boyer and his critics was the equal of that between the Earps and the Clantons, the warring clans that finally met in mortal combat at the OK Corral. Why? It wasn't as if one camp supported the Earps, and the other the Clantons. In that regard they were both on the same side. So what was the huffing and puffing all about? Peppercorn guessed that it had to do with proprietorship, with the desire to be sole gatekeeper of Wyatt Earp's memory.

As Hugh O'Brian had observed, it was Stuart N. Lake's biography, *Wyatt Earp: Frontier Marshal*, that had been responsible for establishing Earp's reputation in the first place. Lake was no historian, but had been near historic types, having worked in President Teddy Roosevelt's press office. Now Roosevelt had been one of Owen Wister's closest friends, so there was a direct line between Wister's hero, the Virginian, and Lake's. Neither would have looked out of place sitting with King Arthur at the Round Table. In short, they were several degrees removed from reality. Having created the legend of Wyatt Earp, Lake naturally became its chief custodian. As such he was consulted by Hollywood big shots decades before the producers of Hugh O'Brian's TV series approached him. In 1939 *Frontier Marshal* was made into a movie with none other than Randolph Scott playing the peerless Earp. Back then Josephine was still alive, and a bit miffed at Lake's presumption. She sought a lawyer who would help her contest the custody of Wyatt's memory in court, but never found one. As a goodwill gesture Lake arranged for her to be hired as a technical advisor by Twentieth Century-Fox. It was a job Josephine took seriously. But after her death in 1944, Lake was unchallengeable – until Glenn Boyer arrived on the scene.

Inspired by Lake's book, Boyer became an enthusiast, indefatigable researcher, and finally an expert on Tombstone's righter of wrongs (collecting testimony from Earp's surviving relatives, as well as from those who remembered conversations with eyewitnesses). Although Lake's book was presented as if it came straight from the horse's mouth, Boyer's investigations revealed that its author had actually done a lot of neighing on his own account. So Boyer set about separating the wheat from the chaff. His own books presented an unvarnished new portrait of Wyatt Earp. The truth and nothing but the truth. Or so he said. Thus Boyer supplanted Lake, and became the man to consult if you wanted the inside story on Earp.

Now the process was being repeated. Young guns were publishing their own biographies of Earp, and they had the aging alpha male in their sights. How ironic it was, they said, that Boyer had done to Josephine precisely what he claimed Lake had done to Wyatt. Reputable historians, they said, did not play fast and loose with the truth. Peppercorn had to admit a certain sympathy with this argument (though whether Wyatt Earp and the Gunfight at the OK Corral qualified as history was another matter). However, there was something faintly self-righteous, even puritanical, about the rhetoric of Boyer's critics, prompting Peppercorn to regard them as Roundheads. In which case, Boyer had to be a Cavalier. Peppercorn fancied that, when the chips were down, he would be one too.

But this did not stop him being a bit of a Roundhead when it came to the photographic portrait in his bathroom. There were certain facts Peppercorn felt he needed to know, such as the name of the photographer. The movie *Tombstone* offered an answer, in that it showed a feisty Josephine posing in C. S. Fly's studio moments before the Earps and the Clantons started shooting at one another in the yard outside. But this logical supposition was dependent upon two preconditions: that the photograph really was of Josephine, and that the original had been taken in Tombstone no later than 1881. Even then there was a problem: C. S. Fly's stamp was missing from every known copy, of which there was no shortage. One of them, Peppercorn discovered, had been auctioned recently at Sotheby's in New York for close to $3,000. He contacted Kate Smolenski of Sotherby's Photography Department, and learned that the picture had been auctioned not once but twice. Ms Smolenski sent him both catalogues. In the first the photograph was credited to 'Anonymous', and its subject identified as being 'Josephine Marcus Earp, at one time wife of Western lawman Wyatt Earp.' But in the second catalogue the sitter was as anonymous as the photographer. Despite this disavowal bids had risen to just short of $4,000, which said a lot about either the quality of the photograph or the tenacity of the belief that it really was Mrs Earp.

So what had happened between the two sales (separated by a mere eighteen months) to set off alarm bells at

Sotheby's? There had been no sensational revelations, no discoveries or confessions, but there had been a continuous series of articles questioning Boyer's identification. Their authors argued that most available evidence – hairstyle, pose, facial expression, format – suggested a date of 1914 rather than 1880 or 1881 (which accorded with the date of the image's copyright). Against that, there was no documentation, nothing but Boyer's say-so. Perhaps if any of the doubters could have explained the meaning of 'Kaloma', that enigmatic word embossed not only on his but on every mount, Peppercorn might have been more impressed by their unanimous conclusion. For the moment, at any rate, he decided to give Josephine (and Boyer) the benefit of the doubt (though he had to admit the doubt still existed).

One thing was certain. The photographer, whoever he was, knew what he was doing. Had the knack. Was able to make his subject seem equally imperial and available (and, oh boy, did Peppercorn want to avail himself of her charms). She looked back at him, head in the air, with an expression of utter disdain, every inch the Empress Josephine. But her visible breasts told a different story. Made it impossible for any man, be he Emperor or mere Cavalier, to say, 'Not tonight, Josephine.'

Peppercorn's admiration for the craft of the unknown photographer also contained a measure of professional envy. At the start of his own career, years before he hit upon photojournalism, Saltzman had urged him to try his hand at glamour photography, citing a friend who was making an excellent living by snapping naked beauties in exotic locations. Peppercorn had gone so far as to call a few modelling agencies, but in the end chickened out – it had felt too much like pimping. An even greater obstacle was a lack of the easy grace required to persuade non-professionals to strip. If only I'd been more like Willy Ronis, he thought. He'd read a story recently about how the nonagenarian Parisian photographer had casually asked a female interviewer from France Inter to pose for him in the nude, even while her tape recorder was still running. The question was broadcast to the entire French nation, as well as her bold, 'Pourquoi pas?' Peppercorn still recalled the difficulty he'd experienced in convincing Lady Antonia Fraser to remove even her coat for a shoot in his studio. He winced at the memory, and wondered where his cousin was now.

The answer came more quickly than expected. When he spoke to his son later that afternoon, he discovered that Saltzman had paid an unexpected visit to Desert Hot Springs the previous day. His son said it had been a bit embarrassing because he'd shown all his fellow workers the infamous images of Saltzman's calamity, but fortunately none had let on. A few days later Peppercorn received a letter from his cousin giving his side of the visit. It was more expansive – and descriptive – than any of its predecessors. Saltzman even wrote about some of the personalities he'd encountered on his travels, including Virginia Campbell, Gary Cooper's co-star. He told of the promise he'd made to visit her Chelsea home, and wondered if Peppercorn could be persuaded to keep it on his behalf. Pourquoi pas?

Virginia Campbell made it seem that Christmas had come early, that she had been waiting all year for Professor Saltzman's call, and that Peppercorn would be a more than adequate substitute. She even had him half-convinced that she truly remembered meeting his cousin in Oklahoma City.

'He was a single gentleman?' she said. 'Right,' he said. 'And you are single too?' she said. 'Right again,' he said. 'Darling,' she said, 'you must come over to meet us very soon. Are you free on Wednesday? We'll have a little party. I'll invite my daughter of course. You'll hit it off, I'm sure. Haven't we? You sound like such a darling man.'

Wednesday came and Peppercorn drove to Chelsea, wondering if he looked like a darling man too. Virginia Campbell certainly greeted him as if he did. Her daughter was made of sterner stuff, but softened when Peppercorn spoke of his son far away in California. 'Don't you think my daughter is beautiful, Mr Peppercorn?' said Virginia. 'The nurses all thought so in the hospital where she was born. They'd just take one look at her and cry, "Bellissima!" So that's what we called her. And so she remained, until she decided she wasn't worthy of the name, and shortened it to Bel. As for her surname, you have to look to one of her husbands for that. I forget which exactly.' 'The father of your grandchildren,' said her daughter. 'Of course,' said her mother. 'How many husbands were there?' asked Peppercorn. 'Only three,' said Bel, 'though I did marry one of them twice.' 'And what is your surname?' he said. 'Stahr,' she said, spelling it out.

Peppercorn mentioned his single attempt at matrimony and its tragic conclusion. Then he spoke of his disreputable cousin, Professor emeritus Saltzman, whose locum tenens he was. He told her about Saltzman's fall, his vanishing act, and his slow reappearance (not in the flesh, but in the form of letters). His most recent, Peppercorn added, had been full of the characters he'd bumped into and the stories they'd recounted. Virginia Campbell was undoubtedly its star, but there was a strong supporting cast, led by 'Doc' Holladay of

Fort Dodge. One of the colourful tales the faux Doc had told Saltzman concerned a real doctor named Tremaine. Peppercorn couldn't tell if he'd aroused the interest of his new acquaintance or not, but elected to proceed as if he had.

The doctor served at Fort Dodge longer than any other, but his service had come to an abrupt end after a visit to Chicago. It seemed that he had checked into a hotel where another of the fort's serving officers was staying with his wife. Whether Dr Tremaine and Captain Smith socialized is not known. What is known, despite an army cover-up, is that Captain Smith surprised the doctor and Mrs Smith in a compromising situation, and shot the doctor twice. Dr Tremaine, who was not badly wounded, later insisted that he was only acting as Mrs Smith's physician, while Mrs Smith swore that she was merely seeking a second opinion – about what, she did not specify. There were no prizes for guessing why the story had appealed to Saltzman. But it seemed to strike a chord in Bel Stahr too. 'How amazing,' she said, 'the exact same thing happened to Ginny's grandparents. Only in that case the doctor didn't get wounded. He died. And my great-grandfather got off scot-free. They had – maybe still have – a strange sense of justice in Louisiana, which is where my mother's family hails from.' 'Don't rush to judgement,' said Peppercorn. 'Eadweard Muybridge, father of stop-motion photography and of the movies too, some say, murdered his wife's lover and was acquitted by a jury in California.' 'Is there anything inside your head other than facts?' said Bel. 'A lot of desires,' said Peppercorn, 'mostly unspoken.' 'You'd better hurry up and give them voice,' said Bel. 'You're not getting any younger.'

She was right about that. When he was but a fortnight

older Peppercorn asked her out for a meal. 'Is this a date?'
she said. 'Maybe,' he said. 'What shall I wear?' she said.
'Nothing for preference,' he said, 'otherwise something
tight.' He booked a table at Moro in Exmouth Market,
where her son was working as a chef. But the night before,
she cancelled. 'My daughter's sitter has called in sick,' she
said, 'would you mind coming here instead? I'm not a bad
cook.' She lived in Chelsea, not far from her mother. Access
to her house was through a gate in a wall, like something
out of *The Secret Garden*. 'Come straight through to the
kitchen,' she said, via the entryphone. She stood to greet
him when he entered the room. The first thing he noticed
about her was that she was stark naked. 'I didn't have anything tight to wear,' she said. Peppercorn admired her style,
and the grands tétons.

'If you'll excuse me for a minute,' she said, 'I'll just go
and say goodnight to my daughter.' When she returned she
was wrapped in a kimono, which did little to conceal the fact
that she was still naked beneath. He asked if she had heard
of her namesake, Belle Starr, Bandit Queen of Oklahoma.
'No,' she said, 'but no doubt you're going to tell me all about
her. What is it with you and the Wild West?' 'Don't knock
it,' he said, 'it's my Shangri-La, the lost world of my childhood.' After he had recited the story of Belle Starr's short
life and mysterious end, she said, 'Maybe it's my mother you
should be courting, if courting you are. After all, she's the
one who co-starred in a Western with Gary Cooper. My only
claim upon your attention is that I once met John Wayne.'

'That's good enough for me,' said Peppercorn. 'It happened because my grandmother got very sick,' said Bel. 'She
was my father's mother. And he felt duty-bound to see her

before she died. He left my brother with Ginny in Rome, and took me to California with him. We stayed in the Beverly Hills Hotel. One afternoon we went to visit some of his friends in an exclusive neighbourhood. I don't remember who they were, but I do remember that their house was full of Central American artefacts. They also had a daughter the same age as me. We were sent outside to play, but she probably thought that I was a bore. Anyway, she said, "Do you want to go and meet John Wayne?" I didn't know who John Wayne was, but I said yes. So we walked down the street. And there he was standing in his front yard. In person he was just like he was on the screen. A real giant. But graceful, and gracious. "Good afternoon, Mr Wayne," said my new friend. "Well, lookee who's here," he said. I was introduced as a girl from Rome, who only spoke Italian, which wasn't true of course. "Bojourno," he said. "Amo la bella Italia." As I told you, he was graciousness personified.' 'Do you remember what he was wearing?' said Peppercorn. 'He looked like a cowboy,' said Bel, 'but it's possible that costumes he wore in movies I saw afterwards have replaced the original.'

'He also impressed Bob Dylan,' said Peppercorn, 'who isn't easily impressed. In the early days of his fame he was taken to meet Wayne, who was shooting a war movie. "I never would have dreamed," Dylan wrote, "that I'd be standing there on a battleship, somewhere in the Pacific, singing for the great cowboy John Wayne." He said there was no man in the movies who could stand shoulder to shoulder with him.'

'Goddamit, Peppercorn,' said Bel, 'are you ever going to touch my breasts?' When they finally made love Peppercorn found himself uncannily aroused by the fact that he was but one remove from John Wayne. It was a detail he chose not to share with his new intimate. Taking advantage of this intimacy he asked if he could photograph her in the nude. 'Sure,' she said, 'so long as I can paint you in a similar state.' 'No way,' he said. 'When you step aside from a mirror the image disappears. But your painting will be a permanent reminder that I am not Charles Atlas.' 'You vain prick,' she said. 'I'll do it, if only to prove that I'm free from such unbecoming egotism. And all you have to do in return is photograph my new paintings, then email them to my dealer in Atlanta.' In fact Peppercorn did sit, but fully clothed. 'I'll try to explain what I'm after,' said Bel. 'When I was a little girl growing up in that old palace in Rome, I had a dream, and in that dream I saw a beam of light illuminating specks of dust. It lasted but a split second, and I have been trying to catch that light ever since. That moment of illumination, that moment when the thing I am looking at comes to life. So you see, it doesn't make much difference whether it's you or a potato on that chair.' And that, Peppercorn supposed, summed up the distinction between a painting – or a photograph – and a portrait.

By the spring of the following year Peppercorn's son had moved north to Santa Cruz. 'The town where he was born,' said Peppercorn to Bel Stahr, 'in his parents' salad days.' Father and son still spoke daily. A week or so before Pesach, the latter mentioned that an amateur production of *HMS Pinafore* was soon to open at the Wharf Theater in Monterey. 'Would you like me to check it out for you?' the young man said, knowing of his father's interest. 'Let's all go,' said Bel. 'You can see the show, and spend Seder night with your son.' Suddenly the old fire rekindled in Peppercorn's belly. 'Why stop in Monterey?' he said. 'Why not follow Josephine's trail all the way to Tombstone?' He resumed his lapsed friendship with the deputy editor of *Terra Incognita*. She informed him that the magazine had recently run a feature on Santa Fe. 'But,' she added, 'the rest of Arizona and New Mexico are still up for grabs.' So he proposed a photo-essay on the cowboy towns of the Wild West – places that existed simultaneously in the collective movie-memory and on the map – and the more remote redoubts of the Apache, the Navajo, the Hopi and the Zuni. 'Sold,' said his friend.

Peppercorn knew that Glenn Boyer lived somewhere in the territory. Maybe they could even pay him a courtesy call. He found Boyer's email address, and sent out a feeler. 'Why not drop by?' Boyer replied. 'It isn't expensive. You merely take us – as the price of admission – to McMahon's Cigar Bar for steaks, and it doesn't ever run over a hundred dollars a person, including cigars. My wife Jane doesn't smoke, so it's relatively inexpensive. If you bring your mistress, it is obviously more expensive. Seriously, I would like to meet you. What the hell? If you can stand it, I can.' 'Great,' replied Peppercorn, 'I'll be with you in about ten days. As a matter of fact I will be travelling with my mistress. How did you guess?' 'Peppercorn,' replied Boyer, 'anyone who travels without their mistress, or someone's mistress, or a wife that knows how to be a mistress, or anyhow a woman, is a fit subject for a sanity hearing. Get in touch when you are in range.'

Now there were four of them; Peppercorn and the Kid, plus Bel Stahr and her daughter, known to Peppercorn as the Starlet. 'There was once an advertisement that began with the line, "Free with every trip to California. A new you . . .",' said Bel. 'Only in your case I don't think it's California that has made the difference. I think it's being with your son.' 'And what is the new me like?' said Peppercorn. 'Like a man who no longer has toothache,' said Bel.

Cavity-free Peppercorn purchased tickets for *HMS Pinafore*. As he drove his crew down Highway 1 at the appointed hour, he described Josephine's adventurous early years. Nearing Monterey the sun dripped into the Pacific like yolk into mayonnaise. There were grey whales out there, swimming to Alaska with their newborn calves.

On the wharf they could hear seals bark. The interior of the theatre was lined with unvarnished redwood, but the voices they heard were sweeter. The first ones belonged to the sailors, who belted out 'We Sail the Ocean Blue'. They stood in a row sashaying their tushes, as if they were members of the Village People rather than the Queen's Navee. Spookily, several of them really were military men, working in the Arabic Department of the Defense Language Institute. What role had Josephine been given in the 1879 production? Not only were her memoirs silent on the subject, but so was everyone and everything else: there was no sign of her name in any of the surviving ephemera. Some claimed this proved that the whole episode was a fantasy, others pointed out that a runaway would most likely adopt a false identity. Given that she could neither sing nor dance – by her own admission – Boyer thought it probable she had been cast as the lowliest (but loveliest) member of just such a chorus line.

How neat it would have been if she had played the heroine, whose name was also Josephine. She had the looks, but not the lungs. In Monterey it was the other way around. Captain Corcoran's daughter resembled a man in drag, but sang like a nightingale. Her makeup was overemphatic, and her blonde curls looked suspiciously like a wig. A dogcollar of flesh swaddled her neck. But as soon as she opened her mouth her unfortunate appearance was forgotten. Her's was the sweetest voice of all.

'Heavy the sorrow that bows the head,' she sang, 'When love is alive and hope is dead!' Hope was dead because her would-be lover came from the lower decks and the lower orders, and was therefore untouchable. Knowing this, she rejected rather than embraced Ralph Rackstraw when he pressed his suit, reminding him of the class system's eternal verities: 'Refrain, audacious tar, / Remember what you are.' Ill-born Ralph could never be her destined mate. That role was reserved for Sir Joseph Porter, First Lord of the Admiralty. Heartbroken, the poor lad resolved to take his leave of life, and pointed a loaded pistol at his head. 'Be warned, my messmates all / Who love in rank above you – / For Josephine I fall!' At which point the femme fatale reappeared crying, 'Ah! stay your hand – I love you!' Finally, in an extraordinary reversal of fortune, it was revealed that Ralph was actually high born and Captain Corcoran of lowly birth. As a result, their roles on ship were reversed with immediate effect. Since Corcoran was now a mere seaman his daughter was no longer an acceptable match for Sir Joseph, thus leaving her free to marry Ralph, who cared not a fig for convention.

After taking their collective bow, the cast formed a guard of honour for the departing audience. What Peppercorn wanted to know was why Americans, both ancient and modern, were so crazy about Gilbert and Sullivan. 'Maybe it has something to do with the way the pair mock the British way of life,' said the show's director (and its buxom Buttercup). 'They enable us to feel superior for once. Over here young men rise on account of merit, not accident of birth, or so we like to think. Take Vincent van Joolen, our Ralph. Were he English he'd probably be working all day in a blacking factory. But because he's American he's risen so far in his chosen profession – the Navy, believe it or not – that he's in line to command a real battleship, not just HMS *Pinafore*. On top of that the words of the operetta are in English, not Italian or German, the songs are funny and memorable, and the ending's happy.'

'Tell me,' said Bel, as they drove back to Santa Cruz, 'did you pick up Josephine's spoor?' 'In her memoirs she thanked Gilbert and Sullivan for saving her from such a respectable spouse as Sir Joseph Porter,' said Peppercorn. 'So it's possible she saw the courtship between her name-sake and the handsome upstart as a model for her romance with Wyatt. In which case, it was indeed the trailhead.'

Because time was limited (the Starlet had to return to school) they flew to Phoenix, but not before spending Seder night with the Kid's godparents in San Francisco. At the beginning of the service (which, as always, took the form of a meal), the head of the household – in this instance Professor Baumgarten – reminded one and all that he was required by the Torah (not once, but four times) to pass on the story of the Exodus from Egypt. Nor did it suffice to merely repeat the oft-told tale as if it were something that had happened long ago. No, he had to tell it in such a way that caused his listeners to feel as though they too had been there, and themselves gone forth from Egypt. 'Do you know,' said the Kid to Bel, as they chewed on bitter herbs, 'I think my dad had a similar end in view when he schooled me in the legends of the Wild West. He showed me the films of John Ford so many times I began to think of them as home movies.' The meal ended with the traditional exclamation: 'Next year in Jerusalem!' 'At least Phoenix is in the right direction,' said Peppercorn.

'Back in the saddle again . . .' crooned Gene Autry, '. . . riding the range once more . . . toting my old .44 . . . where you sleep out every night . . . and the only law is right . . . back in the saddle again.' Newly landed Peppercorn and Co. gleefully echoed his words. Only they weren't exactly in the saddle, more like in a Pontiac. Nor did they exactly spend their first night under the stars either. No, they checked into the Arizona Biltmore, which rose from the Phoenician desert like some Mayan city state, complete with temple-like structures (whose walls were likewise covered with recurring patterns), ornamental pools and numerous ball courts. Who actually built the complex remained the subject of some controversy: Albert Chase McArthur Jr. was the architect of record, but many believed the guiding hand belonged to his mentor, Frank Lloyd Wright (a renowned admirer of pre-Columbian design). What was beyond dispute was the fact that the former sought the advice of the latter. Visiting the site, Wright was astonished by the desert (which he saw as a 'vast battleground of titanic natural forces'), and remained in situ for the duration.

Peppercorn's party stayed but one night. As with sacrificial victims, nothing was denied them: pan-seared scarlet snapper was proffered, and they were invited to have their own skins anointed with a mixture of cactus-flower syrup, honey, citrus-infused oils, native grains and yogurt. But instead of having his still-beating heart ripped from his body when he checked out, Peppercorn merely had his wallet surgically removed.

Frank Lloyd Wright wasn't the only genius to be ravished by the landscape and native cultures of the Southwest. Throughout the 1920s a trip to Indian territory was de rigueur for a hip artistic type in search of authenticity. Even D. H. Lawrence came. Peppercorn and his wife had long ago sought out the ranch where he lived at San Christobel (near Taos), high in the Carson Forest. The Ponderosa it wasn't, but it did have panoramic views over a swooning plateau garnished with purple sage. A winding path through the woods led to the evocative white sanctuary where the writer's ashes were kept. 'You've got to de-bunk the Indian, as you've got to de-bunk the Cowboy,' his living hand had written. 'When you've de-bunked the Cowboy, there's not much left. But the Indian bunk is not the Indian's invention. It is ours.' Was that true? Another question to answer as Peppercorn and Co. followed the trail of Josephine Marcus Earp to Tombstone and beyond.

First stop was Sedona, midway between Phoenix and the Grand Canyon, whose cyclopean red rocks were supposed to possess untapped spiritual powers. Cathedral Rock, for instance, was said to be just the thing for those requiring the 'calming introspection of a feminine vortex'. Max Ernst attempted to establish a studio in Sedona, but found his talents redundant. The town was too much like a figment of Salvador Dali's imagination. Peppercorn and Co. entered it on Chapel Road, which began with conventional places of

worship but ended with an erstwhile petrol station that had
been converted into the consulting rooms of a psychic
reader. 'No thanks,' said Peppercorn, 'our future already
has a blueprint. It's called a map.'

Next morning they attached themselves to a corona of
sunworshippers awaiting the dawn at Yavapai Point, on the
southern rim of a chasm measureless to man. Peppercorn
attempted to adopt the pose of a jaded paparazzi anticipat-
ing the appearance of Anita Ekberg, but as the jagged
horizon was slowly saturated with cadmium yellow, he auto-
matically raised his camera to his eye and watched through
the viewfinder as the first rays of the sun vivified the Grand
Canyon's infinite cavities.

They were observed in turn by the earlybirds: Roman-
nosed ravens (who came and went talking of Edgar Allan
Poe), and a singular western bluebird that sagely nodded its
gorgeous head before helping itself to the breakfast special.
In historic Cameron (one gas station, one general store and
a trading post that also provided accommodation and food)
the plat du jour was frybread, best described as a doughnut
the size of a dinner plate. The only other habitations in the
vicinity were trailers, which had fine desert views but neither electricity nor running water.

The villages of the Hopi had a longer tenure; indeed, one of
them was said to be the oldest continuously inhabited settlement on the North American continent. As soon as Peppercorn
and Co. entered old Oraibi they knew it was the truth. Balanced upon a dusty escarpment on the edge of nowhere the
village looked like it had been transplanted from Tibet; its
houses were dilapidated, its streets and plazas deserted, in fact
the place was practically a ruin. It explained why the Hopi,

alone among the first nations, had been left undisturbed.

At last they came upon a man who seemed to be Oraibi's sole inhabitant. He was sanding an unpainted Kachina doll, and invited them back to his house to see more. The pieces were laid out on a table in the corner of his one-room home (walls of stone, roof of chipboard). Those he had not made himself had been made by members of his immediate family. They had all been painted with dyes extracted from rock. The dominant colours were red, yellow and blue. All were for sale, though the seller was insistent that they were religious artefacts that just happened to be works of art. His house was without electricity or water. The man's wife explained that latrines were located at the edge of the mesa. They were holes in the ground. When one hole became full, it was covered, and another hole dug.

Walpi was in better shape. As Peppercorn's party strolled to the edge of the mesa, where it ended in a three-hundred-foot sheer drop, they were accosted by a man who wanted to know where they were from. He was short but muscular, his biceps bulging from the sleeves of his white T-shirt. His brown face was framed by long, greying hair tied in a ponytail. He knew Europe, he said, having served time with the army in Germany. 'Sprechen sie Deutsch?' he asked. 'She does,' said Peppercorn, nodding towards Bel Stahr. They were separated by her daughter and his son. 'See,' noted Ponytail, 'we have formed the shape of a bow with linguists at either end.'

Beside Bel there was something that could have been mistaken for a parched bush. Closer inspection revealed that its dead leaves were really feathers. 'What's that?' she asked, pointing at the object of enquiry and thereby committing a major faux pas. 'Never point,' snapped Ponytail. 'If you point there is no point. Better to ask in silence with this . . .' He hit the left side of his chest with his fist. 'Those feathers are our prayers. When the white man first came here he tried to make the turkey a sacred bird, serving him up at Christmas and at Thanksgiving, but he was telling us nothing we did not already know. For us the turkey has always been a sacred bird. That is why we use his feathers to address the gods. The eagle too, which the white man took to make the symbol of the country that he stole from us.' A russet whelp seemed unimpressed by this explanation. It stretched out its neck and gobbled up all the prayers it could reach.

'Do you speak English at home,' said Peppercorn, 'or your own language?' 'I am a resident of the universe,' said Ponytail, 'so it makes no difference whether I speak English, German, or Shoshonean.' As he continued he opened his hand to reveal a silver key, which he began to revolve hypnotically between his thumb and forefinger. 'What you need are words that will open the door to the inner world. And when you have found them you will have access to this . . .' So saying he snatched the key, made a fist, and once again struck his heart.

Ponytail's nephew appeared, a friendly, open boy, who was obviously not as sharp as he should have been. He informed the strangers that he was a member of the Road Runner Clan (like his uncle), and a dancer; as a matter of fact, he would be performing on the morrow. He begged them to attend. Alas, they were forced to decline. But many summers before, at Shungopovi on Second Mesa, Peppercorn had seen the Hopi bid farewell to the Kachinas, supernatural beings who spent six months among their acolytes, and the rest of the year in the San Francisco Mountains (distant, but still visible on the western horizon). Then the plaza was full. A dozen Kachina lookalikes were standing in its centre, having already formed a diagonal line. They wore square masks over their faces, feathered headdresses, capes hanging from their shoulders, and brightly coloured kilts. On the topmost roofs of the corner houses golden eagles were chained. They spread their wings to rise on the wind, only to be jerked back by their leg irons. On that wild afternoon, when lightning flickered along the horizon and sweat oozed from the stratosphere, it was not so very hard to suspend disbelief.

Unlike the Hopi, who possessed nothing the Europeans wanted, their neighbours were invaded and did fight back. Famously belligerent, the Navajo held their own until the arrival of Kit Carson (first of the famous Indian-fighters, after whom the forest where D. H. Lawrence sat out eternity was named). Not long ago Peppercorn had been surprised to discover five newly published books, each telling the same story about Carson. It seemed that in 1849 he had been persuaded by the army to track down a renegade band of Jicarilla Apaches who had murdered an emigrant and kidnapped his bride. Carson succeeded in finding them, but was too late to save poor Mrs White, who was discovered with an arrow piercing her left breast (which was still warm to the touch). Among her possessions was a well-thumbed copy of *Kit Carson: The Prince of the Gold Hunters*.

Carson was unfamiliar with its contents, and would have remained so (being illiterate) had one of his companions not read the dime novel to him. What he heard occasioned him great upset. The cause was not the fact that his fictional alter ego was better looking, taller (the real Carson was a bantam at 5 ft 4 in.), and more articulate, but that he had triumphed where the real Carson had failed, and had rescued a comely damsel from her savage captors. Ever after, or so he avowed in his (dictated) autobiography, he felt shame for the false comfort this particular scrape must have offered its most eager reader, who so shortly afterwards became a rudely disillusioned corpse.

How to account for a diverse quintet of writers happening simultaneously upon the same event? Coincidence, or zeitgeist? Peppercorn decided it had to be the latter, because the episode illuminated the precise moment when reality met myth, when the west met the Western. But there was a further twist: who could say that the figure looking aghast at his false representation was any more real? Wasn't the Kit Carson who found the bloodied copy of *The Prince of the Gold Hunters* also a figure out of a book? Didn't that mean every fact was really a fiction? Peppercorn knew what Saltzman would have replied: Welcome to the club. But before he could formulate his own response the zeitgeist changed again. More recently still he had found a sixth book that repeated the same story. This time it was a cautionary tale, meant to demonstrate the limits of American power. From such a point of view Carson's war against the Navajo was a metaphor for the invasion of Iraq. Though this probably didn't make the Navajo feel any better about their defeat.

Navajoland, which included Monument Valley and had Canyon de Chelly as its sacred heart, was considered impregnable. Kit Carson lost but one man in taking it, because his strategy was not bloody engagement but starvation. To emphasize the finality of its defenders' expulsion he ordered the felling of all their orchards, most especially the ancient peach trees, an act of spiteful vandalism for which the Navajo have yet to forgive him.

The defeated Navajo were exiled from their ancestral lands, but were granted the right of return in 1868. Nearly forty years later, seven Navajo horsemen and their dogs rode through the canyon. Their passage was recorded by Edward Curtis, in a photograph that showed tiny figures lost in a majestic landscape. So potent was the image that the actual canyon seemed incomplete to Peppercorn without that long-gone caravan. A second photograph showed a line of Navajo braves riding away from the camera towards a range of dark mountains. Curtis called it 'The Vanishing Race'. He was too pessimistic. In the intervening years the Navajo had multi-plied, rather than vanished, and their sacred canyon had once again become a vision of pastoral beauty, with fields of corn and groves of peaches all growing out of the red soil in the lee of its roseate walls.

As the Canyon de Chelly was to the Navajo, so was Monument Valley to Peppercorn. Okay, he had no physical purchase upon it, no freehold or leasehold, nor any moral or ancestral claim. No ancient Peppercorn had ever lived there, nor any modern one (save himself) even set foot in it. Yet he was bound to it more even than to Jerusalem (to which he was at least linked by the story of his people). He was bound to it by the innumerable Westerns he had watched in his younger days, many of which had become embedded in his memory. Of these, none were so great as the movies John Ford had directed there. The fact that the events they depicted had not happened was irrelevant to Peppercorn. The power of their telling made him feel that they had. Without those stories Monument Valley would still have ravished his eye – but it would have been sterile, a terrestrial Mars.

Just how John Ford had first discovered the valley's existence was not entirely certain. In the 1930s it was far removed from civilization, served by neither railroad nor road. The usual story was that Harry Goulding, proprietor of a trading post and lodge in the neighbourhood, had gone to Hollywood to drum up new business for himself and his landlords. In this version John Ford was supposed to have taken one look at his photographs, chartered a plane, and flown there the next day to confirm the area as a location for *Stagecoach*. Written out of this scenario was John Wetherill, another lodge-owner, who may well have played a greater role than Goulding. What the hell, thought Peppercorn; either way, Ford arrived. There he found the perfect locus for a series of epic battles: between truth and legend, between civilization (plus its laws) and the wilderness (with

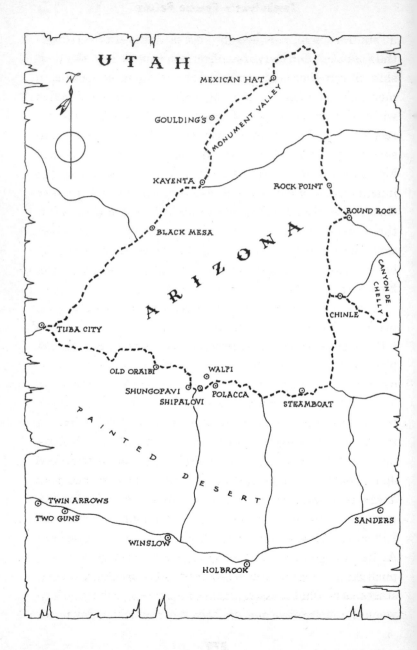

all its freedoms), between the representatives of the one –
the Paleface – and the personification of the other – the Red-
skin. Surely there could be no more fitting place for such a
monumental dialectic than this devil's punchbowl filled
with gigantic monoliths of magenta and cinnabar, itself a
result of the eternal conflict between earth and water, con-
solidation and upheaval. The Navajo continued to rule over
Monument Valley, of course, but Ford took possession of it
imaginatively, and it was in Ford's world of light and shadow
that Peppercorn had settled. So when he came upon it for
the second time in his life it felt like coming home. Darkness
was approaching, and Goulding's Lodge remained open for
business after all these years. If it was good enough for John
Ford it was good enough for Peppercorn.

Next morning Peppercorn steered the Pontiac down the
precipitous dirt road to the valley floor. It was like entering
a three-dimensional representation of his memory, the one
place on earth where he remained forever young, where he
could witness the several ages of Peppercorn already lived.
There he was with his father, as clear as day, watching a
black-and-white stagecoach bounce across the valley floor, at
its reins Andy Devine, on its roof the young John Wayne,
picking off the wild Apaches. And in his memory it remained
John Wayne, even though he had long since learned that
Yakima Canutt or some other stuntman had doubled for him
in all the Monument Valley scenes. As if reading his mind the
Kid stuck his head out of the window and cried, 'Apaches!'
At once Peppercorn unleashed the Pontiac's horsepower,
pushing it along the same dirt road taken by the immortal
stagecoach. Phhht, phhht went the arrows. Pshaw, pshaw
went the answering bullets from the Kid. 'Slow down, for

God's sake,' said Bel. But there was no stopping Peppercorn, as he and his son re-enacted the coach's perilous journey.

However, departure from Monument Valley was delayed because Peppercorn had still not figured out a way of photographing it. In Andre de Toth's *Indian Fighter*, Kirk Douglas – who fought both against and for the Indian – befriended a meek protégé of Matthew Brady. To be more accurate, he took to the man, but not to his newfangled art. When the latter positioned his tripod high above a gorgeous river, the Westerner advised the Easterner against releasing the shutter. 'Why ever not?' exclaimed the photographer (as Peppercorn recalled). 'I want people in the East to see the beauty of the West. Unable to resist its charms they will cross the continent, bringing the benefits of civilization with them.' 'That's exactly why I don't want you to take the picture,' said Douglas. 'To me the West is like a woman, my woman, and I don't intend to share her with anyone.' How right he was, thought Peppercorn. Nowadays, Ford's fine and private place displays her charms for the dubious purpose of selling automobiles and God knows what else. Could Peppercorn make the land seem virginal again?

As he considered possibilities he recalled the extraordinary solution arrived at by a French photographer named Frederic Brenner. His picture was a beauty, but it was also a box of tricks. Panoramic in size, it was essentially a dyptich. On the left was a small band of Jews, got up to look as if they had just crossed the Sinai. Their leader, their rabbi, was cradling their portable homeland, the Sefer Torah. They stood in a V-formation, with four figures on either side, the apex being guarded by a ninth Jew on horseback. Behind them, rising vertically from the valley floor, were the great buttes. The Jews were poised at the rim of a two-lane blacktop. Opposite them, though only visible as reflections in the wing mirror of an SUV, was a matching group of Navajo. The two peoples had been attending a meeting – say, rather, a spiritual conclave – in Canyon de Chelly, where notes on exile and return were compared. That there were similarities between the experience of the two nations was beyond dispute. But Peppercorn felt a little uneasy about the way Brenner had placed the Jews centre stage, and represented the Navajo as ghosts in the wings. This was Navajoland, after all. But whatever his reservations he had to admit that the photograph bore Brenner's stamp.

Peppercorn had still reached no conclusion about how to stamp his own signature upon the landscape when the weather decided the matter. Dark clouds encircled the buttes with alarming rapidity, discharging both fire and water. Peppercorn's companions retreated to the car and insisted that he join them. 'The Kid is half a man,' said Bel, 'but still too young to be an orphan.' Peppercorn was about to abandon his position when the sun suddenly shook off the clouds and torched the mesas. Between the burning silhouettes of East Mitten and Merrick Butte a rainbow grew. Peppercorn couldn't capture the lightning, but he caught the rainbow.

Before the Navajo and the Hopi there had been the Anasazi, the Sinagua and the Hohokam (meaning 'those who have disappeared'). They may have all gone, but the Southwest was full of evidence that they had once existed: spectacular ruins such as Montezuma's Castle, Casa Grande and Mesa Verde. To reach Mesa Verde from Monument Valley, Peppercorn and Co. were required to scoot across the high Colorado plateau. Entering the Ute tribal lands they noted a huge, rust-coloured cloud ahead of them – except that it couldn't be a cloud, as it arose from the earth. Nor was it smoke or fog. To tell the truth, it looked like some plague from one of Cecil B. DeMille's biblical extravaganzas. Eventually it engulfed them, and they were transported to a world drained of colour. It was almost as if they had gone back in time, had become an element in a sepia photograph. If so, it was an image in the process of disintegration; millions of microscopic dots were on the move, hurling themselves against the windshield. None of the travellers had ever seen one before, but they recognized it as a dust storm. Only in Cortez did it blow itself out. By the time they completed the ascent to Mesa Verde the sky was immaculate.

Unfortunately, the Anasazi took no account of Peppercorn's fear of heights when constructing their sandstone villages in vertical clefts, beneath overhanging cliffs with vertiginous gradients. Nevertheless, he managed to enter a few, the largest of these being the so-called Cliff Palace. In its heyday (circa 1300) it had accommodated more than two hundred souls within a multitude of buildings (some square, some round), made from sandstone blocks the size and colour of a crusty loaf. Caught in the last light of day, the structures glowed like honey on toast.

No one could say for sure just why the Anasazi abandoned Mesa Verde or where they went afterwards, but Peppercorn and Co. followed one conjectured route down to the pueblos of New Mexico. In the Visitors Center at Zuni a devout Christian woman addressed the seated custodian: 'May I share something with you? You said before that you and your people believe in the Great Creator. Well, I do too. We are the same really. We both believe in the Great Creator. I'd like to leave you a booklet about my religion. I'd be very happy if you would read it.' Its title was *Eternal Life*. As if Christianity weren't already a prominent presence on the pueblo. But from that woman's point of view, it was the wrong sort of Christianity.

Inside Our Lady of Guadalupe, Peppercorn and Co. were greeted by a tall man with longish black hair, turquoise earrings, a pair of thick spectacles and paint-spattered overalls. 'Ken Seowtewa,' he said, extending his hand. 'I am a Catholic,' he added. 'Once I was an altar boy, now I am creating the altarpiece.' He pointed to a huge canvas, something like ten feet by seven, upon which Christ was depicted as a Zuni rain god. Flanking it were two buffalo heads, the relics of St Homer and St Omer, both barbecued in 1972 to celebrate the church's rededication. Ken revealed something of its history, which went back to 1629, and almost came to an end in 1820, when Mexico recalled its priests. 'Father Niles Kraft initiated the restoration in 1966,' he said, 'and invited Alex Seowtewa, my father, to donate his skills to the cause. Alex had been schooled in the traditions of the Zuni by his maternal grandfather, so he had a sense of what had been on the walls when the church was new – not Christian devils, but Zuni ogres, whose job was the same: to discipline those who strayed. Alex offered to restore them in all their fearsome glory. Father Kraft liked the idea, but thought the images should be more positive. My father considered this suggestion for a long time, then in February 1970 began work on representing the festival of Sha La Ko, which is the Zuni equivalent of Christmas. And that was just the beginning. Seven years later I joined my father in the project. Until then I had been something of a rebel, and came close to breaking his heart. But when I began to work alongside him my eyes were opened, as was my heart. My father has been called the Michelangelo of the Southwest, and I am proud to be known as his assistant. Every day we meet here early in the morning to sort out our schedule, and discuss any new ideas. Then we set to work. Together we have covered the walls with scenes of Zuni life. Now my own son, Joshua, is helping us complete the task.' The boy waved from the scaffolding, high above their heads.

'Your English actor Ben Kingsley came here and made a film about the murals,' Ken continued. 'And many other famous people have travelled here just to see them, including Jacqueline Onassis and Marlon Brando. Recently I showed them to the UN ambassador from Luxembourg. I have also written about the work for a magazine published by the Smithsonian. A local man pirated it and is selling copies, which his customers bring here and ask me to sign. I complained to him, and he chased me off like a little boy. He is also a lawyer and not a Zuni. Now he has put my article on the Web, and claims that donations sent to him will go towards the mural. But we have not seen a penny. He obviously shares the belief that Indians were put upon this earth only to be cheated. Look around you. Do our achievements not merit more respect?'

The back and two side walls had been divided horizontally. The lower sections accommodated framed portraits of saints and other iconic figures, done in the neocolonial style. They had a dismal appearance, as though they had been varnished with tobacco juice. Above them, however, were life-size lines of dancing Kachinas, painted in rainbow hues of red, yellow and blue. 'When all else is complete,' said Ken, 'the area above the altar will be painted with a summer sunset, with orange clouds, through which Jesus will appear. Rays of light will pour from him, and fall upon our village as a blessing.' 'Amen,' said Peppercorn.

Founded like Oraibi in the year dot, Acoma was already old when the Spaniards arrived. The first to reach its impregnable summit complained breathlessly that the climb had almost killed him. Acoma was not known as Sky City for nothing. Peppercorn, Bel and their offspring made their ascent in the company of a local guide. Once there she led them along streets with views of eternity at either end. Women emerged from the mud pueblos to sell their distinctive pots decorated with black and white geometric designs, or teasingly hot tamales. There were kivas where the old religion was practised, and another seventeenth-century mission where Catholicism was preached. Like Ken Seowtewa, their guide saw no conflict in following both creeds, in praying to a portrait of St Joseph as if he were the god of rain. Whatever the weather, nothing grew on the bald rock, so everything had to be carried up from the valley some four hundred feet below (itself no Garden of Eden), including wood for warmth. Consequently, the air was full of the sweet scent of smouldering cedar. Next morning it would be full of snowflakes.

'If you ever plan to motor west . . .' sang Nat King Cole, '. . . travel my way, take the highway that's the best . . . get your kicks on Route 66 . . . you'll see Amarillo, Gallup, New Mexico . . .' It was in Gallup that the overworked Pontiac pulled up in the forecourt of the El Rancho, surely the platonic ideal of all motels: neon without, signed photos of movie stars within (having been founded by D. W. Griffith's less famous brother, the Hollywood connection was its birthright). Their bedheads were wagon wheels.

It was just as well the place was such a hoot, because it looked as though Peppercorn et al. would be trapped there indefinitely. A truck had jackknifed in the unexpected blizzard and blocked the interstate. The breakfast room filled with travellers waiting for the road to reopen.

Peppercorn half expected to see Saltzman among them, but didn't. He listened to the conversations the newcomers struck up with the locals, and before long was privy to the medical history of most of Gallup's citizenry. The restaurant was convivial, the coffee pot dark and deep, but they had promises to keep, and miles to go before they slept, so they loaded up the Pontiac and (bypassing the obstruction) lit out for warmer climes.

Peppercorn had added old Mesilla to the itinerary at the last minute, on account of something Philip French, the film critic, had written in one of his reviews. Praising an exuberant movie set in an Italian restaurant, French had concluded by comparing the experience to a meal he'd enjoyed at Lorenzo's in Mesilla, New Mexico. This was sufficient recommendation for Peppercorn. 'You're crazy,' said Bel, as they hurtled down Highway 25 (pausing only to gas up at Truth or Consequences). 'Look, the man knows his films, and he loves Westerns,' said Peppercorn. 'Why should I doubt his judgement when it comes to restaurants?'

After a boisterous night in Mesilla – first station on Billy the Kid's Via Dolorosa, but that is another story – they drove west to Lordsburg. Peppercorn was aware (thanks to a post-card from his cousin) that John Ford had shot the final scenes of *Stagecoach* not there, but on a ranch in greater Los Angeles. He stopped anyway, feeling it his duty to pay proper homage. The real Lordsburg turned out to be little more than a ghost town, its motels boarded up, its liquor store (a plaster-cast wigwam) all but deserted. Nothing like the rowdy place where the Ringo Kid finally caught up with the killers of his brother. (There were three of them, and only

one of him, but righteousness prevailed on that dusty street.) Peppercorn père et fils prepared to re-enact a reduced version of the shootout. As he ceded the role of the Ringo Kid to his son, it crossed Peppercorn's mind that they were also participating in an older, Oedipal drama. At the very least the process of eclipse was commencing, whereby the son would eventually outshine his father. To Peppercorn's surprise he didn't mind one bit. If he could no longer play the Ringo Kid, there was always Rooster Cogburn.

In the old days the road west of Lordsburg would have been a place of maximum danger, for it encroached upon the territory of the Chiricahua Apaches, whose most famous warrior was the dread Geronimo. However, Geronimo was never their chief. The hereditary leader to whom he bowed was Naiche, son of Cochise (who bowed to no one). Cochise had initially tolerated the Americans. However, in 1861 the Chiricahua were accused of abducting a white boy. Cochise and several of his relatives approached an army post to protest their innocence, but were immediately seized as hostages. Cochise escaped, but the others were hanged. Thereafter Cochise chose resistance. For the remainder of the 1860s no soldier or settler was safe from his attentions. During a sixteen-month period, his men attacked twenty-two stagecoaches and slaughtered all their drivers.

Nowadays, travelling Interstate 10 was a much safer proposition. It was even possible to visit the great chief's stronghold in the Dragoon Mountains without a cavalry escort. The detour took them past the portals of ranches, past bone-dry river beds (where an unlucky motorist could drown in a summer storm), past the Cochise Country Store (whose rusty facade featured a miner and his over-loaded

mule en route to riches), and its neighbour, the white clap-
board Cochise Hotel (both empty and locked, alas).

Eventually they entered a wooded valley stacked with
stands of madroño, oak, juniper and manzanita, one among
many canyons, all protected by soaring ramparts of granite.
This was where Cochise went to ground. In life his enemies
could never hold him, in death too he had evaded them.
Somewhere in this untamed wilderness his body was buried,
forever the hidden genius loci.

Cochise died in 1874, but Geronimo was still on the war-
path when Josephine travelled to Tombstone. Who knows,
thought Peppercorn, perhaps he was the one who scared the
living daylights out of the future Mrs Earp, and (if only temporarily) drove her into the arms of the wrong man? Though
it was also possible that Josephine had dreamed up the whole
episode in order to disguise sexual attraction and capitulation
as gratitude. Either way, Geronimo went on to frighten many
more pilgrims before surrendering to General Crook in 1886.
Seeing photographs of that historic event displayed upon the

wall of C. S. Fly's reconstructed studio in Tombstone reminded Peppercorn that he had once assisted his cousin in writing a lecture about them. As far as Peppercorn could recall, Fly had somehow obtained permission from the General to follow the troops and record the event, both for posterity and – Fly hoped – prosperity. Fly by name, fly by nature. But he had some talent too, Peppercorn noted, and an eye for composition. Several photographs showed the same scene from different angles for no other reason than artistry. Although Geronimo was always outnumbered by soldiers, there was never any doubt as to who was the centre of attention, whose presence was the most powerful. Thus did Fly make his fall the more poignant. There were other images taken in plein air – such as that of a man strung up from a telegraph pole in Tombstone – but most were obtained in the studio and printed as cartes de visite. Peppercorn's portrait of Josephine Marcus was not among them, nor did it bear any resemblance to Fly's other work, which betrayed no interest in either erotica or darkroom trickery.

Outside Fly's studio were two rows of mannequins facing one another. All the figures were men, all were dressed in the style of the 1880s, and the majority were armed. They represented the nine combatants who had participated in the infamous gunfight upon which Tombstone now depended for its livelihood. On the one side were the three Earp brothers – Wyatt, Morgan and Virgil – plus Doc Holliday; and on the other Ike and Billy Clanton, Tom and Frank McLaury and Billy Claiborne. They were positioned not in the OK Corral itself, but in the vacant lot where the gunfight actually occurred. In her memoirs Josephine called it 'the gunfight west of Fly's house'.

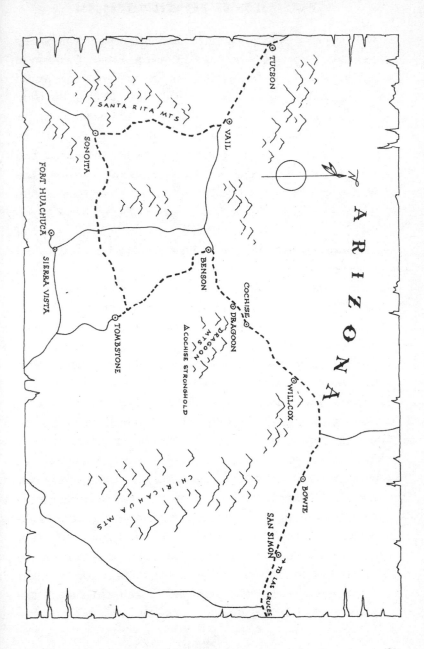

Although her mother had acted in a Western with one of the Hollywood greats, Bel Stahr knew next to nothing about the genre or the events they immortalized. She had not even seen *My Darling Clementine*. 'So,' she said, 'what happened here?' 'God knows,' said Peppercorn. 'According to the movies it was a simple matter of good versus bad, Wyatt Earp the lawman, being the goodie-in-chief, and Ike Clanton the cowboy, a pejorative term in those pre-Virginian days, the very epitome of evil. But chroniclers are more various. Some have even swung to the opposite extreme, seeing the Earps as cold-blooded killers, card sharps and whoremasters. Others have seen it in political terms: rural, anarchistic Democrats against urban, orderly (though not necessarily honest) Republicans. Still others point the finger at Johnny Behan, claiming that he engineered the whole tragedy just to get even with the man who stole his girl. Tombstone's Trojan War, they call it. But the consensus seems to be that Wyatt Earp was an honourable man, though never a sea-green incorruptible, doing what had to be done. A mensch.'

Conveniently placed around the corner was G. F. Spangenberg's Pioneer Gun Shop, which made the proud claim that 'we catered the Gunfight at the OK Corral'. Peppercorn knew it was wrong, but he went in. God forgive him, the Kid followed his example. 'Howdy,' said the proprietor. An old-timer was buying ammo for his equally decrepit Winchester. He looked longingly at a new pump-action on the rack. 'A year ago you would'a sold me that beauty for certain sure,' he said. 'But these shoulders have gotten too old to take the recoil.' 'No need to worry bout that,' said the proprietor, 'it's powered by gas.' The old-timer shook his head sadly. 'Not in this lifetime,' he said. 'I'm losin my touch, and my grip on things. Look at this scar. I was trying to open somethin, but opened up my hand instead. Nearly cut it right off.' He left with his shells. 'What can I get you gentlemen?' said the proprietor. Were it possible Peppercorn would have bought a revolver, if only to impress the Kid and make his cousin green with envy.

As Peppercorn led his party along Allen Street, it seemed to him that he and the Kid were the only males in town not armed with Colt .45s at their hips, and not dressed in the style of either Wyatt Earp or Doc Holliday. He also noted that every other shop on Allen was a photographer's studio offering the same service: portraits in the style of C. S. Fly. Passers-by were invited to step inside and dress up as an Earp, a Clanton or a working girl from the Bird Cage Theater (the next stop of Peppercorn's itinerary). Why not us, he thought? Failing to persuade his companions to support the profession to which he belonged, he pushed them into the premises of Jeff Lawrence, chosen at random. The photographer's assistant, a woman from Bath, of all places (near where the Peppercorns had once lived), escorted them to the back of the store where there were rows of sand-coloured dusters, waistcoats, black gabardines and the varied plumage of soiled doves. There were hillocks of holsters, a platoon of boots, boxes of Stetsons, and sufficient pistols and rifles to start a revolution.

Peppercorn and the Kid tried on black hats and long gabardines, but rejected them instantly, thinking they looked more like orthodox Jewboys than reckless cowboys. In the end they went for simplicity: just the hats and the weapons. Likewise, Bel Stahr and the Starlet declined the opportunity to dress up as whores, preferring the rougher

garb of cowgirls. The photographer arranged them as a group (with the Kid cradling a shotgun centre stage), then got behind his camera. It stood on a tripod and had a bellows, but there the resemblance to C. S. Fly's model ended. No glass plates, darkrooms or corrosive chemicals for Mr Lawrence; his camera was connected to a computer, which printed the end product moments after he had clicked the shutter. Looking at it in the street, Bel Stahr said, 'What if some future researcher finds this in a junk shop and decides that I'm not Bel Stahr, but Belle Starr and you lot are . . .' Peppercorn filled in the blanks. 'Her husband (any one of four), her son Eddie, whom many suspected of being his mother's unknown assassin, and daughter Pearl, who ran a successful brothel in Fort Smith, Arkansas.' 'Exactly,' said Bel. 'What if people mistake us for that unsavoury bunch?' 'Then we'll have a good laugh at their folly,' said Peppercorn, 'wherever we are.'

Nearer the Bird Cage, Peppercorn purchased a copy of *True West* magazine from a news-stand, because his portrait of Josephine was on its cover. Above the photograph was the question: 'Is this Mrs Wyatt Earp?' On the whole, the magazine thought not. The same photograph was also featured on the front page of a 'special historical issue' of *The Tombstone Epitaph* (founded 1880). It was used (with the permission of G. G. Boyer, Peppercorn noted) to illustrate an article called 'Tombstone's Pioneering Prostitutes', but did not go so far as to claim that Josephine Marcus had ever been – God forbid – a fallen angel or a soiled dove. The photograph appeared yet again in the basement of the Bird Cage, with a less than polite caption.

Opened in 1881, with a frontage not unlike that of the

Theatre Royal in London's Haymarket, it remained so round the clock for eight years, until a flood shut down the mine that was Tombstone's raison d'être. The old pleasure palace stayed sealed for nearly half a century after that, until it was reopened in the 1930s as one of the West's historic landmarks. 'That accounts for the stink of decay,' said Bel. If ever a place smelled haunted, it was the Bird Cage. No wonder half of its visitors claimed to have experienced paranormal activity, or seen actual ghosts.

Fourteen life-size cages were suspended from the ceiling of the dance hall. They were empty now, of course, but had once contained prostitutes. At the far end of the hall was a stage, with a mildewed pelmet and drapes. On either side were boxes, inhabited only by plaster casts of long-dead sybarites. Downstairs there were cribs for other whores. One in particular attracted Peppercorn's attention, because of the notice attached to it: 'This bordello room was used by Sarah Josephine Marcus in 1881. She worked under the name of Sadie Jo and Shady Sadie. Note the license of ill fame. It was in this room where many romantic encounters with her future husband Wyatt Earp were carried on. Note: Wyatt signed her license. At the time she was engaged to Sheriff Johnny Behan who frowned on her work as a prostitute.' ('Frowned on', thought Peppercorn, where did they get that phrase?) His photograph was also displayed with this unequivocal assertion: 'Josephine as taken by Camillus S. Fly in 1881 when she worked in the Bird Cage Theater. It was a gift to Johnny Behan her live-in lover until she met Wyatt Earp. The photo was concealed until after his death in 1912.' 'Is it true?' said Bel. 'It's true like the caption describing the homunculus upstairs as one of only two mermen in the United States is true,' said Peppercorn.

It was time to seek out the man most likely to know the truth: Glenn G. Boyer, the colossus of Tucson. So Peppercorn drove across cattle country to his door, and thereby fulfilled Dr Helman's prescription. Boyer issued a belly laugh when they told him they'd come from Tombstone. 'Do you still have your wallets?' he said. 'Probably not. The only place there that deals an honest hand is Spangenberg's.' 'Mine was long gone,' said Peppercorn. 'Went that first day in Phoenix.' 'We'd be happy to put you up overnight in our guest house,' said Boyer. 'We only recently moved in, so you'd have to share it with some packing cases. Beyond that inconvenience, the room rate is superior, and my wife is a memorable cook.' 'It's a kind offer,' said Peppercorn, 'but we've got to be back in Phoenix tonight for a dawn flight to San Francisco.' 'At least stay to have a beer or two,' said Boyer.

They entered the house. 'This is Jane Candia Coleman, the writer,' Boyer said, introducing his wife, 'yet to win the Pulitzer, due to the judges' preference for mediocrities, but nominated several times already.' Their former residence, a ranch – just across the border in Rodeo, New Mexico – had been placed on the market. It consisted of two large houses, eighty acres of land, a stall barn, a swimming pool and about a hundred large trees. Its asking price was on a par with the value of Peppercorn's Victorian terrace (with its tiny garden) in St Albans. 'It would make one hell of a fine horse property,' said Boyer, 'and has the potential to be a fair-size dude operation.' If only I weren't frightened of the creatures, thought Peppercorn, picturing himself leading a chain of city slickers into the wilderness. Of all the livestock, only two dogs had migrated to Tucson with their owners. One of these, however, was a massive English mastiff, the picture of melancholia, to which the Starlet immediately gave her heart. 'Lucky for her Cisco has already had his breakfast,' said Boyer (though, in truth, the dog gave no sign of being anything other than a perfect gentleman, albeit rather elderly). The Starlet was handed a flannel to mop up the drool as it overflowed his great jaws.

Peppercorn told Boyer the curious way he had acquired his photograph of Josephine, and asked him how he had made the identification. 'When I was in the air force, back in the mid-fifties, I found myself stationed in Yuma,' Boyer said. 'There were no shortage of bars, but I patronized an adobe cantina run by a former beauty named Carmelita Mayhew – the widow of a mining man, if I remember correctly – who still had more spirit in her than a bottle of home-brewed tequila. By then I was already interested in Wyatt Earp, and figured she may have a story or two to tell. And I knew enough about women to know that if you treat an old beauty as if she were still a young beauty, she'll look kindly upon any requests for a favour. So I asked her if she had ever met Wyatt Earp. "You betcha," she said. Used to accompany him to the race track over at Harqua Hala. "Tell me about him," I said. She went one better and told me about Josie. Turned out they were bosom buddies. One day she showed me a photograph – *the* photograph – saying, "That's her when she was young." It was the first time I'd ever set eyes upon Wyatt Earp's dark lady, and I could hardly believe what I was seeing. Carmelita explained, with a wicked twinkle in her eye, that Johnny Behan had got her "bombed on wine", and persuaded her to pose in the altogether. Of course, Carmelita held on to the original, but let me make a copy. Maybe I would've kept it to myself if it hadn't been for a remarkable coincidence. A member of the family sent me an oval portrait of Josie, obviously taken from a locket, and the two likenesses were a match. Naturally this will always be insufficient proof for some. They continue to claim that the picture is of a young woman named Kaloma, or someone else, or that it is of no one in particular. Take your pick. If it isn't Josie, it ought to be.'

Quoting D. H. Lawrence's opinion that the cowboy was bunkum, Peppercorn wondered if anything of Wyatt Earp had survived Boyer's debunking. 'All I did was to show that he wasn't a saint,' said Boyer, 'not that he wasn't a man. And a pretty good one at that. He preferred to subdue his opponents with his fists or his gun butt, but if he had to use the other end of it, he used the other end of it.' 'You approve of guns?' said Bel. 'Let me tell you a story,' said Boyer. 'In Dodge City, not so long ago, a killer stole a state trooper's gun and shot him with it. Did he get away? Did he hell. Before he had the chance to even turn around four bystanders cut him down. As my good friend puts it, "Every bullet you fire is a little victory for liberty." And any potential robber would be well advised to keep clear of this property. There are concealed weapons everywhere. As a matter of fact, I've got three guns hidden about my person as we speak.' Bel began to look him up and down, whereupon he let out another guffaw. 'It's a joke,' he said.

But the laughter subsided when he spoke about his enemies, those knaves who disparaged his working methods. 'To them, history wasn't history unless it was backed by documentation, which was a joke,' said Boyer, 'because none of them are real historians. Anyway, what would these people have me do with all the first-hand accounts and second-hand stories I have collected? Consign them to the junk heap because there is no corroborating evidence, or make them public?' 'Sounds to me like they're just jealous,' said Bel, 'jealous of you, and jealous that you got there before they did.' 'You should read some of the things they write about him,' said Jane. 'One even threatened to kill me,' said Boyer. 'It's true,' said his wife, 'these people are fanatics, they are absolutely crazy.' 'I can't prove a connection,' said Boyer, 'but not long after the threat was made some ill-intentioned individual cut right through my brake cables.' Peppercorn had read articles in which the couple were portrayed as uncultured bigots, with a penchant for homophobic gutter talk. Peppercorn didn't believe a word of it. Watching Jane discuss her collection of Apache baskets, Zuni bowls and Hopi pots with Bel made such pieces seem more like character assassination than honest reporting. She explained that she had travelled from reservation to reservation, buying from the makers themselves. 'Sometimes the tribal elders would stare at me and insist that I had Indian blood in me,' Jane said. 'I told them I wished that I had, but that I hadn't.' She also expressed interest in Bel's work, and asked for an invite to her next show in Atlanta.

Boyer, meanwhile, left the room, returning with two fat socks like Santa Claus. In the one was the revolver that had once belonged to Nicholas, the Earp clan's paterfamilias. In the other was nothing less than the Colt .45 Wyatt Earp had exercised at the OK Corral. 'This gun killed at least two men,' Boyer assured his audience, as he plucked it from its woollen sock and handed it direct to the Kid. Without thinking, the Kid cocked the weapon and began to squeeze the trigger; then he paused, fearful that he might have damaged such a rare artefact.

'Don't be shy,' said Boyer. 'The gun doesn't matter. If there's something your heart says do, then do that something, and let the thing bear the consequences.' So the Kid pulled the trigger, and Ike Clanton's ghost jumped.

When they departed Boyer squeezed Bel Stahr's shoulder. 'You're a doll,' he said. 'There's something of John Wayne about him,' she concluded afterwards (and she should know, having met the great man). 'He's big, but he can be gentle too. You feel he'd be good with horses and women.' On the flight back to San Francisco Bel said: 'Well, is she as great as Glenn said she was?' 'I'd put it this way,' said Peppercorn, looking up from his copy of *Stories from Mesa Country*, 'as Annie Proulx is to Wyoming, as Larry McMurtry is to Texas, so Jane Candia Coleman is to Arizona.'

Among the many responsibilities of Professor Baumgarten, the Kid's godfather, was putting together a new edition of Thomas Carlyle's complete works. One of his colleagues in this project was Mark Engel. Although Carlyle's house in Cheyne Row was around the corner from Bel's, Peppercorn had no particular interest in the writer. What was of interest was the fact that Mark Engel's father had been the producer of *My*

Darling Clementine. And so a few days after Peppercorn's return from Tombstone, the indefatigable Professor B arranged for him to meet Engel at a Chinese restaurant in Santa Cruz. Engel told Peppercorn that his father had served under Ford during World War II, when both men were involved in making propaganda films for the OSS – not in the studios, of course, but at the front. In fact, they had first worked together at Pearl Harbor early in '43, and their paths had crossed occasionally thereafter. When hostilities were concluded, Samuel Engel had returned to his former life as a Hollywood producer and scriptwriter, and unexpectedly resumed a working relationship with Ford. His son recalled dinner-time descriptions of the daily struggles between producer and director, the one wanting more complexity, the other less – disdaining the analytical.

Peppercorn replied that nonetheless the movie that emerged from this dialectic offered a glimpse of perfection. Ford had known Wyatt Earp in Hollywood's early days, where the old lawman had finally fetched up, and claimed to have followed his description of the immortal gunfight to the letter. Bullshit. He even got the year wrong. No, the movie's perfection resided in artistry, not historical accuracy. Once you'd seen Henry Fonda as Wyatt Earp, everyone else – even Hugh O'Brian – seemed an impostor. Because the movie was a work of art, it illuminated the year of its making, 1946, rather than the year in which it was supposedly set. And this was where the conflict between Mark Engel's father and John Ford bore fruit. Ford may have offered token resistance to Freudian notions of ego and id, but he put them on the screen anyway, in the contrasting shapes of Earp and Doc Holliday. The one was a straightforward soul of abounding natural grace; the other half in love with death, and able to quote Hamlet's most famous soliloquy verbatim – especially the lines on suicide. So powerful were both personalities that sometimes you wondered which of them the film was really about. Then you realized that the conflict was actually between two sides of a single personality: the Prince, and the Lord of Misrule. In reality, Doc Holliday had survived the shoot-out, but Ford had killed him off. Why? Peppercorn believed that he had been chastened by what had been done to the Jews in Europe by cultured but murderous men, and had elected to rid Earp of his dark and self-destructive side – his European side – once and for all: to ensure that he left Tombstone a cleaner man than he entered it, an American through and through. 'Forget the indefinite article,' said Peppercorn. 'Fonda's Wyatt Earp was Mr America 1946.'

When he thought about it afterwards, Peppercorn realized that Earp was America's weathervane. Fonda's Earp was essentially FDR's man, a bit of a gambler, but mainly a New Dealer. Hugh O'Brian's Earp was firmly of the Eisenhower era, a Plain (or rather Great Plains) Dealer. But when John Ford revisited Wyatt Earp in *Cheyenne Autumn*, he had Jimmy Stewart play him as a cynical despoiler of his own reputation. It was no coincidence that the bitterest of those scenes were shot days after JFK's assassination. Unfortunately, John Wayne never played Wyatt Earp, but like John Ford he claimed to have met the man himself and, having seen him walk the walk, took Earp's characteristic gait as his own. Anyway, Wayne's ghost strode through the Reagan years with a swagger that reflected America's rediscovered self-confidence. What else could the Congressional

Gold Medal awarded him a month before his death say but 'John Wayne, American'? By contrast, Kevin Costner's 1994 Earp was more modest, more of an American Everyman. There had been attempts to cast George W. Bush as Earp ('Dubya at the OK Corral'), but with little conviction. America still awaited its new Wyatt.

The night after his dinner with Mark Engel, Peppercorn rented a video of *My Darling Clementine* and watched it with Bel. She loved the movie, but was less impressed by Peppercorn's theory. 'Had Ford been as upset by the fate of European Jewry as you think he was,' she said, 'why did he deny Earp his Jewish wife? Unless . . .' She paused for a moment. 'Has it ever occurred to you that Josephine Marcus Earp might be another of Glenn's jokes,' she added, 'a non-existent stowaway with faked documentation, photograph, memoirs, and all?' Peppercorn did not try to convince Bel otherwise, but as soon as it was light the following day he drove her to the Hills of Eternity, a Jewish cemetery not far from San Francisco. They got out of the car and he led her among the graves, until he found the tombstone he was seeking. On it were inscribed the names of Wyatt and Josephine Earp. 'That looks pretty real to me,' he said. Then he added, 'In order to die, one has first to live.'

Now it happened that Professor Baumgarten's wife, Sheila, was related by marriage to an artist named Maury Lapp, and one of Maury Lapp's friends was an older painter named Louis Siegrist. Now this Louis Siegrist had a wife, and her name was Edna Stoddart, another artist. The main thing about Edna Stoddart was that she was the niece of Josephine Marcus Earp. And Edna liked her aunt, and was very like her aunt. When she married for the first time the newlyweds honeymooned with Josephine and Wyatt in Alaska. In her memoirs Josephine described her niece skipping out of doors, and dancing her way along the beach. Josephine knew how she felt, because that was how she had felt. 'The same feeling still sometimes overcomes me,' she wrote, 'even at my age. It was a wonderful life.'

Edna's ended in Mexico in 1966, a month shy of her seventy-fifth birthday. Louis Siegrist buried her there. When the coffin entered the churchyard, it was reported, myriad small birds took to the air and began to sing, as if one of her own paintings had sprung to life. It did not occur to Siegrist that there would be anything wrong about giving his wife a Christian burial, because Edna had concealed her Jewishness throughout her married life. She had also hidden the fact that she was a grandmother, passing off her grandchildren as the inheritance of second marriages. Siegrist only discovered the truth when one of them wrote him a letter of condolence. Edna died before Lapp befriended Siegrist, but the former was well acquainted with her executrixes. Knowing of Peppercorn's interest in Josephine, Professor Baumgarten's wife mooted a brunch at her relative's house, at which all could meet.

Maury Lapp lived in Santa Rosa, where Luther Burbank created the golden nectarine, and Charles Schultz doodled 'Peanuts' into existence. Lapp had a frosting of white hair, and an equally white goatee. He looked like a Bundist. His paintings were cityscapes: railroad yards, canals, streets, factories, all infused with a sort of dreamy realism, or so Peppercorn thought. He knew better than to ask Bel her opinion of them, but he liked them well enough. Edna's executrixes were two middle-aged women introduced as

Laurellee and Suzanne. Laurellee was an elegant redhead with a figure like Audrey Hepburn. Suzanne was grey-haired, more like a schoolmarm than a movie star. Peppercorn lazily assumed they were a couple: a temperamental thoroughbred, and a careful rider. Only gradually did it dawn on him that they were sisters. Their father and Siegrist

had been great friends and neighbours, and it was through him they had inherited their joint role in Edna's afterlife. As well as being a painter, Edna was a devout recorder of her own existence. The sisters had donated thirty volumes of her diaries to the Smithsonian (keeping one back for themselves). But they had retained many of Edna's paintings, a few of which they brought along to show Peppercorn. The pictures were like illustrations to lost or unwritten fairy tales, teeming with brightly coloured creatures both familiar and exotic. One of the most striking images portrayed an angel beneath a crescent moon. A halo crowned her corn-coloured hair. Resting on one hand was a white bird. In the other she held a yellow apple. To her left a small devil hovered sinisterly. Laurellee said he had the features of Louis Siegrist. The more Peppercorn looked at the angel the more it reminded him of Josephine in her veil that veiled nothing. The sisters also had some photographs of Edna, taken by Johan Hagemeyer. She had been a fine-looking woman, and she was not afraid of the camera. For God's sake, she looked like Josephine forty years on. Bel, who knew about faces, agreed. Peppercorn did the sums. Edna would have been twenty-two in 1914, when the photograph had been copyrighted (if not taken). Close enough. Moreover she'd been a student at art schools in San Francisco and Berkeley, where there would have been no shortage of photographers more than willing to take such a portrait. Or perhaps she just looked a lot like her Auntie Josephine.

As Edna's executrixes prepared to depart, Laurellee let drop that she was an actress. 'I've done a few movies,' she said, 'but usually I work with uncompromising playwrights in small theatres.' She named a few of the writers, of whom one, inevitably, was Leslie Brody, author of *Quiet, Wyatt!*.

On the first Friday after Peppercorn's return from America, Dr Helman resumed his weekly visits. As he uncorked the bottle of Zinfandel he heard a movement overhead. 'Is there someone in the bathroom?' he said. Peppercorn said that there was. Then Dr Helman noticed that the table had been laid for three. 'I took your advice,' said Peppercorn, 'though it wasn't Josephine I found.' When Bel descended the stairs, Dr Helman raised his glass and sang, 'Beloved, come and meet the Bride, Bid welcome to the Sabbath-tide!'

The Kid returned from America in midsummer. Not long

afterwards, Boyer sent Peppercorn an email: 'Sometime during the night of the 21st or morning of the 22nd Cisco gave up the ghost,' he wrote. 'He hadn't been well, wasn't eating right, and seemed to have arthritis. Besides, mastiffs don't live long. He was my big, awkward, stumbly boy with the loving heart. I will never have another mastiff, but I'm glad I had him, and wish I could bring him back for another few years. He may have lasted longer if we'd stayed out in the country, at a somewhat higher altitude. Equally, this may be true of me.' 'The Starlet wept when I told her that Cisco had gone the way of Old Shep,' wrote Peppercorn. 'In fact we were all uncannily upset. As far as I know there is only one palliative for grief. To get back in the saddle again.'

True Tales of the
WILD WEST N°5

The True Voice
of America

If a man has no future, thought Saltzman, he'd better enjoy living in the past. Highway 1 was perfect for such a man, especially the seventy-mile stretch between Big Sur and Santa Cruz. Whereas parts of Kansas were fixed in the fifties, this bit of California remained loyal to the sixties. Saltzman was a veteran of that era – just – arriving in the fall of '69 to do graduate work at UCSC. Too late for the Summer of Love, but in plenty of time for Altamont, where the Rolling Stones sang 'Sympathy for the Devil', while Hells Angels murdered a fan. He had spent another year at Santa Cruz as a visiting lecturer in the early 80s, and frequently went back for conferences. He had many friends there but, feeling more like the Wandering Jew than a tenured professor, wanted to visit but one, the one who had since died.

About forty miles south of Santa Cruz, Saltzman took a left and entered a strip of road cut between stunted coastal pines. He drove until he reached the park ranger's hut. The ranger within expressed admiration for his 1961 Ford Falcon, remarking upon its reupholstered bench seats and its body newly resprayed. Saltzman said he was just the delivery boy, and handed over the day fee. Then he drove to land's end and once again gazed upon Point Lobos. The sky was as blue as purity, though there was fog banked menacingly offshore, like an army of ghosts. He walked up the slope to his right until he reached a promontory amid stands of Monterey cypresses. They are like me, thought Saltzman, bent backwards by invisible forces, but not yet on the deck. Peering down he saw jagged granite peaks, and white water roiling in the cove. An observer would be justified in thinking him lachrymose, but it was only the wind whipping in off the waves that made his eyes water.

Despite the dominant wind section and the incessant percussion of the breakers, he could still hear the knock-knock as sea otters, floating face up among the kelp, smashed abalone shells on their chests. Even louder was the guttural bark of a sea lion, whose slick head had just broken the surface. Other heads followed suit, creating a gruff chorus. On the strand spotted seals snoozed, and probably snored, beside the blanched boles of whole trees. Sleek as guided missiles, cormorants took to the air, leaving behind flat rocks sporting toupees of guano. Pelicans flew in elegant formation until one or another, attracted by a flash of silver below, broke ranks and executed a kamikaze dive. Somewhere among all this voracious and vociferous life, perhaps moving with the waves, perhaps floating on a thread of fog, or perhaps lost among the grains of sand, were the ashes of Charles Neider.

Saltzman hadn't been there when his friend's ashes were scattered, but he had taken leave of him at his Princeton home in March 2001. By then the prostate cancer that killed him on Independence Day had invaded his bones, and he was effectively bed-ridden. Dying by increments in his living room, he still remained part of the whole, with books, newspapers and telephone all to hand. His curiosity was insatiable, his dignity infallible. Light from the late winter sun saturated everything save for the bed, which was protected by an open black umbrella. Although in the shadow of death, Neider claimed not to fear it. Observing the sceptical look on his wife's face, he agreed that his nearest and dearest might not second his words, nevertheless he repeated them: he did not begrudge death, because life had not begrudged him.

The part of his life's work that had first attracted Saltzman's attention was the authorship of a novel called *The Authentic Death of Hendry Jones*. Its title (as well as its hero) derived from *The Authentic Life of Billy the Kid* by Pat Garrett, the man who simultaneously ended his subject's career and his habit of breathing. Neider had originally meant to set his book in New Mexico, on account of it being Billy's own stamping ground. He actually moved to Taos in 1954 to conduct research, but was driven out before he could properly start by persistent storms of red dust. He travelled to California to lick his wounds, discovered Point Lobos, fell in love with the place, and decided to relocate his book. Billy the Kid remained the model for his hero, but traces of a local desperado named Tiburcio Vasquez were thrown into the mix. Señor Vasquez was one of those road agents with an appreciation of the need to butter up the press. Like Jesse James in another neck of the woods, he became known as a friend to the poor, an even better friend to ladies, and a defender of the oppressed.

Unlike the myth-hungry hacks, Neider took the word 'authentic' he had used in his title very seriously indeed. He wanted to know what it would be like to live half your life in the saddle, so he rented a cabin in the backcountry and rode for days on end through canyon and chaparral. He became a little gun crazy. In order to fully appreciate the feel, action, resonance and recoil of a Colt .45, he wore one in an old-fashioned rig and sometimes shot off rounds in a narrow canyon. When he did so he took his life into his hands, for the bullets ricocheted unpredictably off its walls, deadly as direct fire. Deafness was another hazard, on account of the thunderous discharge. On top of that, the shells were expensive. So when it came to target practice Neider favoured a lighter weapon. One day he took a pot shot with a .22 at what looked like a bull skunk. It was at an impossible distance, but the creature keeled right over. Only afterwards did he discover that the animal – a badger, not a bull skunk – had been dispatched by a bullet that had entered the brain via a nostril. Word got around, and the locals began pestering him to use his legendary marksmanship on their behalf. One offered him $20 for every feral cat he plugged. He explained that his shot had been a fluke, one in a billion, but his listeners favoured legend over fact. Just like Doc Baker's listeners in the book that emerged from Neider's labours.

It opened, Saltzman recalled, pretty much where he was now standing. Doc Baker (its narrator) was pointing out the cypress beneath which he and some other gang members had buried their leader, Hendry Jones (universally known as the Kid). The tree was on the prow of the promontory, and a risky proposition for tourists who came from God knows where to see the Kid's grave, so the authorities set up a stone marker by a safer tree. Even then, there were plenty who refused to believe that he was buried beside either. On the contrary, they managed to convince themselves that he lived still, and had fled to Mexico, where the son of a gun continued to raise merry Cain. Doc Baker had no patience for them. He was telling the truth, and those not interested in hearing it could 'run along to the stores and pick up one of the little books full of lies about the Kid's life, written by some smart alec Easterner that never sat in a Western saddle, never smelt good horseflesh or a campfire dying in the hills, and yet is ready to tell the country all about the Kid. I was there and I know what happened.'

You may conclude from the above that Neider himself was a true man of the West – in which case, you would be jumping to the wrong conclusion. Neider was a Method writer, just as Marlon Brando (who acquired the movie rights to his book) was a Method actor. Though raised partly in Richmond, Virginia, where he was wont to camp beside Civil War trenches, Neider was actually born in Odessa, like that other tough Jew-on-a-horse, Isaac Babel.

Brando's movie differed from Neider's novel in many ways. For one thing, it was called *One-Eyed Jacks*. For another, its hero wasn't named Hendry but Rio. And these were by no means the only liberties taken by Brando. Doc Baker wouldn't have stood for it, but Neider was more amused than angered by the movie star's indifference to authenticity. Besides, he knew that Brando had the right to do as he damn well pleased. Saltzman remembered his friend using those very words, and was ready to swear he could hear their echo yet.

They were first spoken on a summer's evening twenty years or more ago, while they were enjoying a barbecue up the coast at New Brighton. It was the Pacific that had quenched the fiery sun, but it could just as easily have been the Aegean, for the combination of red wine, roasting meat and the resinous sweat of pines gave their dialogue a platonic flavour. 'On account of the vast distance between the shooting script and its source, I was not encouraged to visit the set,' Neider had said, 'which didn't stop the man who had the first shot at writing it from coming around in hope of picking my brain for free. Sam Peckinpah got to be famous later for making some particularly violent films, but in those days he was grandly respectful and always called me "Master". I liked being called Master, and having my brain picked, what was left of it.' 'I always felt *Pat Garrett and Billy the Kid* was closer in spirit and fact to *The Authentic Death of Hendry Jones* than was *One-Eyed Jacks*,' said Saltzman. 'Now I know why.' 'Maybe so,' said Neider.

One day, when the filming was well advanced, Neider got a call from Brando's father, inviting him to view some rushes. Brando junior, Neider noted, had stuck his pistol in the wide cummerbund that encircled his waist. Brando senior asked his opinion. 'First time he'd draw that gun he'd blow his balls off,' observed Neider. 'Talk to him about it,' urged Brando senior. 'He admires you. You're the only one he'll listen to.' Brando junior didn't, of course. Nevertheless, Neider's final assessment of the movie was characteristically generous: 'It has a romantic, perhaps adolescent, bitter-sweetness that distinguishes it from other Westerns.'

Of course, some vestiges of the epic confrontation between Billy the Kid and Pat Garrett survived even Brando's reworking. In the movie there was the same initial comradeship between hunted and hunter, friendship that turned finally to enmity. The big difference was that it was the hunted who turned pursuer, and the hunted who won the climactic shoot-out. Rio (ex Hendry, ex Billy) ended the movie not dead and buried as both history and legend demanded – not to mention the book upon which the film was based – but galloping across the white sands of Carmel Bay, while his pregnant lover (also mounted) waved hopefully after him.

Neider wrote other books besides, including several about Antarctica. He also arranged and edited *The Autobiography of Mark Twain*, and was as pleased as Punch when it was placed forty-third by a panel of Modern Library judges on a list of the hundred best non-fiction books in English of the twentieth century. 'Life did not begrudge you, old friend,' murmured Saltzman to himself, 'but it's fucked me over good and proper. If there are any, and you have their ear, perhaps you could ask the powers that be to do me a good turn for once.'

Not waiting for an answer, Saltzman sped past familiar landmarks: Sand City, Fort Ord's firing ranges, the PG&E power plant at Moss Landing, artichoke fields around Castroville, and then the straight run to Santa Cruz. No one knew he was coming, and no one knew he was there, so he was pretty confident that the crowd gathered at the junction of Union and Chestnut was not waiting for him. But if not him, who? He parked the car and went to find out. Overhead lights began to flash red and crossing bells to sound. Traffic backed up. The sidewalk vibrated. It was either an earthquake or a train. It was a train, but no ordinary one. The first Saltzman saw of it were the flags atop the locomotive. Has campaigning for the next election already begun? he wondered. He figured it must be carrying a presidential candidate at the very least. When it stopped the welcoming committee, most of whom held flags of their own, assembled around its open-ended caboose. Above their heads, the train's flags continued to flap and crack like captive kites. First to step forward was the Mayor of Santa Cruz. He cleared his throat, then welcomed no aspirant but the President of the United States to his city. This brought forth the man himself. Taking his place beside the Mayor he waved to his fellow patriots and delivered an impromptu address. It commenced with a promise to put an end to war, continued with a tribute to the spirit of the pioneering cowboy, and concluded with a hymn to the beautiful land those heroes had inherited.

The war in Iraq was in full swing, but the President was not George W. Bush. What Saltzman was witnessing, he discovered, was a re-enactment of the twenty-sixth President's one and only visit to Santa Cruz, which had taken place a century before. As a matter of fact, that original visit was well worth celebrating. So beguiled had Theodore Roosevelt been by this western Eden with its colossal trees and bottomless chasms that, directly upon his return to Washington, he proposed numerous laws to protect it. Thanks to them the Santa Cruz Big Trees & Pacific Railway Company was able to duplicate the President's ride exactly.

Being in no hurry, Saltzman boarded the train with the multitude. It pulled out of the old depot and left the city via a short tunnel, emerging among the shady redwood groves of Rincon Gorge, at the bottom of which flowed the San Lorenzo, still bubbling with winter rain. While the train progressed Teddy greeted all the passengers personally, breaking off occasionally to exclaim 'Bully!' as yet another natural wonder

imposed itself upon his vision. Like Ermal Walden Williamson, the man who would be John Wayne, Michael Cawelti undoubtedly looked the part, with his full-moon specs, bristling moustache, topper and frock coat. His Secretary of the Navy (also on board) was somewhat less scrupulous, having failed to conceal a diamond ear-stud and a grey ponytail.

As well as being a convincing lookalike, Mr Cawelti was reputed to be something of a Teddy Roosevelt scholar, having spent seven years or more researching his subject. So when he extended his hand, Saltzman had a question ready: 'Did the President recall staying at the Occidental Hotel in Buffalo, Wyoming?' 'My good sir,' replied the President, 'I hear from your accent that you are an Englishman. But even a stranger like yourself, if he has travelled any distance in this great country of ours, will be aware that there is hardly a hotel in which I did not stay. Is there another question I could answer?' There was the one that Peppercorn had asked him, not so very long ago: 'Does the name Stuart N. Lake mean anything to you?' 'This is the second time you have found me wanting,' replied the President. He looked at his Secretary of the Navy. 'Do we know the gentleman?' he asked. The Secretary shook his head. 'It seems that we do not know the gentleman,' replied the President. 'Should we?' 'I have been told that he once worked in your press office as a burnisher of reputations,' said Saltzman. 'But his greater claim to fame was the invention of Wyatt Earp. Using the Virginian as his model, he turned the old chancer from an ambiguous – if not plain dubious – character into an impeccable gentleman, and an unbending upholder of the law.' At that the President's face lit up.

'Bully!' he cried. 'You have read Owen Wister's magnificent novel. Being a sea-green incorruptible myself, I must declare an interest. I am its dedicatee.'

'As a professor emeritus of American Studies you are not telling me anything I don't already know,' said Saltzman. 'Just as I already know that you and Wister both were weedy patricians from the East, rehabilitated by spells in Wyoming and the Dakotas. But even as you grew more manly, the pair of you saw that the honest way of life that had restored your own equilibrium was vanishing. You refused to regard this as an inevitable outcome of manifest destiny, but rather as a national tragedy. The cowboy, as far as you and Wister were concerned, was no dying breed but a continuing necessity, a moral exemplar sans pareil. Both of you began to proselytize on his behalf.'

Roosevelt's big chance came in 1898, with the outbreak of the Spanish–American War. He immediately stood down as Assistant Secretary of the Navy, and formed an irregular regiment called the Rough Riders (a strange brew of Ivy-League romantics, glee-club singers, gunslingers, and Texas Rangers), pinching the name from Buffalo Bill, whose travelling show was correctly titled, Wild West & Congress of Rough Riders of the World. Roosevelt's men trained enthusiastically, impressed the authorities, and were shipped from San Antonio to Cuba to join the fighting. Their moment of glory arrived at the Battle of San Juan Hill, where they secured victory with an inspirational charge – or so Roose-velt later claimed. Like-minded Frederic Remington (Roosevelt's friend as well as Wister's) covered the war for arch-belligerent William Randolph Hearst. His painting of the heroic scene added to Roosevelt's lustre. Buffalo Bill went further, offering not just one scene, but a re-enactment of the entire battle, thereby restoring the Rough Riders to their proper place. Unlike Roosevelt, Buffalo Bill saw nothing to salvage from the advance of progress but spectacle. He was an impresario of ghosts, all condemned to relive their finest hours. Scott Fitzgerald understood this very well when he characterized Tom Buchanan, Gatsby's nemesis, as 'forever seeking . . . the dramatic turbulence of some irrecoverable football game.' But Roosevelt moved on, becoming McKinley's running mate in the presidential election, and replacement after his assassination in 1901.

By then Wister was shaping the book that probably did more for the cowboy than even Roosevelt. Had the Virginian only wooed and won his schoolmarm, it would have sufficed. Had he only impressed her Eastern relatives, it would have sufficed. Had he only been gifted a ranch and made it prosper, it would have sufficed. But he did more. He could see which way the wind was blowing, and he could smell the smoke upon it. He knew that the locomotives required coal, and that the railroad would pay him handsomely to mine the seams that lay beneath his land. Thus the cowboy, without compromising character, became an entrepreneur and capitalist. As well as, it goes without saying, a Roosevelt supporter. His successors, two-fisted capitalists to a man, dig for oil. And not just in America.

'If I catch your drift aright, sir,' said the President, 'you are holding me and my fellow enthusiasts responsible for the behaviour of future presidents, in particular that of the forty-third. Have I hit the nail on the head?' 'Not squarely,' said Saltzman. 'You cannot be blamed if others traduce your example. Wister's political philosophy may have verged on the fascist, but, as Walter says in *The Big Lebowski*, at least it's an ethos. Now it's a sentiment on a road map, which urges the rest of the free world to follow America's example and "Cowboy Up". But did that copy-writer know of what he wrote? Had he served in Afghanistan or Iraq? I doubt it. Your warmongering, however, always had a measure of authenticity. The Battle of San Juan Hill may not have occurred exactly as you described it, but there's no denying you were there. In short, you and Wister were men of your time. The forty-third President, however, is an anachronism. No, he is worse than that. He is, if you will, a re-enactor. And his role model is President Roosevelt – Theodore, not Franklin, of course. Mr Cawelti, you are doing a fine job, re-enacting him here, among the redwoods he saved. But Mr Bush is making a real hash of it in the White House. Having an actor there was bad enough, but a re-enactor is a disaster. Nineteenth-century scenarios do not play well in the twenty-first.' 'That may be,' said the twenty-sixth, 'but it is not permissible for one President to speak ill of another.'

So saying, he took his leave of Saltzman and proceeded along the aisle, pumping flesh as he went. Still high on his own verbosity, the ex-professor was remembering, for the first time in months, how much he enjoyed the bluff and counter-bluff of educated debate. The realization only made him regret his folly the more bitterly.

At the beginning of the twentieth century, the Henry Cowell State Park, where the train finally screeched to a halt, had been a fashionable resort known as Big Trees. It was here, among the arboreal wonders, that Teddy Roosevelt redux delivered a speech that made him sound like the American apostle of Dr Astrov from Anton Chekhov's *Uncle Vanya*. 'Cut down one of these giants,' said the re-enactor, describing an arc with his finger, 'and you cannot take its place. Nature was its architect, and we owe it to ourselves and our children's children to preserve them . . . We should see to it that no man for speculative purposes or for mere temporary use destroys the groves of great trees. Where the individual and associations cannot preserve them, then the State, and if necessary the nation, should step in and see to their preservation. We should keep the trees as we should keep great stretches of wilderness, as a heritage for our children's children to preserve them for use, and for the sake of the nation hereafter.' After the President had concluded, the Mayor announced that his honoured guest would prefer to walk through the trees unaccompanied. 'Yes,' said Roosevelt, as he was swallowed by the shade of the deep, dark forest, 'that I love you not the less, but the trees more!'

The following day Saltzman dropped off the Ford Falcon at an address on K Street in Sacramento. 'What next?' he thought.

He had heard of Sutter's Fort (Sacramento's seed) and, learning that he was within a block of it, decided upon a visit. Johann Augustus Sutter was a Swiss-born entrepreneur who became an American citizen, but (circa 1840) chose to seek his fortune in California (then part of Mexico). In exchange for swearing allegiance to the (ever-changing) President of Mexico, he was granted a parcel of land in the fertile valley watered by two rivers, the Americanos and the eponymous Sacramento. With land came responsibility. Sutter was expected to secure the estate and its hinterland from the Russians at Fort Ross. This he did by exerting his authority over the troublesome indigenous population and (so it was said) 'converting them into a peaceable and industrious people'. He was also required to report the presence of strangers, especially Americans, to the authorities (which he did). But Sutter's sympathies remained with the United States, and he looked forward to the day when California would become part of the Union, which explains why the fort still bears his name.

Early visitors were greeted by a stockade standing alone in a lush valley at the confluence of the two rivers; later visitors found it at the junction of K and L Streets, swallowed whole by California's capital. What they could see had been saved for posterity by the Native Sons of the Golden West, who purchased the site in 1890. By then all that remained upright was Sutter's house. The rest had to be reconstructed from old plans. Volunteers rebuilt and whitewashed its outer walls, and replaced the bastion at the end nearest to where Saltzman stood. Since its original construction predated California's independence, the fort was, in the name of verisimilitude, flying the Mexican flag.

Saltzman entered via a wooden gate and crossed an invisible time threshold that transported him back some hundred and fifty years. 'The fort', wrote an early witness, 'is a quadrangular adobe structure, mounting 12 pieces of artillery . . . and capable of admitting a garrison of a thousand men; this, at present, consists of 40 Indians, in uniform – one of whom was always found on duty at the gate . . . The inner wall is formed into buildings comprising the common quarters, with blacksmith, and other workshops; the dwelling house, with a large distillery house, and other

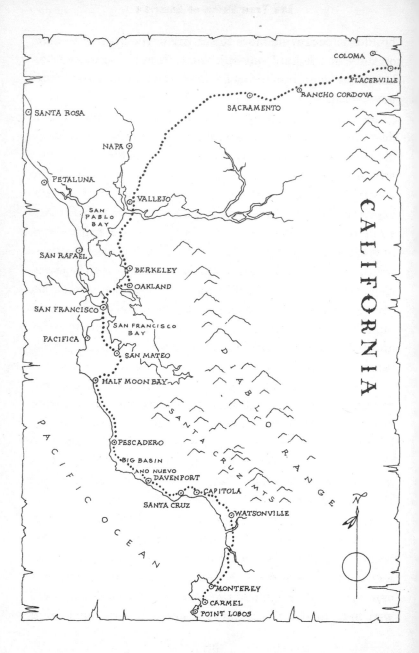

buildings, occupying more the centre of the area.' The man on duty at the gate was still there (though he looked too blonde to be an Indian). His fellow troopers, however, were nowhere in sight.

As far as Saltzman could see, the fort's only other defender was a woman wearing a blue bonnet, a modest blouse, a hooped skirt and thick, schoolmarmish specs. She was standing behind a counter in a modest pavilion and waving invitingly. When Saltzman reached her she explained that she was manning the fur trapper's display while the fur trapper was away doing what fur trappers do best. She had no expertise in the cruel tools of his trade, which were on display behind her, but she had a bit of experience when it came to furs and was happy to share it. Shaded by canvas, Saltzman settled on a stone bench. She held aloft a dark pelt and asked him to guess its provenance, and the use to which it was put. 'Beaver,' he said, 'much favoured in the manufacture of top hats.'

'This one's harder,' she said, picking up a skin whose colours were a mix of vanilla, coffee and chocolate. 'You're right,' said Saltzman. She smiled. 'Raccoons were usually left alone,' she said, 'because no one could think of a use for their hides. So they were laughing until one unlucky day – unlucky for them, that is – a playwright penned a drama about a congressman from Tennessee. To give the character some stage presence he provided him with a unique prop: a coonskin hat. The real congressman from Tennessee – better known to you and me as Davy Crockett, king of the wild frontier – was persuaded to pose for a portrait sporting one. For the first and last time, I reckon. Why would he be wanting a fur hat in the hot and humid forests of his home state? Well, the play was a hit, and a fashion craze was born, which was good news for everyone except the raccoons.' She stroked the fur dreamily. 'Same thing happened when Fess Parker played Davy Crockett in the fifties,' she continued. 'Sent the price of raccoon tails into orbit.'

Saltzman remembered how badly he had wanted one of those hats, but neither his mother nor Peppercorn's had been prepared to give their sons the necessary permission. He demanded a reason for the denial, and was told that it was unlucky to wear a dead animal on your head. He wanted to know how come it was okay for his grandmother to drape a fox-fur stole – face and feet still attached – around her shoulders. Because she didn't wear it on her head, was the answer. Perhaps if my mother had been less superstitious, thought Saltzman, I wouldn't have felt the need to assert my manhood at every opportunity, and spiked my own career.

When the fur trapper unexpectedly reappeared, the woman departed without a further word. Her replacement was wearing a linen shirt laced to the throat, high boots and a leather hat. He looked as though he knew of what he spoke. Not for him the cissified furs – he meant to show off the masculine stuff, how the traps did their work. 'I always use a "live" trap in my demonstrations,' he said, forcing back the jaws of something that could be a shark's dentures. 'By "live" I mean one that has a spring and sharp teeth. Being "live" means being dangerous.' He gave Saltzman a searching look, the sort patented by the latter's mother and his psychiatrist. 'I'm going to give you some good advice,' said the trapper. 'Never do what I am doing. Never put your fingers between the teeth of a "live" trap. Never.'

He began to explain what happened when an ill-starred quadruped did something equally incautious with one of its four feet. Saltzman's imagination was assisted suddenly by the irrefutable clang of jaws snapping shut. 'At this juncture the unfortunate creature has two choices,' continued the grim-visaged fur trapper. 'It can either await death – which comes via starvation, if it's unlucky, or a coup de grâce, if it's not – or bite through its own limb.' The fur-trapper paused, his face turning white. He had been too slow, and the trap had closed on his thumb. Saltzman could clearly see the man's blood seeping through its teeth.

The fur trapper continued his silent attempt to free the tortured extremity, his eyes growing wider with undischarged pain. But it was not a one-man job. 'Would you like some help?' asked Saltzman. 'Do you know, I think I would,' the fur-trapper replied quietly (almost sarcastically). 'What would you have me do?' said Saltzman. 'Press your hand down hard on the latch,' the other replied. Saltzman complied. There came a metallic twang, a human sigh, and the iron jaws relaxed their grip. The trapper quickly prised them apart. By some miracle his thumb was still attached to his hand. Saltzman learned a second lesson from the incident, a lesson well known to Sigmund Freud and Captain Hook: the past was not pacified territory; it remained dangerous, and possessed a damaging bite. Look out the windscreen my boy, thought Saltzman, and not into the rear-view mirror.

Saltzman was standing at the crossroads, not knowing which way to turn, when his cellphone rang unexpectedly. Looking at the display he was astonished to see that the caller was Mae Fairweather, an erstwhile colleague and a bloody-minded feminist who hated his guts. Even so, he looked forward to hearing her voice again. He pressed the green button, but the voice that greeted him was not hers. The unknown woman clearly did not know who he was, either. 'Is that NS?' she enquired. 'Speaking,' he said. 'Can I ask what the initials stand for?' she said. 'Noah Saltzman,' he said. 'Thank goodness for that,' she said, 'I was worried they might be shorthand for Mr Nasty or even National Socialist.' 'Why are you calling?' he said. 'I picked up this cellphone in the parking lot,' she said, 'and I'm trying to trace its owner so that I can return it.' 'Well, I can tell you that it is the property of Professor Mae Fairweather,' he said, 'Dean of the Department of Media Studies at the University of St Albans.' 'Would St Albans be in Great Britain?' she said. 'It would,' he said. 'In that case,' she said, 'Professor Fairweather is a long way from home.' 'Where is she?' he said. 'In Sacramento,' she said. 'Me too,' he said. 'Is that coincidence,' she said, 'or are you travelling companions?' 'Coincidence,' he said. 'Look,' she said, 'I found this thing no more than twenty minutes ago. The parking lot belongs to Mercy Hospital, so there's every chance that your friend is still inside. Where are you right now?' 'Standing at the junction of Alhambra and Folsom,' he said. 'Why, you're practically here already,' she said. 'If you come over right now you could maybe point her out to me.' What the hell, thought Saltzman, could be the Good Samaritan looks like Meg Ryan. She texted a photograph so that he would recognize her when he arrived. The woman, Saltzman saw, would never be mistaken for Meg Ryan. Her name, she had told him, was Letty.

When Saltzman found her she also showed signs of

having expected better. Too bad, he thought, we can't all be Tom Hanks. Letty was wearing a nurse's uniform and smoking a Lucky Strike. She offered Saltzman one. 'They're a life-saver when you work in the Emergency Room,' she said. 'Sacramento is more law-abiding than most American cities – one murder and four rapes in an average week – but there are still enough domestics to make you sick to the stomach.' Her shift was due to start in twenty minutes. 'If your friend doesn't turn up in that time,' she said, 'take the phone and mail it to her home address.'

About two minutes after Letty went to work Mae Fairweather appeared. Her right wrist was in a plaster cast. 'Saltzman,' she cried, 'what the fuck are you doing here? Though, to tell you the truth, I'm almost glad to see you. How did you know I was at Mercy?' He told her about Letty. 'You must have passed her in the corridor,' he said. 'What did she look like?' Fairweather asked. 'A bit like Miss Piggy,' he said, 'but with astounding breasts.' 'Are you trying to wind me up?' she said. Saltzman ignored the question and asked one of his own. 'What happened to you?' 'A stupid fall,' she said. 'I put my right arm out to break it, and broke my wrist instead. Not that I knew it at once. But after a couple of days I realized it was more than a sprain. So I here I am. I can tell you, Saltzman, when I discovered that I had chosen a pro-life hospital with a papal ban on contraceptives I was about ready to take my fracture elsewhere.' 'But you didn't,' said Saltzman. 'As you can see,' said Fairweather.

She asked Saltzman what he'd been up to since his own little stumble. 'Driving,' he said, 'a lot of driving.' 'Would a little more be a terrible chore?' said Fairweather. 'I've been commissioned to write a sequel to *Sexing Up Monroe*. My publishers are crazy about the new title, *Marilyn at Aulis*. Its subject is the making of her last movie, which was also the unmaking of her. In my book, Arthur Miller is the new Menelaus and John Huston the new Agamemnon. Of course, Marilyn wasn't actually sacrificed by either on the set of *The Misfits*, but the bad opinion of powerful men can be as effective as a knife to the throat. I was on my way to check out some of the locations they used when one of the gods stuck out his big foot, and over I went. After the doctor told me I couldn't drive for weeks, I thought that was the end of the trail. But it seems that a benign female deity, seeing my predicament, guided you here to make amends.' 'Why should I do you a favour?' said Saltzman. 'I've been told that your voice was among the loudest calling for my suspension.' 'It could be equally loud in calls for your reinstatement,' said Fairweather. 'Back at the USA you're already known as Bill Clinton by some. With my help you could become the Comeback Kid.' 'I ain't gonna be your chauffeur,' said Saltzman, 'but I'll drive your car, so long as we travel as equals: you in pursuit of your agenda, me in pursuit of mine, which was, you may recall, to save the Department of American Studies.'

The first stop Saltzman added to Fairweather's itinerary was Coloma. Since it was but a few miles off Highway 50, the road they were travelling to Lake Tahoe, his passenger hardly had cause to bellyache. Of course, she did anyway, but only until they arrived. Once there, Fairweather was forced to concede that Coloma had its charms – the chief of them being that it wouldn't consume too much of her precious time. Of its few buildings, only one had a story attached. The story went like this.

At the beginning of 1848, one of Johann Augustus Sutter's employees, a fellow called James Marshall, reported that the sawmill at Coloma would work a lot more efficiently if its tail race were deepened. 'So,' said Sutter, 'go deepen it.' Marshall went back to do just that, and in so doing altered much more than the flow of a river.

On 24 January he returned to the fort, and asked to see his boss in camera. 'Is this what I think it is?' Marshall enquired, displaying two ounces of yellow ore. Sutter consulted the *Encyclopaedia Americana*, tested the sample with nitric acid, and said, 'It is.' He ordered Marshall to keep his mouth shut. Whoops. On first observing the gold, Marshall (old wool hat in hand) had exclaimed, 'Boys, I have got her now.' But those were not, in fact, the words that sparked the rush. The wider world was sceptical, and remained so until December 1848, when President Polk declared the sample kosher. Within a year the population of California had increased by a hundred thousand, of whom 92 per cent were male and 73 per cent were under 40.

Nothing was left of the original mill. However, a reconstruction had been put up at some remove from the American River. It was a long, open-sided structure with a circular blade at its heart, whose vicious teeth looked even more cruel than those that had bitten into the fur trapper's thumb. As it turned out, they chewed up not only Marshall but also the man whose name was ubiquitous.

Where Sutter's Mill once stood was a cairn of stones, washed smooth by the fast-flowing waters that had once powered it. Attached to the pile was a brass panel, commemorating Marshall's find and the 'great rush of argonauts' it eventually precipitated. How sweet it must have looked to Marshall, as he stood in the rain (it rained on 24 January 1848) and stared at those gleamings plucked from the dimpled water. Standing in the same spot on a hot afternoon, Saltzman tried to recapture that moment of happiness. Marshall must have felt, however briefly, that he had found one of the goose's golden eggs, little knowing that contained within it were robber barons and Arcadia's end, the hoop broken, and Crazy Horse dead. Sutter saw more clearly, which is why he told Marshall to hold his tongue, but even he couldn't fully predict or completely avoid the consequences of anarchic greed.

Squatters stole his earth, but that was not the worst of it. The wheels of his mills ceased to move as the men who turned them deserted en masse to join the Forty-niners. Nor were there any left to plant or harvest his remaining fields. 'I am ruined,' he declared as he departed. Like many a dispossessed Indian before and after, Sutter ended up in Washington, petitioning for restitution. He died within sight of the Capitol, two days after Congress had adjourned without considering his case.

After the gold rush, a local magazine chronicling its history asked James Marshall to pen a self-portrait. 'I wish to say that I feel it a duty I owe to myself to retain my likeness,' he replied, 'as it is in fact all I have that I can call my own, and I feel like any other poor wretch – I want something for self. The sale of it may yet keep me from starving, or, it may buy me a dose of medicine in sickness, or pay for the funeral of a – dog – and such is all that I expect, judging from former kindnesses.' Marshall ended his days as a gardener, and was buried at Coloma – but not like a dog. Saltzman didn't know when, but at some point a handsome memorial had been erected above his grave.

Beyond Coloma (itself 2,000 feet above sea level), Highway 50 began to rise with greater purpose, until it peaked at over 7,000 feet. It was at this point that Saltzman and Fairweather were granted their first glimpse of Lake Tahoe. From there they descended 1,000 feet to its western shore, which they skirted for the best part of thirty miles, until they reached the turn for Squaw Valley (site of the 1960 Winter Olympics). The new road followed the Truckee River, which eventually spilled into Donner Lake. There they pulled over, having reached Saltzman's second stop. It had taken the best part of an afternoon to drive the hundred miles from Sacramento to the lake, a distance earlier travellers had required three weeks to cover – if they were lucky. As for those that weren't . . .

Among Saltzman's acquaintances when he'd been a visiting lecturer at UCSC was the writer James D. Houston. They weren't exactly neighbours – Saltzman lived on 9th Avenue and Houston on East Cliff Drive – but were divided only by Schwan Lake (though everyone called it a lagoon). The former had a view of the Pacific from the attic where he worked, but the latter had a whole vista from his front porch. Saltzman recalled sitting there one afternoon when the sun was going down, sipping Bonny Doon's finest, and contemplating the little yachts with their pot-bellied spinnakers all scooting into the harbour. To his right was the lagoon, its flat surface serving as a landing-strip for incoming ducks and geese. Tall eucalyptus lined its banks, each tree with a full complement of cormorants, upright like black sentinels.

'Saltzman,' said Houston, 'ain't we the lucky ones? We

get hungry, so we go to Shoppers Corner or, if we fancy Chinese, to O'Mei. For sure, we don't have to go down yonder to the lagoon and grub about for mussels or abalone – not that it isn't fun to do so once in a while, but every day? Not on your nelly. Isn't that what you English say? We get invited to spend a year at a foreign university, so we book a plane ticket and, hey presto, we're there within the day.'

Houston paused, gave Saltzman a look like he was a lumberjack assessing a redwood, took a gulp of wine, and continued. 'Do you know who Patty Reed was?' he said. 'Don't think I do,' said Saltzman. 'Well,' said Houston, 'back in 1920 she was living in this house and, of an evening, sitting on this very porch, just like we are doing now. And yet getting here damn near killed her. You see, Saltzman, Patty was the daughter of James Reed, one of the leaders of the Donner party. You've heard of the Donner party, I suppose?' His supposition was spot on.

Saltzman knew that its leading lights were two farmers and a furniture manufacturer: the Donner brothers (Jacob and George) and their neighbour, the aforementioned James Reed. They departed Springfield, Illinois, for California in April 1846 (just about the time President Polk was fixing to wrest control of that promised land from Mexico) like biblical patriarchs, their caravan peopled with wives, numerous offspring, mothers-in-law and all manner of kin (not to mention teamsters and other servants). Behind them trailed their kine. If only the poor saps hadn't been such greenhorns, clueless as to what travails they might have to face. En route they gathered other families, equally clueless. But what did it matter? Just beyond the next horizon was that cornucopia called California. By the time it pulled into Fort

Laramie, Wyoming, the line of wagons was a village on wheels.

Some say it was at Fort Laramie that Reed first enquired about a new short cut being advertised by a scout named Lansford Hastings, who immodestly called it the Hastings Cutoff. They say that Reed was cautioned against taking it by a seasoned mountain man, whose firm advice was to keep to the California Trail. At a fork in the road called Parting of the Ways a majority followed the mountain man's counsel (and were glad that they did), while the remainder, led by George Donner, peeled away to the south-west in the direction of Fort Bridger. Numbered among the latter were Donner's brother and James Reed.

The reformulated Donner party bought supplies at Fort Bridger, and there are some who say it was Jim Bridger himself who recommended the Hastings Cutoff. Lansford Hastings, who was supposedly waiting for them at the fort, had already departed at the head of a long wagon train, so George Donner decided to risk continuing the journey without him. Twenty wagons set off from Fort Bridger on the last day of July. The journey to the Great Salt Lake should have taken no more than a week, but the badly navigated prairie schooners kept beaching in blind canyons, and it lasted nearly a month. And that was the easy bit. After that the alkali wastes of Utah and Nevada nearly did for them altogether. Human nature also took a turn for the worse, what with shootings, stabbings, fornications, robberies, mysterious disappearances, mock trials and the banishment of James Reed (who left his family and rode ahead to Sutter's Fort, where he awaited his family with increasing anxiety – when he wasn't off fighting the Mexicans, that is).

Meanwhile, the emigrants tottered on until they reached Donner Lake (called Truckee then). Their wagons were ruined and bare, their livestock either dead of exhaustion or stolen by aboriginals, and their bellies as empty as their wagons. Moreover, their leader was stuck six miles back on Alder Creek fixing a broken axle. For all that, it was still only Hallowe'en, and crossing the Sierras was hardly an unreasonable expectation. On All Saints' Day they gathered their remaining strength (and their remaining possessions) and began the ascent. However, they fell back exhausted. Having rested for a day they made a second assault, but got no further. They slept in anticipation of a third attempt, but that night their luck – never good – finally ran out. They awoke to find themselves buried by one of the worst blizzards in the region's history.

That's when their troubles really began.

Saltzman tried to picture the scene, but found it impossible. How could anyone imagine the process of freezing to death in a place where summer-folk were swimming, sailing, or skimming over the lake's shimmering surface on water skis? So he hiked with Fairweather into the gloomier reaches of the Donner Memorial State Park – full of straggly pines and man-sized thistles – where they found a brass plaque bolted to a giant boulder that listed the names of all who were compelled to winter there. Of those, forty-eight survived the ordeal and forty-two perished. Some of the latter, so it was claimed, were buried in situ. But they weren't: according to recent archeological evidence there were no human remains in the vicinity. Saltzman also happened to know that eight of the names in the deficit column did not rightly belong there, the persons concerned having left this world en route. It seemed that even words cast in bronze were not infallible. 'Why have you brought me to this morbid place?' asked Fairweather. 'Sorry to deny you victim status,' said Saltzman, 'but this visit is not about you. It's about gathering more evidence to support my thesis that all history – particularly that history relating to the Wild West – is little more than speculation, shadows glimpsed in a glass darkly.' Everyone knew that cannibalism had taken place here, but even that incontrovertible fact was now being questioned by some archeologists.

And yet Saltzman was moved to be there. Why? On account of a novel written by his old buddy, James D. Houston. Beginning in 1920, with Patty Reed (by then 82) sitting on her porch and contemplating the tide's eternal ebb and flow (as Saltzman and Houston had done in their time), *Snow Mountain Passage* went on to recount the Donner party's star-crossed journey from her point of view. Somehow, Houston managed to make real not only the stoical calm of an old woman looking back, but also the precocious sensibility of an eight-year-old, open to wild adventure and incredible privation. It was through young Patty's eyes that Saltzman saw the snow-bound emigrants who, having realized that there would be neither escape nor rescue, build shelters from whatever materials were at hand. He saw the decline and death of many as cold and hunger took their toll. He even had an inkling of the bodily needs that compelled a child to devour a beloved dog; the first time unwittingly, the second time knowingly. Young as she was, she understood that hunger was transgressive, that it recognized no boundaries. She knew that eating the family pet was no different from eating a family member, and yet she did it with something like relish, as did many of the other survivors (and it wasn't, perhaps, only quadrupeds they were enjoying). All Saltzman had to do was shut his eyes to see Patty standing in line with her siblings, while her frantic mother served up the dog's ears, neck, tongue, even his eyes. So weak were the survivors when succour finally showed up that it required four separate expeditions (called Reliefs) before all were brought down safely to Sutter's Fort, a process that lasted from mid February until mid April. Not many families out-lasted the ordeal entire; the Reeds were among the lucky ones. But Mae Fairweather hadn't read Houston's book, and needed enlightening as to what had (or may have) happened there.

Her education began at the Pioneer Monument, higher than a house, which was a bronze statue of an emigrant family. Professor Fairweather was not amused. The man stood straight-backed, his right hand shielding his eyes as he looked towards the future. Sheltering beneath his raised arm (but also leaning towards that unknown future) was his wife, an infant clutched to her breast. Cowering behind the man's leg was a daughter. A tablet attached to the statue's base explained his boldness and her trepidation: 'Virile to risk and find: kindly withal and a ready help. Facing the brunt of fate. Indomitable – unafraid.' '"Virile to risk and find",' said Fairweather. 'What the fuck does that mean?' Saltzman chose to define 'the brunt of fate' instead, explain-ing that the height of the statue's base – exactly twenty-two feet – was the precise amount of snow required to transform a starving emigrant into a cannibal. 'And you can bet your life that Mr Virility up there was first in line when his wife and daughters were the plat du jour,' said Fairweather.

The museum merely confirmed her prejudices. Ghost-hunters frequently reported a sudden drop in the temperature, and an oppressive atmosphere of gloom in certain sections of the museum, especially those parts where gruesome artefacts relating to the Donner party's dietary habits were stored. Not Mae Fairweather. Her temperature rose to fever pitch. 'My God,' she cried, 'where was charity, where was any sense of community or commonwealth? The nearest these people came to both was cannibalism. And it seems that it wasn't just Mr Virility outside who ate his better half. In Japan there is an earwig called the *Anechura harmandi* that has turned female sacrifice into a lifestyle. Having weaned her nymphs the dam then permits the little pigs to devour her in toto. If I have understood this place correctly, *Homo sapiens* behaves likewise in extremity.'

Saltzman's mother knew nothing about Japanese earwigs, but she behaved like one anyway, regarding any uneaten food as an offence against her own flesh. Young Saltzman rebelled sullenly by chewing but never swallowing, by storing the residue in his cheeks until it was safe to spit it out. He did the same at cheder, where he was compelled to spend his Sunday mornings, being force-fed Hebrew. Peppercorn, in the same class, was equally non-compliant. They spent the remainder of the day in each other's company. One Sunday Saltzman's parents were host and hostess, the next it was the turn of Mr and Mrs Peppercorn. It was the latter who introduced their nephew to *Bonanza*, which became a regular feature of Sunday afternoons thereafter. The show featured Ben Cartwright and his three sons, who were (according to the rarely heard words of its signature tune), 'the friendliest, fightingest, loving band, that ever set foot in the promised land'.

The Cartwrights' promised land was not the one Saltz-man and Peppercorn heard about at cheder, but a big chunk of Nevada. Saltzman knew exactly where it was because an old map appeared at the beginning of each episode, showing the Cartwright ranch atop Lake Tahoe. To the north was Carson City, west was Virginia City and Reno. The ranch was called the Ponderosa as a tribute to the pines that sur-rounded it. While the signature tune galloped towards its climax those trees seemed to self-combust, and flames began to pour from the heart of the map, at which point the four Cartwrights would appear riding towards the camera: Ben's boys were called Adam, Hoss and Little Joe. Adam (the oldest) had a mysterious inner life and a university degree, Hoss was a gentle giant, while Little Joe was young and impetuous. The disparity in temperament, age and size was explained by the fact that they all had different mothers, Ben being three times a widower. Since there was no cur-rent Mrs Cartwright, the family had a Chinese cook.

How unlike the home life of the Saltzman family was that of the Cartwrights. Instead of constant yelling, people spoke politely during mealtimes. What was the word? They *conversed*. No threats were ever issued to coerce the Cartwright boys into emptying their plates. On the contrary, they ate voluntarily and with relish – especially Hoss. (Could Chinese food really have tasted so much better than his mother's?) After the last credits had rolled, the two cousins would run into the garden (or upstairs if it were raining or too dark) to re-enact the episode they had just watched. Their guns looked quite realistic (especially Peppercorn's) but only fired caps, which came in reels, one hundred blackheads per strip of pink skin. When spent, they emerged from behind the hammer like miniature bus tickets – bus tickets for a one-way journey to Boot Hill. Some afternoons, when they were feeling particularly rebellious, Saltzman and Peppercorn secretly planned to run away to Nevada and beg Ben Cartwright to adopt them.

And now, thought Saltzman, here I am. He tried to explain to his uncomprehending passenger why it was so important for him to visit the Ponderosa Ranch Western Studios and Theme Park, which was exactly where the TV map had located it. 'I'm like a salmon driven to return to his spawning ground,' he said. 'But aren't you supposed to be lampooning fake establishments like this,' said Fairweather, 'exposing their essential shallowness?' 'You obviously haven't watched enough wildlife documentaries,' said Saltzman. 'Spawning grounds are shallow.' How could he convey to her that this place was different, that the Ponderosa Ranch Western Studios and Theme Park was a portal back

to his childhood? Its catchphrase spoke directly to him: 'Where Memories . . . become Adventures.'

Incline Village, home of the Theme Park, tipped towards Lake Tahoe. Behind it was the Mount Rose range. The sun was hot overhead, and every step the visitors took raised little dust devils. 'Yuk,' said Fairweather, after they had paid the entrance fee, 'it's like penetrating America's collective consciousness. Isn't that what that filthy patient-fucker called it?' 'The collective unconscious,' said Saltzman, 'Jung called it the collective unconscious.' But he had to concede that Fairweather was right either way: all Main Streets looked alike – this one, the one at Melody Ranch, even the one at Deadwood. All had saloons with swing doors, men dressed to kill, cantinas, hardware stores, gunsmiths, blacksmiths, photographers.

Lingering outside Professor Hargrove's Old Time Photo Studio, ex-Professor Saltzman thought of a way to ensure that Fairweather would keep her part of the bargain. If one photo had brought him down, then another could help restore his fortune. But how could he persuade Fairweather to pose alongside him?

'Has it crossed your mind that all the men here are certifiably insane?' she said. 'They lock up lunatics who think they are Napoleon or Jesus Christ, so why not these arrested juveniles?' 'You wouldn't want to be stuck here, then?' he said. 'God forbid,' she said. 'Play your cards right,' he said, shaking the car keys in her face, 'and it won't happen.' 'What do you want me to do?' she said. He told her. 'It's not enough for you to be known as a pervert,' she said, 'now you want a reputation as a blackmailer too.' 'If that's what it takes,' he said. That's exactly what it took, though (in truth) Fairweather offered far less resistance than he had anticipated.

There was a short line inside Professor Hargrove's studio, though the six people ahead of Saltzman and Fairweather turned out to be a single group. While the Professor was still busy with earlier customers the sextet was offered a choice: 'Pioneer or barfly?' Having opted for the former, the six were directed towards a chrome coat-rail from which hung an array of dusters, dungarees and denims. Tattered felt hats, worn boots, chaps, plus an arsenal of handguns and rifles, were also available as accessories. Having turned themselves into their real (or wished-for) ancestors, the ersatz pioneers were placed in or around a covered wagon. When posed the same question, Saltzman said, 'Barfly.'

Professor Fairweather's usual attire was a Nicaraguan smock and baggy jeans, which Salltzman thought of as a feminist burka. He was therefore somewhat surprised when she accepted without demur the only garment available for women in the barfly wardrobe: a saloon-girl's working attire. He was even more surprised when she emerged from behind a screen wearing it. The low-cut dress was tight around the bust and waist, and rode high above the knee. When she hiked it up he glimpsed the black garter around her thigh. 'My God,' said Saltzman, 'the sisters should see you now.' 'And if they could,' she said, 'they'd understand that I was trying to get under the skin of Marilyn, to learn how it felt to be the object of a sad sack's lascivious gaze.' Saltzman, for his part, was wearing a long black coat, a wide-brimmed black hat, a fancy waistcoat and some weaponry. The pair posed before the bar, with the long mirror and the glasses behind them. In the resulting image

Professor Fairweather looked convincingly like a two-dollar whore, but Saltzman was a lousy Doc Holliday. If it weren't for the Colt .45 at his hip, he'd have been a dead ringer for Isaac Bashevis Singer's Gimpel the Fool. But it hardly mattered what he looked like. It was Professor Fairweather's appearance that was his ticket home.

A Gene Autry lookalike with a stoical horse was performing with his lasso when Saltzman and Fairweather emerged into the sunlight. Between tricks he addressed his audience. 'Just because all they watch on TV is *Power Rangers*,' he said, 'it doesn't mean that cowboys don't live on in the hearts of little boys. You'll see the truth of what I'm sayin when I call for assistance.' Sure enough, at least twenty youngsters, all of whom were already dressed for the part, raised their hands. 'What did I tell you?' he said. 'Boys,' snorted Fairweather, 'always boys.' But she was wrong. They passed a father who was patiently teaching his daughter (of about seven) the art of the quick-draw. True, she was wearing a pink holster packed with pink-handled pistols, but her mind was on the job. 'Okay,' said her father, 'drop your arms down to your sides.' He examined her as a tailor might. 'Your holster's too low,' he said eventually. 'You never want it at arm's length. Better to have it so that the handle rests between the elbow and the wrist.' 'Mummy says it looks nice where it is,' answered the girl. 'Sweetie, we're talking about a weapon, not some fashion accessory,' her father said (not unkindly). 'If you leave the holster where it is you'll have to snatch for those guns. Try it my way and you'll find they practically jump into your hands.' What do you know, he was right. 'That's my gal,' he said, patting her head. The masterclass seemed strangely famil-iar to Saltzman, and then he recalled why: hadn't Joey received similar advice from Shane in that seminal movie of his childhood?

Saltzman and Fairweather left Main Street and passed a white-steepled church (said to date back to 1871), which was licenced to conduct marriages (and probably funerals too). Attached to it was a small graveyard that contained but three crosses: one each for Ben, Hoss and Little Joe. Since they never really lived the dates given were those of the deceased stars who had played them (less a century), two of whom were actually Jewish. Adam was the last of the Cartwrights and, presumably, still going strong. What a strange decision, thought Saltzman, to admit death to Arcadia.

But there was no hint of it at the Ponderosa itself. 'Noth-ing has changed since Ben and the boys left,' said a guide. 'Look, even their hats and jackets are hanging on the rack, awaiting their return.' Saltzman wandered off alone, towards the dining table he remembered so well. It had been laid for dinner, with fine china and silver cutlery. Opposite was the fireplace, whose inner walls were charred black in an effort at verisimilitude. 'If you ask me, that's where they roasted the three Mrs Cartwrights,' said Fairweather, 'when the winters were particularly bitter, and other food scarce. To lose two wives is carelessness, but to lose a third has to be murder.' Near the fireplace stood a pair of leather armchairs. Saltzman had to admit, if only to himself, that they made the ranch feel more like a gentleman's club (no ladies permitted) than the home of four red-blooded males. The rear wall of the great room had been removed and space made for the director and camera crew, plaster casts of whom could been seen through observation panels. Racks of spotlights were suspended from the ceiling. Saltzman waited in vain for someone to cry, 'Camera! Lights! Action!' For the lights to blaze again, for the camera to roll, and for Adam or Little Joe to burst upon the scene with news of . . .

'Have you seen this?' asked Fairweather, as they left the building. She was gesticulating towards a brass plaque, which looked just like a regular historical marker – except that it honoured the Ponderosa, and the pioneer spirit that had made its existence possible. 'What existence are they talking about?' said Fairweather. 'This is a fine lunacy that cannot distinguish between a genuine National Monument and a tacky stage set. All grist to your mill, eh, Saltzman?' She was right, of course, but Saltzman felt he owed it to his former, more innocent, self to spare the Ponderosa the strictures of deconstruction.

Whacked by a day on the road, Saltzman and Fairweather checked into the Cal Neva, so called because it straddled the state line. The fact that gambling was legal in at least half of the hotel was probably what attracted Frank Sinatra's interest, when he bought it back in 1960. Unfortunately, his chum Sam Giancana decided to come down from Chicago to see how his protégé was getting on. That was in the autumn of 1963. The local authorities took umbrage at the presence of such a prominent mobster in their parish, so they pulled the plug on Sinatra. He promptly took umbrage, shut the place down, and left in a huff. Some years later, the resort reopened under new management. Nonetheless, Sinatra's presence remained in the Celebrity Showcase, whose walls were filled with paparazzi-style photographs of Marilyn Monroe, Sammy Davis Jr. and Dean Martin. Sinatra himself was featured almost doubled with laughter, and sporting a natty Cal Neva skullcap topped off with a Star of David. Beside him, though not attached, was a woman whose decolletage went all the way to China. This room has an uncanny atmosphere, mused Saltzman, the uncanny atmosphere of a space illuminated by light from long-extinguished stars. But Fairweather at least seemed revitalized by the afterglow, especially that emanating from Monroe. Unable to take notes because of her injury, she spoke her thoughts into a dictaphone.

Later that night she knocked on Saltzman's door. 'I'll agree to sex,' he said, 'but only on condition that cameras are outlawed.' 'You won't be such a smartass when you hear what I've just discovered with a little light Googling,' she said. 'It seems that the Ponderosa ain't even the Ponderosa, that ol Ben and his boys never ate so much as a crumb from its table, or ever rested their weary butts in its gentlemen-only armchairs. In short, no episodes of *Bonanza* were shot there. Not a single one. The Theme Park's raison d'être was to provide fans with a place of pilgrimage and its owners with a source of revenue. Ben, Hoss and Little Joe were in on the act, and would stop by once in a while to pose for photos and press the flesh. But when all is said and done, what we just visited was nothing more than the replica of a studio set, a fucking fabrication, a rip-off. You were taken in, Saltzman, taken in by a great big ol doll's house. If you want proof, check out the credits at the end of any episode, the last words of which are always the same: "Filmed at Paramount Studios, Hollywood." Sleep well, sucker.'

Saltzman knew Virginia City primarily as the den of iniquity the Cartwright boys visited when they wanted to punch something other than a cow. But in the course of his reading he had also become familiar with the curious way these imaginary visitations had saved the real metropolis from dereliction. Like Deadwood, Virginia City began life as yet another mining camp. Tents fluttered like white flags on the slopes of its rugged valleys and ravines, while their residents tunnelled into the rock below. In 1859 two such types (O'Reilly and McLaughlin) hit the jackpot. A third miner (Comstock) muscled in on the act, claiming that O'Reilly and McLaughlin had been working on his property. Thereafter the find would be known as the Comstock Lode, and the tents as Virginia City. Mansions sprouted overnight like mushrooms, as did millionaires. President Lincoln made Nevada a state in 1864 (though there was hardly a soul in it outside Virginia City) because he needed its votes and Comstock's bullion to save the Union. By the 1870s Virginia City had a population of thirty thousand. These needy souls were serviced by a hundred saloons, innumerable brothels and six churches. And the best was yet to come. Deep down in the Consolidated Virginia Mine a new seam was struck, making 1873 the year of the Big Bonanza. Two years later, Virginia City was ablaze. It may have been built upon silver and gold, but its walls were made of resinous timber. The competing fire companies fought each other more effectively than they fought the flames, which had a wolfish appetite for wood. No matter. The Bonanza Barons rebuilt the city with money-to-burn extravagance, and this time they built it to last. They built it of brick. The new castles, mansions, hotels, saloons, shops, offices and whore-houses all lasted. The ore, however, didn't. Everyone who could afford it moved to San Francisco, arriving in good time for the earthquake. The less wealthy population of Virginia City remained but dwindled, until only a thousand were left. Then, exactly a century after the discovery of the Comstock Lode, the Four Horsemen of the Renaissance showed up, in the shape of the Cartwrights, Ben, Adam, Hoss and Little Joe, and a new bonanza began. This time round the mother lode was tourists, who came expecting to see what was already familiar from television.

They were not disappointed (even though TV's Virginia City, like the Ponderosa, was actually a studio set in Hollywood). Thanks to tourism, the wheels of fortune in the real Virginia City's saloons and gambling halls began to spin again. Funds were generated, and the most prominent structures renovated. C Street, in particular, stood revealed as a showcase of nineteenth-century commercial architecture. Saltzman reckoned that it was sometimes possible to read a building's original purpose in its present appearance.

He certainly required no prompting to work out that the HQ with a solid shell of red brick (for confidence, even assertiveness), high parapets (for an all-round perspective), and a cast-iron store front (demonstrative of unshakeable integrity), belonged to Nevada's oldest newspaper, the *Territorial Enterprise* (founded in 1858). Or at least it did until it became The Mark Twain Museum (it was while serving as the paper's city editor that Samuel Langhorne Clemens adopted his immortal nom de plume). The newsroom where he penned his copy was downstairs in the basement, and had been preserved entire, with its printing presses, type trays, swivel chairs, graffiti, dust and spiders' webs. Apparently Twain sat in a corner like some dunce. His desk was still there, as was his chair, books, umbrella and sundry paraphernalia. In the bookstore on the ground floor Saltzman even found a copy of Charles Neider's edition of the great man's autobiography.

In the last paragraph of his Introduction, Saltzman's friend had written: 'Not everything that Mark Twain says in this book is gospel fact. He may have thought it was the fact, or he may have invented or forgotten.' Nevertheless, Neider thought that nearly all of it was true 'in the poetic and psychological sense'. So Saltzman sort of believed Twain's version of his eventful life in Virginia City, while suspecting that it contained a whopper or two. It began in 1861 when Orion Clemens (the autobiographer's older brother) was appointed Secretary of the new Territory of Nevada, thanks to the fact that an old school friend was a member of Abraham Lincoln's cabinet. At that time Twain himself was riding with the secessionists, though there was little danger of brother fighting against brother, because the

eternal contrarian's martial enthusiasm lasted but a fortnight, at the end of which period he decided that he was
actually an abolitionist, and a pacifist to boot. So he cast
aside his sabre and booked a seat beside Orion on the stagecoach to Carson City.

Upon arrival, the sensible brother took lodgings, while
the more feckless one decided to chance his hand as a
prospector on the California side of the Sierras. While thus
engaged Samuel Langhorne Clemens (as he was still known)
sent occasional letters to the *Territorial Enterprise*, which
were published under the pen name 'Josh'. They led eventually to the offer of a job as its city editor at $25 per week.
Feeling shunned by Lady Luck, the failed prospector
accepted. At twenty-six he was little older than a printer's
devil, and the paper's owner was even younger. Respect for
their elders was a characteristic of neither. On the contrary,
the new recruit saw it as his civic duty to turn members of
the legislature (which met in Carson City) into laughing
stocks. They replied in kind with a succession of insults as
long and elaborate as a filibuster. 'To save them time,' the
recipient noted in the autobiography, 'I presently began to
sign the letters [i.e. articles], using the Mississippi lead-
man's call, "Mark Twain".'

Twain quickly began to write about subjects other than
politics. For example, he broke the sensational news of what
his paper called, 'A Bloody Massacre Near Carson City.'
Writing with unhealthy gusto, Twain conjured up the image
of a man named Philip Hopkins dashing into the city on
horseback, 'with his throat cut from ear to ear, and bearing
in hand a reeking scalp from which the warm smoking blood
was still dripping, and fell in a dying condition in front of

the Magnolia saloon'. Sheriff Gasberie immediately organized a posse, which galloped to the man's house where a
ghastly spectacle awaited. 'The scalpless corpse of Mrs Hopkins lay across the threshold, with her head split open and
her right hand almost severed from the wrist. Near her head
lay the ax with which the murderous deed had been committed. In one of the bedrooms six of the children were
found, one in bed and the others scattered about the floor.
They were all dead. Their brains had evidently been dashed
out with a club, and every mark about them seemed to have
been made with a blunt instrument.' The eldest daughter
(Twain named her as Mary) was found in the garret, fright-
fully mutilated, with the knife that killed her still
protruding from her corpse. Two of her battered siblings,
the only survivors, pointed an accusing finger at their father.
Twain concluded that the man must have been driven
insane by financial insecurity. Numerous papers picked up
and reprinted the grizzly tale. Their readers were sickened,
but fascinated. The only trouble with the story was that
Twain had invented every word of it. When he confessed,
the duped journals responded with outraged editorials, but
Twain's subsequent apology fell a long way short of abase-
ment: 'I take it all back.' Let it stand as a warning to
pilgrims who want to discover the True West, thought Saltzman. Don't believe a word you read. Double-check
everything. Then check the checker.

Mark Twain remained in Virginia City for more than two
years, but one day suddenly took off. What happened?
Twain offered a mock-heroic explanation in the autobiography, which Saltzman took with a pinch of salt. It seemed
that on an otherwise quiet day in April 1864 a bored Twain

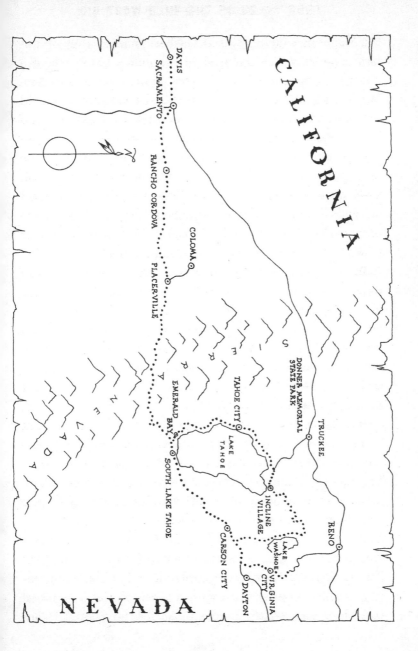

lightheartedly challenged the editor of a rival paper to a duel, confident that the cowardly fellow would never accept. But accept he did. Both men were to be seen practising the following morning, in a typical dry gulch studded with trees and enveloped by mountains. Twain quickly discovered that he couldn't hit a barn door. His second, however, was a dead shot, and to prove it he blew the head off a bird the size of a sparrow at a distance of thirty yards. His rival's second noted the decapitation but not the executioner, and jumped to the wrong conclusion. The duel was duly cancelled. But if the quarrel was resolved peacefully, why the necessity to flee Virginia City? It was because, when Twain returned, he discovered that he had become an outlaw overnight. A new law had made it a criminal offence to challenge another to a duel. The authorities gave Twain a choice: be on the next stage out of town, or face two years in the state pen. Twain took the stage.

For some reason, Twain's shoot-out never attained the status in Virginia City that the Gunfight at the OK Corral had in Tombstone – perhaps because the only fatality was a small bird. It didn't even feature in Twain's own museum, the entire second floor of which was given over to a display of sixteen life-size tableaux depicting significant moments in the history of Virginia City, the bloodier the better. Saltzman and Fairweather went their own ways, but both found themselves attracted to the same tableau, the one entitled 'The Murder of Julia Bulette'.

A plaster cast of the unlucky woman was stretched upon her own bed, covered in naught but a shift. Death rather than sexual abandon was signified by spilt blood, livid marks around the throat, and a ghastly aspect to her mortified face.

'This how you like em, eh, Saltzman,' said Fairweather, 'dead, but still warm enough to fuck?' 'If all women were like you,' he said, 'I guess the answer would have to be "yes".' 'And if all men were like you,' she said, 'I'd have to be dead before I'd let any of em lay a finger on me.' 'I'm relieved to hear that the quality of academic debate has not deteriorated in my absence,' said Saltzman, turning his attention to the caption.

'Slowly and dreadfully, Julia Bulette died,' it gloated, 'finally throttled to extinction by once-friendly hands.' Those hands were attached to the arms of a Frenchman named John Millian (also written Milleian and Melanie). At least, that is what a local court decided, though the evidence was no more than circumstantial. In any event, the verdict sufficed for the hangman, who did his job on 2 May 1868. The place of execution was a ravine on Virginia's City's outskirts, a stone's throw from the Jewish cemetery. Among the witnesses was Mark Twain (by now on the payroll of the *Chicago Republican*). 'I saw it all,' he reported. 'I took exact note of every detail . . . and I never wish to see it again. I can see that stiff, straight corpse hanging there yet, with its black, pillowcased head turned rigidly to one side, and the purple streaks creeping through the hands and driving the fleshy hue of life before them. Ugh!'

Saltzman recalled that Julia Bulette – billed in the museum as Virginia City's favourite whore – had actually featured in an early episode of *Bonanza*, catching the eye of Little Joe (if he remembered aright). No surprise, given that she'd been played by Jane Greer, once one of Hollywood's deadliest femmes fatales. What the real Julia Bulette looked like was unknown, though the museum did display a photograph said to be of her. It seemed a surprising identification. The subject's unflattering dress was divided into two hemispheres by a leather belt that bit deeply into her waist. It had the cut of a uniform, and looked at least a size too big for its wearer. Her hair was parted in the middle and bound severely at the back. The face it framed was square-jawed and devoid of sensuality. A church organist, maybe; a whore, never. The single piece of evidence that she was not only a whore but the Queen of Whores came in the unlikely form of a fireman's helmet with the figure 1 stencilled upon its high forehead (also in the picture). Julia Bulette, it seemed, had been elected an honorary member of fire engine No. 1 (in recognition of 'numerous favors and munificent gifts'). It had been these same firefighters who had escorted her body to the burying ground.

Leaving Fairweather to mourn her fallen sister, Saltzman moved on to a tableau entitled 'The Horrible Story of the Donner Party', which featured a man of feral aspect sitting in a rocking chair before a cold fireplace. A long grey beard covered his chest like some sort of vile bib. Grey hair curtained his shoulders, back and most of his face. At his feet was a zinc bath full of bloodied hands, which reached up like those of the drowned. This was Lewis Keseberg, the last of the Donner party to be saved. The caption introduced him from the point of view of his rescuers: 'Old Keseberg himself presented a most repulsive appearance – no ogre or ghoul feasting in his den could have been more hideous. His beard was of great length . . . while the nails of his fingers were of such a length that they resembled the claws of a wild beast. He was ragged to an indecent degree, exceedingly filthy, and as ferocious as he was filthy. When confronted in his den and discovered in the very act of indulging in his cannibal feast, he roused up and glared upon those who approached him as if he were a hyena.'

Those who approached him were named William Foster, Joseph Sels and John Rhoads, all members of the Fourth Relief. Its leader, Captain William O. Fallon, later recorded their impressions in a journal, according to which Keseberg was discovered not as above but 'lying down amidst the human bones, and beside him a large pan full of fresh liver and lights'. He was asked what had become of his companions, to which he replied that they were all dead, the last to go being Mrs George Donner. 'He ate her body,' added the journal, which was published in the *California Star* on 5 June 1847, 'and found her flesh the best he had ever tasted.' Keseberg further stated that he had obtained at least four pounds of fat from her remains. 'No traces of her person could be found,' concluded that part of the journal. It then proceeded to accuse Keseberg of stealing the dead woman's silver and gold. As if its depiction of Keseberg weren't sufficiently damning, another member of the Fourth Relief, Ned Coffeemeyer, let it be known that the women and children he devoured may not all have died of natural causes. In an attempt to repair his reputation, Keseberg sued Coffeemeyer for slander. He won his case, but was awarded only one dollar in damages and ordered to pay costs. Not exactly a resounding endorsement of his good name.

Yet the main evidence against him was highly unreliable. Capt William O. Fallon, being unlettered, could hardly have written the journal that bore his name. A more likely author was Sheriff George McKinstry Jr., the man who sold the story to the newspaper. There was, by then, a lively market for horrid tales about the Donner party's imagined and unimaginable excesses. This did not prove that the report was a mischievous invention, however; it could just as easily have been a transcription of Fallon's oral testimony. Either way, it should be treated with the same caution as Mark Twain's blood-curdling report of mass murder, to which it bore some resemblance.

That said, Keseberg's reputation appeared irretrievably lost. Among his few present-day supporters was an eccentric academic by the name of Professor David Fenimore, who was prepared, upon request, to adopt the persona of Keseberg and deliver a monologue in his defence. 'I stand accused of the most horrid abominations,' was how it began. 'I have been cursed in the street as a murderer and a thief. I have been stoned by children, and mocked and reviled by their elders. But as God is my judge, I am innocent of any crime. Look at me: I am no "demon". My accusers base their case on second-hand accounts or worse – the fabricated "journal" of an illiterate mountain man, sensational distortions in the press . . . or the self-serving excuses of a few villains wishing to clear their own names . . .' When asked by Saltzman why he did it, Fenimore replied, 'I guess the Donner party is just about the biggest legend here in the Truckee–Tahoe area, sort of like Dick Whittington's cat in London. Our ongoing regional panto, as it were. And I like to give the traditional villain a decent crack of the whip. Call it fair play, if you will.' So who was the real Keseberg: the King Lear type (more sinned against than sinning), or the plaster cast of the 'old cannibal' in the Mark Twain Museum? Who could say? Though it should be pointed out (in the interests of accuracy) that Keseberg was not old at the time of the crossing (being but thirty-two), and that his hair was not grey but blond, as befits a German. Indeed, Fenimore was of the opinion that 'being an immigrant, and a haughty Prussian to boot, proved to his disadvantage in a period of jingoistic national expansion and increasing European immigration'.

But even if he were guilty as charged, Keseberg was still yesterday's monster. Contemporary monsters had far greater appetites. A big seller in the souvenir shops on C Street was a hessian sack, though it was no ordinary hessian sack. Printed on its obverse in red capitals was the following: 'Terrorist Body Bag'. Below that were the faces of Saddam Hussein and Osama bin Laden, both with crosshairs superimposed upon them. Underneath were these directions: 'Locate, Capture, KILL!' Having done that, the sack's owner was instructed to 'Stuff wretched remains in bag. Send to HELL!' Finally, in red and blue type (against a white background) were the words: 'GOD BLESS AMERICA'. Saltzman watched Fairweather gleefully purchase one of the sacks, knowing that she would frame it and hang it in her office as evidence of middle America's bottomless vulgarity. It was hardly Saltzman's cup of tea either, but (despite his academic credentials as a po-mo) he didn't subscribe to Jean Baudrillard's view that the First Gulf War hadn't actually happened, or that Osama bin Laden wasn't a cunt.

Although there was plenty more to keep Saltzman busy, he had to give way to Fairweather's obsessive pursuit of Marilyn Monroe, and in Virginia City they were hot on her trail. Even before leaving St Albans, Fairweather had booked a room at Edith Palmer's Country Inn (which looked down upon C Street from a great height). And not just any old room, but Marilyn's Room: the room she had occupied when shooting scenes for *The Misfits* in nearby Dayton. 'This ranks among the oldest buildings in Virginia City,' said Leisa Findley (who ran the Inn with her childhood sweetheart), as she handed Fairweather the prized key, 'one of the very few to have survived the great fire of 1875.' Space was found for Saltzman in Edith's Room (named in honour of the original innkeeper). It contained a no-nonsense brass bedstead, whereas Marilyn's Room was dominated by a sumptuous divan of powder blue, canopied with matching chiffon. Witnessed by Saltzman the bag-carrier, Fairweather fell upon it and wept.

Like many a biographer before her, Fairweather had become convinced that she alone understood Monroe, so much so that, had she been around at the time, she would certainly have saved her. 'From what?' asked Saltzman. 'I've already told you,' said Fairweather. 'From bloodsuckers like Miller and Huston, who took what they needed from her but who gave nothing back. On the contrary, they bullied her, derided her, undermined her, sacrificed her, and finally left her for dead.' 'To what end?' said Saltzman. 'To what end?' echoed Fairweather. 'Why, so that the world would know such a one as she had danced to their tune.' And so on. Even as he yawned, Saltzman had to admit that Fairweather knew the history – and the prehistory – of *The Misfits* inside out.

'Maybe things are different now,' she said, 'but back in '56 quickie divorces in Nevada were exclusively available to residents. Luckily for out-of-staters who couldn't wait to get shot of their old wives, it only took six weeks to establish residency. Arthur Miller served his time in the desert (his closest neighbour, doing the same, was Saul Bellow). I don't know how the latter passed his days, but Miller wrote a short story with his next wife, Monroe, in mind. Called "The Misfits", it described the types (all anachronistic, a few charismatic) who hung around the local bars and somehow managed to get by with old-fashioned skills and no responsibilities. They called themselves hired hands rather than cowboys, believing that the only real cowboys were the ones they saw on TV. The tale focused upon three of them – misfits all – who, finding no home in the world, chose to stick around in Nevada, an empty place of shifting sand and nada. There they were joined by a woman, who (against all odds) retained an "intact sense of life's sacredness", and looked at the men with "naked wonder in her face even as she was smiling in the way of a grown woman". As I said, Miller wrote it with Marilyn in mind.

'Their marriage began well, but was shaken by Marilyn's ectopic pregnancy, which meant that she would never be able to bear Miller (or anyone else for that matter) a child. Her career would have to be her solace. Miller was a serious writer, I grant you that much. Marilyn was desperate to be taken seriously as an actress. In drama classes she had played Cordelia to her teacher's King Lear. She called that impromptu performance by Russian-born Michael Chekhov the greatest she had ever seen. Her dream was to be Lady Macbeth, alongside Marlon Brando as the regicide. To help her on her way, Miller gave her a gift: a script based upon the story he had written while enduring the purgatory between one marriage and another. Marilyn would star as Roslyn Taber, of course, the girl with that expression of "naked wonder". John Huston, a director Marilyn trusted, was recruited. Expectations were high. Money was raised, a crew enlisted.

'In July 1960 they all flew to Reno to begin shooting. A photograph exists of Marilyn and Miller in their room at Mapes Hotel. Marilyn, with her back to the camera, is looking out of the window. Miller is staring at her, a cigarette drooping from his lips. His hands are at his sides, as if he knows that moving them would be useless, that she is already beyond his reach. The unseen photographer was Inge Morath, the next Mrs Miller. You're not going to convince me that she and Miller weren't making eyes at each other behind Marilyn's back. Anyway, by late August or early September, when Marilyn checked in here, the division between husband and wife had ceased to be metaphorical. They were so far apart, they didn't even sleep under the same roof, let alone in the same bed. In lieu of Miller, Marilyn roomed with Paula Strasberg, of the infamous Actors' Studio. Most commentators – taking their cue from Huston

and Miller, who called her Black Bart and worse – have cast her as the villain, the woman who put big ideas in Marilyn's empty head and thereby ruined her. Take a peek at the photograph that Morath took of the pair if you don't believe me. Strasberg, dressed in a black outfit (which included a veiled hat) and looking like the Angel of Death, seems to be accosting Marilyn, who appears suitably aghast. But Marilyn turned in a great performance, and if Huston and Miller didn't help her, then who did?

'As I see it, the movie's very first scene was designed to increase Marilyn's insecurities and make a mockery of Strasberg's role as her coach. Everyone knew that Marilyn had trouble learning her lines. So what does Huston do? He decides to film Roslyn rehearsing the remarks she has prepared for one of Reno's infamous divorce courts, and getting them repeatedly wrong. Her prompt is Isabelle Steers (played by Thelma Ritter), a good sport, but no intellectual giant; in other words, a travesty of Paula Strasberg. So what happens? The scene turns out to be a self-fulfilling prophecy, of course. Driven half crazy by nocturnal struggles with her lines and her fears, Marilyn begins to show up on set at irregular hours. Some days she never arrives at all. Why blame Strasberg for something that Huston brought upon his own head? Instead of blackening her name, director and writer should have gone down on bended knees and offered thanks to her for getting Marilyn on set at all. And now, Saltzman,' concluded Fairweather, 'your job is to get me to Dayton.'

Saltzman retreated to Edith's Room in order to pinpoint Dayton's whereabouts on a road map. Then, not wishing to appear ignorant before Fairweather, he racked his memory and somewhere found a few spools of *The Misfits* stacked therein.

Having been granted her divorce (despite fluffed lines) Roslyn immediately chanced upon Gay Langland: handsome, charming, at ease with the world, though not, it turned out, with himself. In order to persuade Clark Gable to take the part, Miller had peddled the movie to him as a sort of Western. 'Westerns and the West have always been built on a morally balanced world where evil has a recognizable tag – the black hats – and evil always loses out in the end,' he had explained. 'This is that same world, but it's been dragged out of the nineteenth century into today, when the good guy is also part of the problem.' The problem in this instance being the iron laws of economics, which decreed that men like Langland, who lived for hunting wild horses, could only continue doing what they loved if they sold on their captives as mince, to satisfy the appetites of poodles. Gable played him as a man who lived as though that bitter truth did not exist, so when he got wind that a herd of mustangs had been spotted in the mountains, he reacted with the old excitement. Langland's partner, Guido, was equally keen, but they were only two, and needed a third to make up a team (one to spook, two to rope). The most likely candidate would be a down-at-heel cowboy, and the most likely habitat for that endangered species would be a rodeo. As luck would have it there was one about to begin (ah ha, thought Saltzman) in Dayton. He recalled that the pair, plus Roslyn and Isabelle, had piled into Guido's old auto and headed for the show, where they quickly signed up Perce Howland (played by Montgomery Clift, fresh from socking John Wayne in *Red River*), a middle-ranking bronco-buster.

After his ride, which was almost – but not quite – a success, they repaired to Dayton's one bar, where Roslyn did something no one who saw it was ever likely to forget.

While Saltzman searched for the car keys someone opened his door without knocking, and for a nanosecond he didn't recognize the woman who entered. When he did, his little flutter of excitement dived straight under the bed. As in Professor Hargrove's Old Time Photo Studio, Fairweather had exchanged her feminist uniform for something more flattering. This time it was a cream dress patterned with polka dots, cut low over the chest, and tight around the butt. For once, Saltzman had the good sense to keep his mouth shut, and nor did he raise the subject of her uncharacteristic outfit as they navigated the dozen or so miles downhill to Dayton.

Fairweather wanted to go straight to the bar, and luckily for Saltzman it wasn't hard to find. Dayton was not a boom town, and clearly hadn't been for several decades. It had a few trees, some lawns and a collection of low buildings, but the overall impression was of heat, dust, somnolence and mountains. Downtown consisted of two streets, and the bar stood at their junction. 'One thing's for certain,' said Saltzman as they entered, 'it ain't Happy Hour.' There were maybe five solitary drinkers (all male) plus the barman, but none seemed interested in the new arrivals, or in creating any bonhomie, let alone mayhem. Saltzman ordered a couple of beers, and wondered what was going to happen next.

He did not have long to wait. Fairweather unzipped her bag and removed a wooden bat. Attached to its middle by a line of elastic was a rubber ball. Oh no, thought Saltzman.

Fairweather held the bat horizontal and bounced the ball up in the air a few times, before rotating the bat and whacking it as hard as she was able with her left hand (her right being unavailable, of course). When it snapped back she hit it again. She tried to establish a rhythm, but because she wasn't naturally left-handed she missed too many times. Three of the men looked up from their beers and watched with half-hearted interest. Saltzman wondered if any appreciated the significance of Fairweather's exhibitionism, were aware that she was re-enacting a famous scene from *The Misfits*, a scene that had given their town its one moment of glory? 'Fuck this,' she said, having missed the ball yet again. She switched the paddle to her right hand (plaster cast notwithstanding). The broken wrist surprisingly turned out to be no hindrance, and at last she hit a winning streak. As she shook her backside Monroe-style, one of the spectators was kind enough to issue a wolf-whistle. His reward was a look cold enough to have deep-frozen a stallion's seed. 'Apparently, Marilyn liked to play paddle-ball in the bar between takes (to let off steam, I'd guess),' said Fairweather (still a little breathless), as they walked back to the rental. 'But what does Miller do when he first sees that spontaneous effusion of righteous female frustration? Does he beckon his wife into a quiet room for a few intimate exchanges in private? No, the pander sells her to the world. He fetches Huston, and between them they improvise a new scene that will exploit Marilyn's gyrating backside for all it is worth. It's like Miller is seizing the opportunity to take revenge for that turned back in Mapes Hotel.' 'I know you won't thank me for telling you this,' said Saltzman, as Fairweather stepped into the car, 'but your ass does look kinda hot in that frock.' 'Frankly, my dear,' she said, 'I don't give a damn.'

Right actor, wrong movie, through Saltzman. Dusk was settling over the Nevada desert, the early stars were already visible, and he couldn't help but think of Langland's last words to Roslyn (which were also Clark Gable's to the world, as it happened): 'Just head for that big star straight on. The highway's underneath. It'll take us right home.' By then Roslyn had saved not only his soul, but the lives of the half-dozen horses he and his friends had captured out on the salt flats near Pyramid Lake. Saltzman knew that he could never expect anything comparable from his passenger, but at least she had promised to save his job, and he was pre-pared to settle for that.

Fairweather seemed in a good mood when they reached Virginia City, and surprised Saltzman by suggesting that they had dinner together at one of the numerous joints on C Street before making the ascent to Edith Palmer's Inn. He was even more surprised when she proposed sharing a bottle of Zinfandel. Most surprising of all was the comment as he unlocked the door to his room: 'aren't you going to invite me in for a nightcap?' Saltzman removed two plastic tumblers from the bathroom, and poured a generous measure of bour-bon (from his private stock) in each. Nonetheless, he felt uneasy. 'What do you want of me?' he said. 'Your penis,' she said. 'For a trophy?' he said. She removed the paddle-bat from her bag and, turning her back on him, began to hit the ball. 'Is it true,' she said, 'do you really think I've got a great arse?' What the hell, he thought, and cupped it in his hand. He was still trying to decide whether this was a good career move when Fairweather swung around and bashed him

hard on the temple with her plaster cast. Saltzman stag-
gered backwards, with astonishment nearly as much as
pain. The second blow, however, was definitely more painful
than anything else, and sent him reeling. Three strikes he
was out, or at least down. He wasn't exactly unconscious,
but he wasn't compos mentis either, and could do nothing
to prevent Fairweather from removing his shoes, socks,
Levis and boxers. 'My God, Saltzman,' she commented, 'I've
seen bigger pricks at a circumcision.' A picture of the mohel
and his knife, plus the remembered words, 'I want your
penis', were enough to restore motion to his limbs. Observing the feeble twitches, Fairweather cracked him on the
chin, and any movement immediately ceased. All Saltzman
knew now was that he was very, very tired. He could dimly
hear Fairweather ransacking the room, but it seemed of no
concern to him, and he went to sleep.

It was the word 'Dayton' repeated several times that
awoke him. But it wasn't Fairweather haranguing him for
his sexist behaviour there, because the accent was definitely
American. Perhaps it was Nurse Letty, and he was in her
hospital? The way his head ached made that a distinct possibility. But it was a funny hospital that made you sleep on
the floor, and with your privates exposed. He felt them
before he saw them. The relief of knowing that they were
still attached almost made his headache vanish. Now that
his eyes were open he could see that Fairweather had
switched on the TV, and (unless he was hallucinating) the
person on the screen was his old friend Maureen Droz. The
Dayton she was speaking about was not a place, but a man:
someone called Dayton O. Hyde, who ran something called
the Black Hills Wild Horse Sanctuary. Maureen was obvi-

ously crazy about him, and when he spoke Saltzman kind of understood why. Dayton O. Hyde was like a Gay Langland who fitted in perfectly, who had found his niche beneath that fat star. 'My place is a cowboy's dream,' he told the viewers. 'An unspoilt eleven thousand acres where America's wild horses can run free, instead of ending up in cans as pet food.' There's the sort of man who restores your faith in America, thought Saltzman, the sort phonies like Ronald Reagan and George W. Bush wished they were, and pretended to be. How right it sounded; not President Bush, but Pretender Bush. Dayton O. Hyde even had his own Roslyn, except it was he who'd done the saving. She was a woman from Alabama who had suffered a terrible tragedy – the loss of both husband and daughter – and was whiling away her days as her old mother's unpaid chauffeur. Then, one evening, she had caught a TV feature about the Black Hills Wild Horse Sanctuary – presumably the one Saltzman was watching – and on a sudden impulse had packed a bag, jumped in her car, and made straight for it. Fuck me, thought Saltzman, if I ain't gonna do the same.

He levered himself from the floor to the edge of the bed, and sat there until he felt confident enough to stand. Summoning the strength to dress, he made the distressing discovery that he had nothing to wear, Fairweather having made off with his Levis and his Redbacks, as well as his small collection of underpants. Fortunately, she had been considerate enough to leave his wallet, so he arranged for a local store to deliver replacements. However, the car keys were gone, and with them (he assumed) the car. When Saltzman was at last able to make his way down to the reception desk, Mrs Findley handed him an envelope. 'Your friend left this for you,' she said. Inside was half of a torn photograph, the half that showed him looking like Gimpel the Fool.

Saltzman, a wanderer once more, took a taxi to Carson City. From there he flew to Denver, where he found a connecting flight to Rapid City. Renting a car at the airport (on the understanding that he could return it at his destination), he completed the last fifty miles of his journey to Hot Springs, South Dakota. He showed up at the Black Hills Wild Horse Sanctuary the following morning. The camera had not lied: Dayton O. Hyde looked to have the quiet authority and secret melancholy of Gary Cooper. So enamoured was Saltzman that, had he been asked to serve as his catamite, he would have volunteered gladly. Fortunately, Hyde just needed someone to help drive the old school buses used to transport visitors around the sanctuary. Given Saltzman's previous experience, Hyde offered him the job.

'Saltzman sounds like a family name,' said Hyde. 'I don't want to be addressing your entire ancestry whenever I speak to you. Isn't there something a little more particular I can use?' 'Well, God knows me as Noah ben David,' said Saltzman, 'but you can call me Noah.' 'Then that's what I'll do,' said Dayton O. Hyde. He explained that, although visitors were important, the majority of the sanctuary's income came from renting out locations to movie-makers. 'In fact, some cable company has just finished shooting a biopic of Crazy Horse down by the Cheyenne River,' he said. 'The area used to be the home of the Cheyenne – which is why the river is called what it's called – but they were displaced when the Sioux got squeezed out of Minnesota. I don't need to tell you what happened to the Sioux in due course. But I've been encouraging them to come back, by providing space where they can perform their Sun Dance ceremony. Last year as many as four hundred turned up to watch and participate. I haven't joined in, as yet, but I have sweated with them in their sweat lodges. Damn near killed me.'

'What Dayton is attemptin to do,' said his biggest fan, that woman from Alabama, 'is to create a place where all of us can live in harmony, if only because we are all mutually dependent here: man, beast and land. The Black Hills Wild Horse Sanctuary is like America was before it got spoilt. Dayton knows he can't turn the clock back, but he is tryin to see if the history of the American West could have been written differently.'

That afternoon Hyde took his new recruit to meet the sanctuary's raison d'être. 'Just look at them,' he said, as a small herd galloped past. 'Is it any wonder that our other main source of income is semen from these stallions? There's a lot of call nowadays for the old mustang bloodline,

you see.' Driving back to his HQ over rough terrain, Hyde told Saltzman a story. 'A long time ago I wrote a book about the Shoshone,' he began, 'and learned a little of their language. Okay, I learned one sentence: "There's an antelope on the ridge." I remembered it for thirty years, always hoping that I would have occasion to use it. Then one day, not so long ago, I was out with some Sioux braves and I looked up, and there was an antelope on the ridge. So I pointed to the animal and said, "Bundi dhooya gooha bahai," or words to that effect. The Sioux looked at me as if I had gone mad. In my excitement I had forgotten that they speak Lakota, and don't understand a word of Shoshone. Be warned, Noah, you're going to hear that tale, and many others like it, repeated a thousand times, till you start to wondering what you've done wrong in life to deserve such a fate. Think you can take the punishment?' 'Compared with what I've experienced,' said Saltzman, 'it ain't punishment, it's a reward.'

In order to get to know this backwater visionary better, Saltzman began reading his memoir, *Yamsi: A Year in the Life of a Wilderness Ranch*, which began with these words: 'I am a spring, not a winter man. In spring, a man is filled with dreams and new hopes.' It was the true voice of America.

Billy the Kid Tries to Go Straight

The owl liked the fact that he had unusually long legs (for an owl), which afforded him dominion over land as well as sky. He liked to walk upon the desert sand and observe the rodents he preyed upon scuttle down their holes. But he also enjoyed standing still, especially if he was standing stock-still on the black-top beneath a baking sun after a midsummer storm, feeling the rising steam cleansing his stilts and his tawny feathers. It meant nothing to him that the black-top upon which he stood ran between Lordsburg and a ghost town called Shakespeare.

A middle-aged man travelling south toward spooksville noted something in the north-bound lane, and slowed when he saw it was a single owl taking a sauna. Amid the tendrils of steam the bird gleamed like something newly painted. Ain't that a sight? he thought, and wondered what strange owl was it that walked abroad by daylight. He knew he would find the answer to that, as to most questions, in his ever-present copy of Peterson's *Field Guide to Western Birds*.

He lifted his foot from the brake pedal, allowing the car to resume its forward motion. Almost immediately he saw a beat-up RV travelling fast in the opposite direction. Let's give the driver the benefit of the doubt, and assume that he didn't see the owl, or (if he did) that he expected it to get out of the way pronto. Likewise, the eyewitness turned around hoping to observe the owl aloft, but saw instead a bundle of lifeless feathers knocked indifferently into the ever-encroaching sand.

He pulled off the road and backtracked to the scene of the crime, clutching his well-thumbed birder's bible. The victim of the hit-and-run was prone in the dust, both legs bent double like old drinking straws. One wing was spread fan-like upon the ground, while the other rose perpendicularly and fluttered aimlessly as the hot winds blew. Despite the blinding light its pupils were fully dilated. The surrounding coronas had lost their yellow fire, and were fading fast like a torch with dying batteries. According to Peterson it had to be a burrowing owl. Its solitary mourner fashioned a last hole for it with his bare hands, and gentled it in with his right foot.

Passing the little mound on his return journey he thought of the owls in *Macbeth* and *Julius Caesar*, both of them bad omens. Near Lordsburg he was startled by the sight of the young John Wayne flagging him down. 'It's a mirage, you fool,' he said to himself, 'only a mirage.' Almost too late he realized that it wasn't. He hit the brakes hard,

and skidded to a halt a few feet shy of a startled hitch-hiker.

Unbidden, the young man opened the passenger door. 'I thank you for stopping,' he said. 'Like as not my last ride would've rolled right on over me, like he did the owl. We both saw it plain as day. Sunnin itself on the black-top. But the son of a bitch didn't even slow down. I told him right then that I didn't want any more of his company.' 'Where you going?' asked the driver. 'Along the interstate aways,' replied the hitch-hiker. 'Would old Mesilla suit?' asked the man. 'Like an Armani shirt,' replied the youth. No hayseed, he, thought the man.

'Ham,' said the youth, 'my name is Ham.' 'Short for Hamlet?' asked the driver. 'If only,' replied his new companion, 'but it's just Ham, as in ham sandwich.' 'I'm Noah,' said the man, 'as in the Flood.' It occurred to him then that his namesake was also a birdwatcher, the world's first in fact. Ain't that a nice coincidence? he thought.

The automobile's shadow lengthened as the sun hastened towards the western horizon. Ahead, the Organ Mountains went from apricot through pomegranate to molasses. As the odometer turned, the future grew even darker. 'What were you doin on that road from nowhere?' asked Ham. 'Visiting a ghost town,' replied Noah. 'Did you see any?' asked Ham. 'Not in the flesh,' replied Noah, 'but the Stratford Hotel did feel kinda spooky. They say that Billy the Kid once worked there as a dishwasher.' 'I didn't know that,' said Ham, as if it were a serious gap in his knowledge. 'Are you a Billy the Kidologist?' asked Noah. 'A bit more than that,' replied Ham, 'I *am* Billy the Kid.' 'Oh-oh,' thought Noah. 'That's to say, I'm on my way to Lincoln to play him in the annual re-enactment of his escape from their jail,' added Ham.

'So you're an actor?' asked Noah. 'More of a re-enactor,' replied Ham, 'though in my dreams critics talk of my Billy in the same breath as Paul Newman's. Have you seen it? God! I've taken a few actin classes and know a great performance when I see one. Our teacher had some pretty weird ideas. Claimed that stars like Anthony Hopkins and Robert De Niro prepared for their biggest roles by pretendin to be animals. Next thing, he had us doin the same. Half the class said they were birds and migrated. But then he showed us clips from *The Silence of the Lambs* and *Taxi Driver*, and we could see that there was method in his madness. Hannibal Lector was a cobra, and Travis Bickle a crab. But what manner of creature was my Billy? I tried out a range of man-eaters, from wolf to mountain lion. But none fit the bill. I was at a loss. Until this afternoon, when I saw the owl die. He must have known we were comin straight for him. But he didn't give a fuck. He just stood there cool as you like, starin death in the chops. Caged owls are just the same. Most captive birds fling themselves against the bars of their cages. Not owls. They just sit, apparently indifferent, but always watchin, watchin and waitin for their jailer to make his one mistake. Then they'll have him, quick as a flash. I shall dedicate my performance to that crazy ol owl. With thanks for handin me the key to Billy's character.'

'When is the re-enactment?' asked Noah. 'Tomorrow afternoon,' replied Ham. 'Doesn't give you much time to rehearse,' remarked Noah. 'There ain't much to rehearse,' replied Ham. 'I've a fancy to see the show,' said Noah. 'How about I give you a ride all the way?' 'I ain't queer,' replied Ham. 'Don't go gettin any ideas about me, just because I been talkin about actin and the like.' 'I ain't queer either,' said Noah. He looked at his passenger. Ham was a good-look-ing kid, not a bit like the sleepy-eyed halfwit with jug ears and Habsburg jaw in the famous tintype of Billy. Had Noah been queer he might have been interested. But he wasn't. 'I'm just offering you a ride is all,' he reiterated.

Ham did not respond immediately, as if weighing up the probity of the offer. At length he said, 'To tell you the truth, I ain't so sure about Billy.' 'You think Billy was queer?' asked Noah. 'I'm not sayin he was,' replied Ham, 'and I'm not sayin he wasn't.' 'What makes you think he might've been?' asked Noah. 'First off, he had a thing about his mother,' replied Ham. 'They say he hit his stepfather over the head with a chair when he caught him fiddlin with her. Second, he had a voice like a songbird, and never shied from warbling. Third is Tunstall, the la-di-da rancher who took Billy under his wing. By all accounts the pair became as devoted as turtle doves. They even took lunch together. Most of Billy's killin was done after Tunstall's murder. His clos-est friends (or so they called themselves) noticed that he had become a changed man. They said you could see the alter-ation in his eyes. It would explain an awful lot if they was lovers.' 'It makes sense,' agreed Noah. 'But we ain't gonna go tellin anyone,' said Ham. 'It's our secret,' replied Noah.

His co-conspirator suggested they meet the next morn-ing in the Bean Coffee Shop on Calle de Guadalupe. Neither asked where the other was spending the night. As Ham walked away from the car Noah observed that he had a pecu-liar gait, almost but not quite a limp.

The coffee shop faced a tiny adobe-style movie theatre. Over a wake-me-up espresso Ham explained that he had worn a holster with a replica Colt .45 for two months straight (except when sleeping) to get a feel for what it was like to live with that weight on your hip. During that time he had practised drawing the pistol before a full-length mirror hour upon hour until his fingers bled. When he finally took the rig off to travel to Lincoln, his right leg no longer operated in tandem with his left. The middle-aged man and the unbalanced youth drained their coffee cups and headed for the plaza.

Development had stopped in old Mesilla circa 1881, when the town ordered the Santa Fe Railroad to lay its tracks elsewhere. On account of that decision the plaza had retained its Mexican appearance. Low adobe buildings lined three of its sides, the fourth being occupied by a colonial-style church. At its centre was a bandstand. However, they ventured no further than the junction of Calle de Guadalupe and Calle de Parian. 'See that buildin on your right?' said Ham. 'That's the old courthouse, where Billy the Kid was tried for the murder of Sheriff Jim Brady, found guilty and sentenced to hang. After the verdict was pronounced they took him from the lock-up here to the county jail at Lincoln, where execution was set for May 13.' 'No shit,' said Noah.

The former courthouse was now the Billy the Kid Gift Shop. The odd couple pushed apart its swing doors and entered the dimly lit interior. Standing among the Zuni bowls, the Hopi kachinas and the Navaho sand-paintings, among the Winchesters, the six-guns, the waistcoats and the Stetsons, Ham spoke. 'Forget all this stuff. It is April 13, 1881. You are Judge Warren Bristol, and you are about to pass sentence upon me.' 'I fear I lack the gravitas,' said Noah. 'The word is gavel,' said Ham, 'but you can do it without. All you need say is, "Hang, hang, hang."' Ham made

Noah repeat his line several times, until he could hear the swing of the rope in the sound. All the while Ham stared at him, immobile and unblinking. Like an owl. It gave Noah the creeps.

Back in the daylight, Ham said, 'Now you're the local sheriff, and you ask me to say somethin good about your stinkin jail for the press.' Noah did as directed. Ham looked at him, long and hard, as though he were some sort of verminous prey. 'It's the worst I ever struck,' he said.

Noah had calculated the drive to Lincoln at three hours maximum, putting their estimated time of arrival at 1.30 p.m. 'Well,' he enquired, as they sped across the Chihuahuan Desert, 'did he shoot the sheriff?' 'Sure he did,' replied Ham, 'but Sheriff Brady was a man who needed shootin. Billy had witnessed his close friend's murder, and named the killers, but the man with the tin star was too crooked to lift a finger. So Billy did. His trigger finger.'

The road dipped and bisected the bottom of an extinct sea, now known as the Tularosa Basin. Sand on either side threw back such a penetrating light that Noah began to fear snow-blindness. Mountains encircled the basin with a band of granite, but suddenly the granite didn't seem so solid as the peaks began to shimmy and dance. Noah couldn't decide whether this was on account of the heat or on account of him having a dizzy spell. Either way, he prescribed water, some bottles of which he had picked up at the White Sands National Monument. Each drank a litre without catching breath.

Although Noah could see that Ham was growing impatient, he insisted upon climbing the nearest dune. Ham reluctantly followed. The temperature was over 100, but the

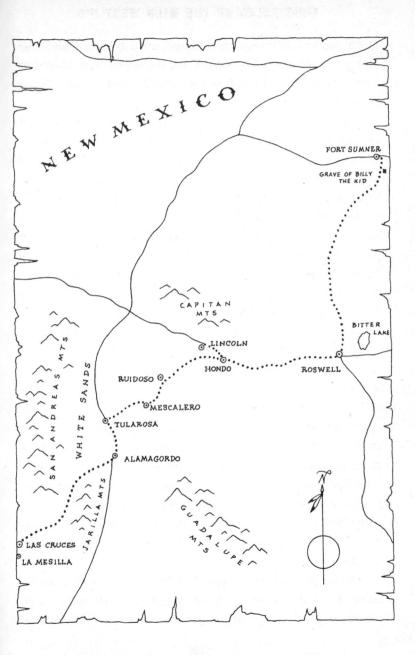

place looked like Antarctica. Only one other person was ascending the hot gypsum, a dude in pressed denims who kept calling a body named Cody. 'Cody!' he cried. 'Cody, come back!' Noah figured that conditions were perfect for a religious experience, for a vision no less. He raised his eyes towards the crest and pictured Buffalo Bill Cody himself galloping over it astride a golden palomino. Down he would come, impressing a glorious new chapter of American history upon the snow-white slope. But all that actually showed was a blonde Shih-tzu.

The next dog Noah saw was a dalmatian. A dead dalmatian. The deceased canine was laid out on scrubland between US 70 and some yucca plants. Its tombstone was a road sign that read, 'Gusty winds may exist'. Dead dogs were hardly a novelty on Indian reservations, even rich ones with casinos, like that of the high-rolling Mescalero Apaches. But this was not a normal dead dog. What caused Noah to look twice, and then stop, was the fact that the corpse was still trailing its collar and lead. Who had dropped it? Who had accidentally abandoned the dog to its fate? Noah conjured up a boy so besotted with Walt Disney's *101 Dalmatians* that he had pestered his parents until they had got him one of his own, on the strict understanding that he take full responsibility for cleaning, feeding and exercising it. All of which he had done unfailingly for years, until that one moment of inattention, until the fall. Now, guilt-stricken, he waited for news of his lost treasure.

'Is there a problem?' asked Ham. Noah gestured toward the dead dog. 'What of it?' asked Ham. 'I want to see if there's an ID tag attached to the collar,' explained Noah, opening the driver's door. 'Shut it,' said Ham. 'You're not goin near that fuckin dog.' His threatening tone drew emphasis from the fact that he was pointing his replica Colt .45 at Noah's belly button. 'You know what,' said Noah, 'you make a pretty convincing Billy.' Ham shrugged, and lowered the pistol.

Noah prodded the corpse gingerly, having heard that dalmatians could be mean bastards, much given to biting strangers for no reason. But this one's jaws, rabid or otherwise, were clamped for good. He unbuckled the collar, from which a brass disc hung. Engraved upon it was an address in Ruidoso, which at first sight looked like Sudden Death Drive. 'Why do we need to go there in person?' demanded Ham. 'Why shouldn't we?' said Noah. 'Ruidoso is on the way.' 'Okay,' said Ham, 'so long as we just deliver the bad news and exit. No counselling, or anything like that.'

'Tough break, kid,' Noah imagined himself saying as the door to 2929 Sudderth Drive began to open. Only it wasn't a boy who was doing the opening but a full-grown woman wearing cutoffs and a white tank top. 'Yes?' she said. Not having prepared for this eventuality, Noah was lost for words. He just handed over the dog tag, collar and lead. 'Where did you get these?' she asked. 'From your dog, ma'am,' he replied. 'Where is Kodak?' she asked. 'Kodak is dead, ma'am,' replied Noah. 'How?' she asked. 'Hit and run, ma'am,' replied Noah, 'out on US 70.' 'Are you a member of the Highway Patrol?' she asked. 'No, ma'am,' Noah replied. 'Then why are you talking like Broderick Crawford?' she asked. 'Lack of imagination,' Noah replied.

'Was the dog facing north or south?' she asked. 'North,' replied Noah. 'Then Kodak was on his way home when it happened,' she concluded. 'From where?' Noah inquired.

'You'll have to ask my husband that,' she replied. 'Three days ago we had the mother of all fights, which ended – nothing resolved – with him taking off in the RV accompanied by Kodak in the back. Where he went I cannot say.' Ham, left in the car, hit the horn hard. 'My, he's an impatient one,' remarked the woman. 'Let him stew,' said Noah.

Many of the houses on Sudderth Drive, he had noticed on arrival, also accommodated galleries, 2929 being no exception. Above its picture window the name Camillus Twentyman had been painted. 'You are Mrs Twentyman?' he asked. 'For the moment,' she said. 'And you are?' 'Call me Noah,' he replied, extending his hand. 'Tell me, Noah,' she said, 'are you familiar with my husband's photographs?' 'As it happens I am,' he replied. There was a lot of wildlife stuff, animals and birds going about their business, and numerous cowboys going about theirs. Most recorders of these American role models found inspiration in conflict – man versus nature, or man versus beast – but Twentyman preferred the domestic: intimate scenes captured in small rooms. One or two of the cowboys were even pictured in the buff. So great was Twentyman's distaste for the picturesque that he shunned colour, and worked exclusively in black and white. Hence Kodak the Dalmatian, thought Noah, as the penny dropped.

'Why don't you step inside?' asked Mrs Twentyman invitingly. 'My husband might be an asshole, but he's a talented asshole.' 'Some other time,' said Noah. 'Ham in the car there is playin Billy in the show the boys are puttin on in Lincoln, and I have a sort of responsibility to get him there in good time.' 'How's that for a coincidence,' exclaimed Mrs Twentyman, 'Cam will be there too. At least, he's been commissioned by Condé Nast to take some photos of all the play-actin. I suppose I ought to tell him about poor Kodak. Any chance of you offerin me a ride?'

'Who's she?' asked Ham, none too happy about his demotion to the back seat. 'Someone you need to cultivate,' replied Noah. 'Her old man is a world-famous photographer, and you're on the list of people he may be shootin for one of the glossies. Who knows? He could make you a star.' Unimpressed, Ham fixed Mrs Twentyman with an owlish stare. 'Your son is beginning to creep me out,' she said. 'Don't mind him,' replied Noah, 'he's just gettin in character. And he ain't my son.' Nevertheless, it occurred to him that fate or chance had replicated the perfect family in his old Volvo. And he liked what it looked like, and maybe even desired one of his own, though he had got a bit long in the tooth for it.

Fifteen miles short of Lincoln, on a road that wound through thick stands of cottonwood, hidden canyons and lost valleys, they passed the spot where Tunstall was gunned down. 'D'you think it was what we'd now call a hate crime?' asked Noah. 'Was Tunstall really murdered because he was queer?' 'Goddamn it, Noah,' cried Ham, 'that was supposed to be our secret.' 'I'm sure we can trust Mrs Twentyman,' said Noah. 'My lips are sealed,' she said (while making them shine with her tongue). 'Sex had nothing to do with it,' said Ham. 'The real motives were money and power. Two factions were fightin for control of Lincoln, and the fat contracts to supply the army with beef and horses. Tunstall and a lawyer named McSween on the one side, two Irish – Murphy and Dolan – on the other. The main difference was that the Irish had the backing of the big wheels in Santa Fe.

Both Tunstall and McSween went down easily. Only Billy was game enough to spoke their progress. So they hired Pat Garrett to finish the job.' 'Boy,' said Mrs Twentyman, 'you sure have a way with facts. That's the first time I ever understood what the Lincoln County War was about.' For a second or two Ham looked more like a peacock than a burrowing owl.

They drove up and down Lincoln's only street a couple of times, looking out for Twentyman's RV, but saw no sign of it. There were, however, plenty of others, as well as covered wagons, horses hitched to rails and milling crowds. The men and women were mostly dressed in the fashion of the 1880s (though a good number of the former augmented their hip-hugging weaponry with pectoral adornments from Nikon). Twentyman was not to be found among them, either. 'The hell with him,' exclaimed his wife, 'let's go eat.' Noah glanced at his wristwatch. The time was 1.35 p.m. On the nose, he thought.

Ham declined the invitation, thinking it more professional to seek out his director in the vicinity of the Pageant Grounds, where *The Last Escape of Billy the Kid* was due to be performed at 3.00 p.m (rather than in the adjacent courthouse where it really happened).

Meanwhile, Noah and Mrs Twentyman repaired to the Wortley Hotel and Dining Room. 'We're glad that you walked through our door today,' said its proprietor. He showed them to a large oval table, at the head of which sat a life-size plaster cast of a lawman (with a badge pinned to his shirt and a napkin tucked under his collar). 'That's Deputy Ollinger,' said the proprietor, 'he was eatin right here when Billy made his famous bid for freedom. Hearin the commotion he pushed his plate away and ran outside. Once in the street he found himself lookin up at Billy on the courthouse balcony. It was the last thing he saw in this world. Billy almost cut ol Bob in two with a double blast from Ollinger's own shotgun. A lot of our guests like to have their photo taken sittin either side of the unfortunate lawman. I'd be happy to oblige if that's what you folks would like.' 'We'd just like to eat,' said Mrs Twentyman. They both ordered fried chicken.

'Noah, I gotta ask you a question, and I'd be obliged if you'd answer it truthfully,' said Mrs Twentyman. 'Was it you that killed Kodak?' 'No,' said Noah. 'Good,' she replied, 'since you're payin for this meal I wanted to be sure it wasn't some sort of reparation.' 'Why will I be payin?' asked Noah. 'Because this is our first date,' said Mrs Twentyman, 'and you want to make a good impression.' 'But you are a married woman,' observed Noah. 'In name only,' replied Mrs Twentyman. 'I haven't seen my husband's dick in two summers. Okay, he's on the road half the year, but does he have to spend the other half cloistered in his darkroom?' 'Was he always so monkish?' asked Noah. 'God, no!' she replied. 'When we first met, about six years ago, ol Cam had a real persuasive tongue in his head. I had gone to his house to interview him for KCOW, and before I knew how or why it was happening I was in his studio stark naked. The pictures he took that day are all in the gallery, and you missed em, Noah.'

While they ate, cumulonimbus stacked up and filled the blue vaults of afternoon. By 2.30 p.m., when they left the Wortley, there was clearly a storm in the offing. They found Ham in the courthouse, now in costume as well as character, and looking every inch the Kid. He was sitting in the far corner of the upper level, exactly where the original Billy had been cuffed and shackled. Today's the day, Ham was thinking. Ollinger is at lunch, and Charlie Bell is gettin careless. When Noah was near enough Ham dropped a credit card accidentally-on-purpose. Noah bent instinctively to pick it up, whereupon Ham grabbed him from behind, moving so swiftly that Mrs Twentyman didn't even see it happen. Ham's assault wasn't anywhere near as shocking to Noah as the name on the credit card.

'No one knows for sure how Billy got a gun,' said Ham, 'but that's the way the Kid'll be makin his escape this afternoon.' 'It looked pretty convincing to me,' said Mrs Twentyman. 'What is known is that Billy plugged Charlie Bell within moments of gettin the weapon,' said Ham. 'Some say he did it because he was a natural-born killer, others that he was given no choice when Bell made a run for it. Either way, the bullet hole's still in the wall by the stairs.'

Legend has it that this hole was put here by a bullet from Billy the Kid's six-shooter when he escaped.

'Are you nervous?' asked Noah. 'Owls don't have nerves,' replied Ham, 'only instincts.' 'See you in the Pageant Grounds,' said Noah.

Outside a couple of black-and-whites had pulled up near the church. The cops were clearly looking for someone, and that someone turned out to be Mrs Twentyman. Two rookies approached her. 'Mrs Twentyman?' said one. She nodded. 'We have some bad news for you,' said the other, 'perhaps we could go somewhere more private.' 'I already know,' she said, 'the dog is dead.' Both cops looked sheepish, maybe even a little suspicious. 'We need for you to come with us to make the identification,' they said. 'What's there to identify?' she cried. 'He's got a tail, four legs, and a black-and-white coat Cruella De Vil would die for.' 'Mrs Twentyman, we're talking about your husband,' said one of the cops. 'You mean he's also crossed the great divide?' asked Noah. 'We believe so,' replied the other. 'An RV was found near Lordsburg with a body in it. The RV was registered to Mr Twentyman. We think the body's his too. Its end was not what you'd call natural.' 'In which case I have some information you need to hear urgently,' said Noah.

But before he or anyone else could say anything more there was a clap of thunder so loud it seemed as though heaven had gone thermonuclear. This was followed by a cloudburst, the like of which had not been seen since the Deluge. So dramatic were these meteorological phenomena that no one noticed Ham run down the courthouse steps. Unobserved by all, he swooped silently upon Mrs Twentyman like an owl upon its prey. Only when she screamed did anyone take note. Most noteworthy was the fact that he was holding a Colt .45 to her head.

Real or replica? A fair number of spectators assumed the latter, and spontaneously applauded the verisimilitude of the action, as well as the dedication of the cast in braving the elements. Noah alone knew what was at stake, and he only knew the half of it. To make matters worse, the rain and thunder were deafening Ham's most necessary inter-

locutors, meaning that they had no idea what it was he
wanted. And confused cops with loaded weapons never made
for comfortable neighbours. In short, the potential for critical misjudgement was level red.

Eventually, Noah took it upon himself to act as hostage
negotiator. He told the cops Ham wanted Mrs Twentyman
and a getaway car. He volunteered to be its driver. As it happened, his was the only accessible vehicle, because he alone
had availed himself of a parking spot on higher ground. The
rest were already deep in flood water. Some were even
floating. Noah left the cops with a riddle or a mystery. Why
had he said, 'Fort Sumner'?

While they figured out the answer, Noah's Volvo moved
miraculously through the floodwater as if it were a boat. 'So
Twentyman was driving the RV that killed the owl,' he said,
'are you some kind of animal rights nut that you kill a man
for killing an owl?' 'Why do you assume that I'm the perp?'
said Ham. 'The cops say they have a stiff, and you have his
credit card. Makes four to me,' said Noah. 'If I did the dirty
deed,' said Ham, 'it was manslaughter, not murder. So this
ain't no confession of guilt. He picked me up on some country road. The first vehicle to pass in an hour or more. Of
course, I was grateful, but it didn't give him the right to put
his hand on my thigh. I took it right off, and told him I
wasn't no queer. The second time he did it I punched him
hard. That's when the collateral damage occurred, that's
when he offed the owl. The third time I lost patience and
shot him. That set off the dog in the back, which I didn't
know was there. Fuck, it gave me a fright. I tried to calm it,
but the fuckin thing just wouldn't stop barking. So I opened
the back doors, fired off a couple more rounds in the air, and

watched the critter hightail it for the north. The last thing I wanted was for it to come to harm. It never did me any. I'm real real sorry it got killed, Mrs Twentyman. As for your husband, I probably did you a favour.'

Water was gushing from the skies, cascading down the hillsides, washing over Highway 380 and pouring into the Rio Hondo, whose banks had long since burst. 'Where to?' asked Noah, as they approached the junction with the 285 at Roswell. 'Where else but north?' replied Ham. 'North to Billy's grave at Fort Sumner.'

The sky was in a state of perpetual motion, most of it tumultuous. Above Fort Sumner in the early evening there appeared a pair of white thunderheads. They were not identical twins: one was bulbous and veined, like malachite. The other was uniformly grey and had a flat top that dipped at the centre. A white addendum bubbled from the recess. 'I'm no birder,' said Ham, 'but that cloud looks like a bald eagle to me.' 'Are you still in character?' asked Noah. 'You betcha,' replied Ham, touching Noah's cheek with the revolver's cold barrel. Higher even than the towering thunderheads was a ceiling of near-black cloud cover. Between the dark grey and the light was a radiant slash of turquoise. To the east and to the west were curtains of rain falling vertically. It couldn't be said any plainer, thought Noah: All the world's a stage.

Until he nosed around the dalmatian, Noah's inclination had always been to let sleeping dogs lie. Unfortunately, that option was presently unavailable. He didn't want to hurt Ham, but he didn't want Ham to hurt him (and Mrs Twentyman) even more. And that, he knew full well, was the most likely outcome. Following Ham's orders, he drove the car to the Old Fort Sumner Museum, and from there they trooped through ankle-deep water to the authentic grave of Billy the Kid. 'Some folks are of a mind that Pat Garrett never shot Billy the Kid,' said Ham. 'Neither here nor anywhere. They say he lied. They say he shot a man named Barlow instead. They say this is an empty tomb, like that of Jesus Christ. According to them, the Kid lived to be ninety. Only last month some ol boy who claimed he was Billy till his dyin day was exhumed over in Hamilton, Texas, to see if he was who he said he was.' 'Well?' asked Noah. 'The jury's still out,' said Ham.

The black granite stone beneath which Billy's bones may or may not repose was enclosed in a steel cage, not as a final insult but to protect it from over-zealous souvenir hunters. Carved into the stone were three words: 'Truth and History'. 'What the fuck does that mean?' asked Noah. 'It means that the truth must be told,' said Ham, 'to ensure Billy gets a fair deal from history.' 'The truth is that Billy was queer, and so are you,' said Noah. 'The whole way here you were pressed up close against Mrs Twentyman. Her with those skimpy clothes of hers all wet so that they look like a second skin. And all the time there's that intoxicatin mix of female sweat and wet cotton comin off her body that even I can smell. I bet you didn't get a hard-on even once. Why, I bet you didn't even think about havin sex with her at all.'

'Well, I am now,' said Ham, pulling Mrs Twentyman back up to the Museum. He pushed her onto the porch, which afforded some protection from the rain, and made her remove her pants. 'Remember,' he said to Noah, 'owls have eyes in the back of their heads.' Then, watched by a panel of experts painted on the adobe wall (including Billy the Kid, Pat Garrett, Wyatt Earp and Calamity Jane) Ham attempted to prove his manhood. His judges (not forgetting Noah) were unconvinced by his performance, but impressed by the cocked .45. Ham was still trying to penetrate Mrs Twentyman when Noah heard the long-awaited choppers. 'Pat Garrett and the posse are on the way, Ham,' he said. The boy looked up. 'It wasn't impotence,' he said, 'it was stage fright. I don't like bein watched.' He appeared humiliated, and gun-crazy. 'You've a choice,' said Noah. 'You can either end up like Billy and die here, or fuck off to San Francisco.' Ham arose, considered the possibilities, and fucked off.

'I'll tell them you were headin south,' shouted Noah at his back. 'Poor darlin,' said Mrs Twentyman, with something akin to maternal affection, 'd'you think he'll be all right?' It was then that Noah became aware that the rain had slackened. He looked up to the sky and saw a pigeon. It had a blue cap, russet breast and a forked tail. He knew such a pigeon would have no correspondence in his birder's bible, because it was fucking extinct! Then the clouds parted and the low sun spot-lit the eastern hemisphere, setting fire to the clouds and creating a vivid rainbow in the middle distance. Try picturing *that* in fucking black and white, Mr Twentyman, thought Noah, as he kissed his widow on lips that were no longer sealed.

Where the
Wild Things Are

Peppercorn had never been married in a synagogue before. He had wed the first Mrs Peppercorn in a registry office, but had felt his atheism double-crossed by the registrar, who had worn a splinter-sized crucifix in his lapel. So he raised no objections when Bel Stahr requested that her cousin's husband, Rabbi Zachary Siskin, be permitted to bless their union and pronounce them man and wife.

As Peppercorn was to Saltzman, so Bel Stahr was to Ida Siskin. They were bound to one another by blood, history and barely concealed rivalry. To make matters worse, both were painters. 'She has seen me suffer too many times,' said Bel, 'so let her see me happy for once.' Not to be outdone Peppercorn invited his cousin, and was astounded when the prodigal promptly accepted. Nor did he show up at the ceremony in St John's Wood unaccompanied. 'Peppercorn,' he said, 'I'd like you to meet Mrs Twentyman.' The Kid was there too, as was the Starlet, and her older brother. Virginia Campbell was also present, dressed as for the Oscars. Dr Helman acted as Peppercorn's best man.

Standing on the bima of his synagogue beneath the wedding canopy, Rabbi Siskin intoned the required blessings in the holy tongue, then, holding aloft the wine-filled wedding cup, said, 'Now that, before God and in the presence of this congregation, you have entered into the sacred covenant of marriage, a new life begins for you as husband and wife.' He went on to explain the significance of the symbolic act Peppercorn was about to perform (as if those who witnessed him stomp on and shatter the wine glass couldn't have worked it out for themselves – this was a Jewish ceremony after all). Foreboding and ill omen went with the territory. Et in arcadia ego. Even in Eden there were predators. Afterwards they all had a stroll in St James's Park, where a pelican (as if to prove the point) snatched a pigeon from the strand, drowned it in his bill, and swallowed it whole. 'Would you Adam-and-Eve it?' said a passing cockney. The newly-weds slept in Bel Stahr's house. No honeymoon had been planned, so the following morning Peppercorn arose and kissed his bride farewell. His destination, however, was far from his own establishment in St Albans.

'Explain to me again why you are going to Yellowstone,' said Bel. 'If it's wolves you're wanting what's wrong with Whipsnade?' 'There's entertainment in zoos,' said Peppercorn, 'but no enchantment. If I want to experience that ancient thrill, that frisson of fear in the old subconscious, I have to go where the wild things are.' And, shutting the door, he did exactly that.

Within hours of his arrival at Jackson Hole, Wyoming, there was a total eclipse of the moon. Peppercorn watched the show from the porch of the Wagon Wheel Motel, his only companion a storefront Indian. When the moon was suddenly transformed into Mars, into a smoking disc of burnished copper, he half expected his wooden neighbour to start issuing war whoops. As the shadow passed from left to right, the outer rim blushed a deeper red, then regained its normal complexion. By its silvery light Peppercorn glimpsed the rangy silhouette of a coyote loping along Route 89 in the direction of Yellowstone. He bedded down for the night in his cabin by the creek, and dreamed of his dentist, whose name happened to be John Wolffe.

The first European explorers of the American wilderness, if they were wise, hired mountain men as scouts. Peppercorn's guide was better groomed (though he did have a red beard), and wore a khaki uniform with official-looking patches that bore the legend 'Teton Science School'. His name, he said, was Kevin Taylor. He ushered his party into a four-wheel-drive SUV, which advertised its purpose ('Wildlife Expeditions') rather than its destination. Up went Robin (a birdwatcher) from Cheltenham. Peppercorn followed. Next came Tom (an engineer) and his wife Betty (a salty horsewoman) from Santa Monica. Already riding shotgun was Hunter (a local). 'What are those?' asked Robin, pointing to some birds that looked as if they had dipped their heads in one of Sidney Nolan's paint-pots. 'Yellow-headed blackbirds,' answered Kevin, exchanging the forecourt of the Wagon Wheel Motel for the open road.

A few miles shy of Yellowstone, Kevin made an unscheduled stop. He jumped down and scanned a quiet bend of the

Snake River with his binoculars. All Peppercorn could see with his naked eye were two white quills nodding in their inkwells. These were transformed by Kevin's superior vision into a pair of rare whooper swans. 'Note their bills,' he said, as Robin, Tom, Betty and Hunter focused their binoculars on the rarities, 'the yellow base with that distinctive black overlay.' The post-dawn light was still immaculate. Across the river, green meadows rose and fell until they finally broke against the impenetrable cliffs of the Grand Tetons, each lovely peak wrapped in its own stole of snow. And don't imagine that the snow was uniformly white; as the sun climbed it changed from crème de menthe to strawberry to vanilla. The landscape was exquisite, but it was also naggingly familiar, so much so that Peppercorn experienced déjà vu. To his chagrin it was the other Englishman, Robin the Twitcher, who solved the puzzle. 'Isn't this where they filmed *Shane*?' he asked.

He's right, damn him, thought Peppercorn, picturing his younger self in the stalls of his local Gaumont, on London's north-west frontier. He was sitting beside his father watching Shane ride off into those very mountains, while a boy of about his own age (standing more or less where he was standing now) cried, 'Pa's got things for you to do. And mother wants you . . . I know she does . . . Shane . . . Shane . . . Come back!' He listened for an echo, but all he heard was Hunter. 'The set used to be a big tourist attraction,' he was saying, 'still is, for all I know. Haw, haw, haw. It's just on the other side of that rise.' Alas, Shane had yet to reappear, but others had been more responsive to Joey's call. In 1995 wolves returned to Yellowstone (after a sixty-nine-year absence); fourteen in the first winter, a further

seventeen the following January. They went forth and multiplied, and by the time of Peppercorn's visit numbered
nearly 275 (though, as Kevin kept cautioning, there was no
guarantee of seeing a single one). Nevertheless, it was the
possibility of so doing that was the point of the expedition,
the rare chance of witnessing a memory come back to life.

Peppercorn can no longer recollect every detail of the
woodcraft he learned from Kevin, but here are a few samples he does remember. The dominant tree in Yellowstone is
the lodge pole pine. Should you decide to abandon civilization and live in a wigwam, their trunks are the things you'll
need. When seen en masse against a background of snow
they resemble an infinity of bar codes. Some are actually
dead, destroyed by fire, but despite this provocation they
continue to stand. 'Small owls will oftentimes nest in cavities drilled in them by woodpeckers,' said Kevin, 'and
starving elk will oftentimes chew their charred bark.' If you
develop headaches or stomach cramps you'd be better off
with the bark of the willow (whence aspirin). Bears with
aching teeth have been known to use it. There are two sorts
of bears in Yellowstone: the black, and the grizzly. Both will
kill you if you make the wrong move. The trick is not to
make it. But first you have to know your bear. You can't tell
them apart by colour; black bears can be brown, and griz-
zlies can be either black or brown. The black bear has a long
snout, the grizzly a rounder face (like the kind of bear a child
would draw). The grizzly has a lump of muscle between
its shoulder blades, which the black bear lacks. Having
identified your bear to the best of your ability you need to
either look confident or cowed and trust to luck. Forget fairy
stories, wolves are no threat to humanity – only to beasts of

the field, and each other. In fact, their favourite food is elk. They much prefer it to livestock, which offers no sport, having lost the instinct to run for its life. Lupins – scores of which sit upon the grass like candelabra atop green baize, their yellow lights taking fire from the sun – derive their name from the Latin for wolf. As their namesake was falsely accused of bleeding the rancher dry, so the flower was supposed to leach nutrients from the soil. Wolf packs are hierarchical. 'A non-alpha male would never dare lift his leg when peeing,' said Kevin. 'It's more like he's stretching.' 'Geldings are the same,' noted Betty, who knew her horses. 'Good visualization!' cried Kevin. Peppercorn was jealous. He too wanted to win Kevin's approval, though he didn't think he'd go as far as Hunter, who'd picked up something that resembled a stretch of black braid. 'A nice skeet,' he commented, showing his treasure to Kevin. 'From a coyote, do you think?' 'Almost certainly,' said Kevin. 'I saw something pretty cool the other day,' he continued, 'a raven bringing up a pellet from its gizzard. When I examined it, I found a sizable leg bone, probably from a chipmunk.'

By this time it was late morning, and they were gathered at the head of the Lewis River Falls, where the snow was still winter-deep. An immature bald eagle was patrolling the river, on the lookout for lunch. To their right was a stand of dead trees; an osprey was perched on the nearest, its nest balanced precariously on the furthest. 'Oftentimes a bald eagle will watch an osprey catch a fish, and then steal it,' remarked Kevin, 'Doesn't say much for the symbol of our nation, does it?'

Fortunately the group was not expected to trap their own lunch, but were served in the dining room of the Old

Faithful Inn. Just about to celebrate its centenary, it was originally billed as the largest log hotel on earth. In keeping with this boast, the central lobby resembled an attic designed to accommodate a brontosaurus. Peppercorn got vertigo just looking at the four balconies that criss-crossed empty space, nearly eighty feet above his head. Tom (the engineer from Santa Monica) confided that, when he had seen the building years before (on his honeymoon), he had refused to spend a single night beneath its unfeasible roof. During the course of their meal, the birdman of Cheltenham revealed that this was his third try at seeing wolves in the wild, the previous two (in Poland's primeval forests) having ended in failure. Could it be that he was no Robin, but a Jonah?

Kevin suggested skipping dessert in favour of watching Old Faithful erupt. As far as Peppercorn knew, Coleridge had never crossed the Rockies, but managed an eyewitness account anyway: 'And from this chasm, with ceaseless turmoil seething, / As if this earth in fast thick pants were breathing, / A mighty fountain momently was forced . . .' Nor was Old Faithful the only geyser on the block. Hardly! They were standing in the middle of one of Mother Earth's hot spots and the thin crust beneath their feet could barely restrain the molten core within. Accordingly, the landscape around the Upper Geyser Basin looked like some post-holocaust vision of Manhattan, with nothing remaining but a few blasted trees and steaming manhole covers. But even here there was beauty (albeit bizarre): in head-size bubbles that emerged from boiling mudpots and burst with a playful pop, in hot pools tinted turquoise, amber and yellow by algae. As if the internal pressures weren't sufficient, there were the external forces. The Yellowstone Valley had been carved out by the eponymous river. The latter was still at it: you could see its waters at work as they tumbled hundreds of feet into a deep canyon, and then ripped like a log saw between its polychromatic walls. By way of contrast, the Lamar Valley (which they were about to enter) was scooped out in slow motion as glaciers slipped through. The Lamar Valley was where the wolves and bears lived.

They saw their first bear at twilight. Kevin was alerted to its presence neither by tracks nor by droppings, but by autos forming a 'bear jam'. He set up the telescope, and there it was: a honey-brown grizzly muscling on all fours between the river and a row of leafless trees. It was more or less dark before Kevin called it a day. A lot of crying wolf, but no actual wolves. The group left the Park at its north-east exit, up on the Montana side, where spring  was still a distant dream. At Silver Gate they visited the studio of two wild-life photographers, Dan and Cindy Hartman. There were pictures of wolves everywhere. Peppercorn begin to fear that (thanks to their Jonah) this was the closest he was going to get to them. However, they did end with a consolation prize. Approaching Cooke City (one potholed road and a dozen or so buildings) their headlights picked out a strawberry blonde scooting across the snow and into the trees. 'No mistaking that,' observed Kevin, 'a mountain fox. Very rare. I've only ever seen one before.'

A full moon was shining over the Lamar Valley when they re-entered it at 4.30 the following morning. Pushing on, they heard yip-yap howls of coyote as each pack in turn re-marked its boundary. At about 5.00 a.m. they positioned themselves where they could see across meadows, across the winding river, through stands of silver aspen, through thickets of Douglas fir, and on until the ground rushed skywards and became mountain. Look! Another bear – a black grizzly – on the far side of the valley, taking a stroll beneath the aspens. For some reason the elk in the vicinity were spooked, and closer inspection offered an explanation – a second (much larger) grizzly was devouring one of their chums. The tactless beast was flat on its belly, tucking into the late elk's hind leg. The soundtrack was provided by a western meadowlark. A quartet of ravens approached the breakfasting bear, bouncily looking for scraps, but the bear was interested in nothing but the elk (which, according to Kevin, had been killed by wolves in the night). Appetite satisfied, the bear decided enough was enough, and left without paying the bill – whereupon a bald eagle descended and finally a solitary coyote helped itself to what was left.

Dawn came as a mixed blessing. It shoved the temperature to above freezing, but also reminded them that time was running out. Stopping beside Roosevelt Lodge they saw a black bear nosing about. A coyote ran down the adjoining slope, and so surprised the creature that it shinned up the nearest fir, but, realizing on second thoughts that it had nothing to fear, the bear descended and arched its back. This caused the coyote to retreat, only to charge back moments later with reinforcements. However, this time the bear was prepared, and ran directly at its assailants, prompting their immediate flight. No more coyotes, and (it seemed) no wolves either.

Then, out of the blue, there was news. Kevin heard on his walkie-talkie that one had been spotted a little further along the river, mixed in with a herd of buffalo, so they headed in that direction. No one spoke. Tension rose in the vehicle. After a few minutes Kevin stopped, got out, and scanned the vicinity with his binoculars. 'It's there,' he said, 'among the buffalo.' With the naked eye it was impossible to tell the creatures apart. Kevin set up telescopes. Peppercorn let Robin look first and Kevin adjusted the angle. 'It's right in the middle of the lens,' he said. Peppercorn paused, allowing anticipation's adrenaline to boost actuality. The rush eclipsed his adult self and returned him to childhood, to the magical creatures that lurked in dark corners. Kevin's description was more prosaic: Peppercorn was looking at a grey-backed yearling from the Druid Peak pack. The novice predator edged, nose first, towards a lactating cow, which was feeding its tan-coloured calf. Eventually, a great bull decided to intervene. Wolf and buffalo faced up to one another, like Alan Ladd and Jack Palance as Shane and Wilson. The bull terminated the tête-à-tête by lowering its massive head and raising its tail, this being a sign that it was either going to defecate or charge. The wolf decided that it was probably the latter and wisely retreated, walking backwards as if taking its leave of royalty.

Approaching West Thumb, near the Park's southern exit, they joined another 'bear jam', occasioned by a black grizzly wandering among the cars. It crossed the tarmac, then ambled away towards the river. Pulling off the road, they were accosted by some men and women, who had just encountered the bear, face to face. Apparently, they were walking uphill along a footpath while the bear was taking a parallel path downhill. As they crossed, the bear paused, rose, rested its paws on the railings, and examined the strangers. Terrified, they formed a bunch, and the grizzly, losing interest, went on its way. 'You did exactly the right thing,' said Kevin. Listening to their excited chatter, Peppercorn was aware that he was hearing the first performance of an opus that was going to be repeated as long as dinner parties existed. Then it occurred to him that this must have been how storytelling itself began in the very first encounters between wild beasts and fearful humanity. But there was more to it than fear. The return of the wolves might not have healed the world, or even Peppercorn, but it did revive his sense of wonderment, make him realize, with some joy, that it was not entirely a thing of the past.

A List of Useful Books

My Life on the Plains: Or, Personal Experiences with Indians, by General George Armstrong Custer, University of Oklahoma Press, 1962.

A Wounded Thing Must Hide: In Search of Libbie Custer, by Jeremy Poolman, Bloomsbury, 2002.

Exploring with Custer: The 1874 Black Hills Expedition, by Ernest Grafe & Paul Horsted, Golden Valley Press, 2002.

Custer, Terry, and Me, by Glenn G. Boyer, Five Star, 2004.

South Dakota, by T. D. Griffith & Paul Horsted, First Edition, 1994.

Great Plains, by Ian Frazier, Farrar, Straus & Giroux, 1989.

Indian Country, by Peter Matthiessen, Flamingo, 1986.

In the Spirit of Crazy Horse, by Peter Matthiessen, Penguin, 1992.

Blood and Thunder, by Hampton Sides, Little, Brown, 2006.

Fodor's Indian America, by Jamake Highwater, Fodor, 1976.

Crazy Horse, by Larry McMurtry, Viking, 1999.

Bury My Heart at Wounded Knee, by Dee Brown, Picador, 1975.

The Indian and the White Man, ed. Wilcomb E. Washburn, Anchor Books, 1964.

Book of the Hopi, by Frank Waters, Ballantine, 1963.

Wild Bill Hickok, by Richard O'Connor, Longmeadow Press, 1996.

Heroes by the Dozen, by Henry B. Jameson, Shadinger-Wilson, 1961.

Buffalo Bill Wild West Annual: Number Five, by Arthur Croom and Denis McLoughlin, Boardman, 1953.

The Oregon Trail, by Francis Parkman, The Folio Society, 1973.

Pathfinder: John Charles Fremont and the Course of American Empire, by Tom Chaffin, Hill and Wang, 2002.

The Misfits: Story of a Shoot, by Arthur Miller and Serge Toubiana, Phaidon, 2000.

Snow Mountain Passage, by James D. Houston, Knopf, 2001.

Spring Street Summer: A Journey of Rediscovery, by Christopher Hudson, Viking, 1992.

Color Country: Touring the Colorado Plateau, by Susan M. Neider, Gibbs Smith, 2002.

Print the Legend: Photography and the American West, by Martha A. Sandweiss, Yale, 2002.

Vanishing Breed: Photographs of the Cowboy and the West, by William

A List of Useful Books

Albert Allard, Little, Brown, 1982.

Sights Once Seen: Daguerreotyping Fremont's Last Expedition Through The Rockies, by Robert Shlaer, Museum of New Mexico Press, 2000.

Gone: Photographs of Abandonment on the High Plains, by Steve Fitch, University of New Mexico Press, 2003.

Bad Land: An American Romance, by Jonathan Raban, Picador, 1996.

Close Range; Wyoming Stories, by Annie Proulx, Fourth Estate, 1999.

Bad Dirt: Wyoming Stories 2, by Annie Proulx, Fourth Estate, 2004.

The Virginian, by Owen Wister, Oxford, 1998.

The Autobiography of Mark Twain, ed. Charles Neider, Harper, 1959.

The Authentic Death of Hendry Jones, by Charles Neider, Harper, 1956.

Frontier Fighter: The Autobiography of George W. Coe, Who Fought and Rode with Billy the Kid, ed. Nan Hillary Harrison, University of New Mexico Press, 1951.

The Collected Works of Billy the Kid, by Michael Ondaatje, Vintage, 1996.

Stories from Mesa Country, by Jane Candia Coleman, Swallow Press and University of Ohio Press, 1991.

Moving On, by Jane Candia Coleman, Leisure Books, 1999.

Doc Holliday's Gone, by Jane Candia Coleman, Leisure Books, 2002.

I Married Wyatt Earp: The Recollections of Josephine Sarah Marcus Earp, ed. Glenn G. Boyer, University of Arizona Press, 1997.

Wyatt Earp's Tombstone Vendetta, by Glenn G. Boyer, Talei, 1993.

The Earp Curse, by Glenn G. Boyer, Historical Research Associates, 1999.

And Die in the West: The Story of the OK Corral Gunfight, by Paula Mitchell Marks, University of Oklahoma Press, 1996.

Wyatt Earp: The Life Behind the Legend, by Casey Tefertiller, John Wiley, 1997.

Inventing Wyatt Earp: His Life and Many Legends, by Allen Barra, Carroll & Graf, 1998.

The Illustrated Life & Times of Wyatt Earp, by Bob Boze Bell, Tri Star, 1995.

Apache Days & Tombstone Nights: John Clum's Autobiography 1877–1887, ed. Neil B. Carmony, High-Lonesome Books, 1997.

Geronimo's Surrender: The 1886 CS Fly Photographs, by Jay Van Orden, Arizona Historical Society, 1994.

Geronimo: His Own Story, ed. S. M. Barrett & Frederick W. Turner III, Purnell Book Services, 1970.

The Assassination of Jesse James by the Coward Robert Ford, by Ron Hansen, Norton, 1990.

Desperadoes, by Ron Hansen, Harper, 1997.

Beyond the Law, by Emmett Dalton, Pelican, 2002.

Historical Atlas of the Outlaw West, by Richard Patterson, Johnson Books, 2000.

The West is Still Wild, by Harry Carr, Houghton Mifflin, 1932.

Winning the Wild West: The Epic Saga of the American Frontier 1800–1899, by Page Stegner, The Free Press, 2002.

A LIST OF USEFUL BOOKS

Jewish Life in the American West, ed. Ava F. Kahn, Autry Museum of Western Heritage and University of Washington Press, 2002.

The American West, ed. Jimmy Durham and Richard William Hill, Compton Verney, 2005.

Horizons West: Directing the Western from John Ford to Clint Eastwood, by Jim Kitses, BFI Publishing, 2004.

The BFI Companion to the Western, ed. Edward Buscombe, Andre Deutsch and BFI Publishing, 1988.

Westerns: Aspects of a Movie Genre, by Philip French, Secker and Warburg and BFI Publishing, 1977.

River of Shadows: Eadweard Muybridge and the Technological Wild West, by Rebecca Solnit, Viking, 2003.

America, by Jean Baudrillard (trans. Chris Turner), Verso, 1988.

Wildflowers of Monterey County: A Field Companion, by David J. Gubernick and Vern Yadon, Carmel, 2002.

A Field Guide to Western Birds, by Roger Tory Peterson, Houghton Mifflin, 1969.

Hot Links and Country Flavors: Sausages in American Regional Cooking, by Bruce Aidells and Denis Kelly, Knopf, 1990.

Picture Credits